CU00596961

Building Websites with DotNetNuke 5

Quickly build and deploy your own feature-rich website with DotNetNuke 5, VB.NET, C#, and Silverlight

Michael Washington

Ian Lackey

BIRMINGHAM - MUMBAI

Building Websites with DotNetNuke 5

First published: April 2010

Production Reference: 1310310

Published by Packt Publishing Ltd.
32 Lincoln Road
Olton
Birmingham, B27 6PA, UK.

ISBN 978-1-847199-92-8

www.packtpub.com

Cover Image by John M. Quick (john.m.quick@gmail.com)

Credits

Authors
Michael Washington

Ian Lackey

Reviewers
Rahul Singla

Andrew The

Acquisition Editor
Dilip Venkatesh

Development Editor
Mayuri Kokate

Technical Editor
Smita Solanki

Indexer
Monica Ajmera Mehta

Editorial Team Leader
Aanchal Kumar

Project Team Leader
Lata Basantani

Project Coordinator
Joel Goveya

Proofreader
Lynda Sliwoski

Graphics
Geetanjali Sawant

Production Coordinator
Shantanu Zagade

Cover Work
Shantanu Zagade

About the Authors

Michael Washington is a website developer and an ASP.NET, C#, and Visual Basic programmer. He is a Microsoft MVP in Silverlight. He has served as a DotNetNuke Core member for many years. He is the author of the *Custom Module Development* chapter in *Building Websites with VB.NET and DotNetNuke 4* (Packt Publishing).

He has authored over 100 pages of tutorials on his sites at `http://ADefWebserver.com` and `http://OpenLightGroup.net`, covering DotNetNuke and Silverlight.

He is one of the founding members of the Southern California DotNetNuke Users group (`www.socaldug.org`). He is also the author of *The DotNetNuke 4 Module Development Guide*, as well as numerous popular DotNetNuke modules such as `http://ADefHelpdesk.com`.

He has a son, Zachary, and resides in Los Angeles with his wife, Valerie.

I would like to dedicate this book to my Valerie and my son Zachary. I do it all for you!

Ian Lackey worked as a systems engineer for a St. Louis-based ISP from 1999 to 2002. At that time, he began developing web applications using ASP and migrated to ASP.NET shortly before the 2.0 release. Ian now works as a full-time programmer analyst II for Washington University in St. Louis Medical School - Department of Pediatrics. He also runs a small business, DigitalSnap Inc. (`http://www.digitalsnap.net`) that provides complete DotNetNuke solutions as well as individual modules (`http://www.itlackey.net`).

Currently Ian is involved in community-driven areas such as the OpenLight Group (`http://www.openlightgroup.net`), which manages open source projects including several DotNetNuke modules and many Silverlight-based applications. He will also be speaking at the St. Louis .NET user group (`http://www.ineta.org`) meetings this year.

Ian currently lives in a small town in Illinois, just East of St. Louis, with his wife Julie (`http://www.calljulie.info`) and two daughters, Britney and Brooklynn.

To everyone in my family, especially Loven and my little B's, thank you so much for your love and support through many long nights behind a laptop. You all are my greatest blessing. Love you forever and always.

About the Reviewers

Rahul Singla is a software professional (often filling the additional roles of Business Analyst and Project Manager) based in Karnal (India).

A university topper in his college during graduation and post graduation, he currently operates a software firm, called Imbibe Inc., and a technical training institute, Imbibe Knowledge Enterprise. His work has ranged from developing proof-of-concept JME applications to end-to-end solutions for organizations. He often freelances on medium to large scale projects, has had some popular articles on CodeProject published, and also maintains a CVS account at `drupal.org`.

Particularly fond of sharing his development experiences with his students, he likes to indulge in micro-flying, travelling, and just lying around in his vacant time. Pretty wary of his schedule, and his inability to spend time with his family, his newborn nephew is his new attraction.

You can find more about Rahul at his portal `http://www.rahulsingla.com`. You might also want to check out his technical blog at `http://www.rahulsingla.com/blog`, where you can find free DotNetNuke 4.x/5.x modules. You can contact him at `rs@rahulsingla.com`.

As always, I will dedicate my work first to the Almighty, who gave me the strength, perseverance, and opportunity to reach here, and then to the three most important people in my life, my father, my mother, and Rmi (my brother).

Andrew The ("The" is his last name, pronounced Tay) currently works as a developer and system engineer for the Los Angeles County of Education in Los Angeles, CA. Andrew started programming in Oracle's PL/SQL on Sun Solaris. Since then, he has worked with various platforms, databases, and languages (AIX, Perl, Korn Shell, DB2, HTML, SQL Server, and C#). He now primarily works with the Microsoft stack (Windows, .NET, and SQL Server).

Table of Contents

Preface

The book starts off by giving you a deep understanding of working with basic DotNetNuke sites, guiding you through the features and giving you the confidence to create and manage your site.

After that, you will journey to the heart of DotNetNuke and learn about its core architecture. Always concise, relevant, and practical, you will find out what makes DotNetNuke tick, and from there, you will be ready to customize DotNetNuke. Developers will enjoy the detailed walkthrough of creating new custom modules. Special emphasis is given to using Linq to SQL and Silverlight to invigorate your module development.

You will master all of this as you leap into the development of a DotNetNuke 5 site.

What this book covers

Chapter 1, What is DotNetNuke? explains the meaning and purpose of web portals, what successful web portals have in common, the different types of open source web portals, and also discusses why we selected DotNetNuke. In this chapter, we introduce our fictional client Coffee Connections, and using user stories, gather the requirements to build a site for it.

Chapter 2, Installing DotNetNuke explains how easy it is to set up a DotNetNuke site on your local workstation. This process has become much easier with each release of DNN, and we expect to continue to see improvements in this area as new versions are released. Some of the new features included in the installation wizard allow you to get your site up and running without needing to modify additional settings once the portal is installed.

Chapter 3, Users, Roles, and Pages covers the concepts of users, roles, and pages. This should lay a foundation for the rest of the information we cover in this book. Most of the concepts we will cover will deal with one or all of these items.

Chapter 4, Standard DotNetNuke Modules discusses the administration, common features, and settings of modules in a DotNetNuke portal. This includes how to add modules to a page, how to adjust layout options, and permission modules. It also covers the standard modules that come prepackaged with DotNetNuke, their basic uses as well as situations they may be used in. It gives a brief overview of all of the modules developed by the DotNetNuke team of developers. These modules range from simple content display to fully interactive forums and e-commerce solutions.

After discussing the modules available from the DotNetNuke team, this chapter discusses third-party commercial and open source modules. After covering the pros and cons of using commercial and open source modules, it reviews a brief list of vendors from both of these groups.

Chapter 5, Host and Admin Tools covers a variety of information. It gives you, as the administrator of a DotNetNuke portal, the skills needed to maintain your website.

Chapter 6, Understanding the DotNetNuke Core Architecture explains how the core of DotNetNuke works. It gives a general overview, examining important pieces of the framework, and finally follows a request through its paces.

Chapter 7, Custom Module Development covers many important concepts that you will most likely use in every module you create. In addition to navigation and localization, it also covers exception handling that will aid you in your module development.

Chapter 8, Connecting to the Database explains how to set up our development environment, create controls, and the data access layer.

Chapter 9, Silverlight Coffee Shop Viewer explains the UI and the Silverlight application. It also shows how to package the module so that it can be distributed to another DotNetNuke website.

Chapter 10, Creating Multiple Portals explains how to create multiple portals that can all be hosted from one account. It shows how to create and use templates, how to use the Site Wizard to upgrade your site, and how to manage these portals once they have been set up. Not only will this functionality allow you to create multiple portals, but as all of the information is stored in one database, backing up them is simple.

What you need for this book

- Windows Vista (or higher)
- SQL Server 2005 (or higher)
- Visual Studio 2008 (or higher)
- Expression Blend 3 (or higher)
- DotNetNuke 5.2 (or higher)

Who this book is for

This book has been written for both the beginner wanting to set up a website and also ASP.NET developers with a grasp of VB.NET and C# who want a deeper understanding of how to work with DotNetNuke. To work with the DotNetNuke code, you will need access to Visual Web Developer Express or Visual Studio .NET 2010. No prior knowledge of DotNetNuke is assumed.

Conventions

In this book, you will find a number of styles of text that distinguish between different kinds of information. Here are some examples of these styles, and an explanation of their meaning.

Code words in text are shown as follows: "We will place them in the Coffee Shop Listing folder that is under the `DesktopModules` folder."

A block of code is set as follows:

```
<%@ Control Language="VB"
AutoEventWireup="true"
CodeFile="Settings.ascx.vb"
Inherits="CoffeeShopVB.Settings" %>
```

New terms and **important words** are shown in bold. Words that you see on the screen, in menus or dialog boxes for example, appear in the text like this: "If this option is selected, an additional option **Add to new pages only is displayed** is also shown".

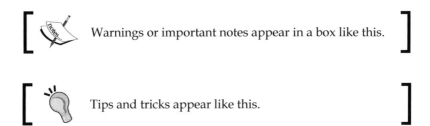

Warnings or important notes appear in a box like this.

Tips and tricks appear like this.

Reader feedback

Feedback from our readers is always welcome. Let us know what you think about this book—what you liked or may have disliked. Reader feedback is important for us to develop titles that you really get the most out of.

To send us general feedback, simply send an e-mail to feedback@packtpub.com, and mention the book title via the subject of your message.

If there is a book that you need and would like to see us publish, please send us a note in the **SUGGEST A TITLE** form on www.packtpub.com or e-mail suggest@packtpub.com.

If there is a topic that you have expertise in and you are interested in either writing or contributing to a book on, see our author guide on www.packtpub.com/authors.

Customer support

Now that you are the proud owner of a Packt book, we have a number of things to help you to get the most from your purchase.

Downloading the example code for the book

Visit http://www.packtpub.com/files/code/9928_Code.zip to directly download the example code.

The downloadable files contain instructions on how to use them.

Errata

Although we have taken every care to ensure the accuracy of our content, mistakes do happen. If you find a mistake in one of our books—maybe a mistake in the text or the code—we would be grateful if you would report this to us. By doing so, you can save other readers from frustration and help us improve subsequent versions of this book. If you find any errata, please report them by visiting http://www.packtpub.com/support, selecting your book, clicking on the **let us know** link, and entering the details of your errata. Once your errata are verified, your submission will be accepted and the errata will be uploaded on our website, or added to any list of existing errata, under the Errata section of that title. Any existing errata can be viewed by selecting your title from http://www.packtpub.com/support.

Piracy

Piracy of copyright material on the Internet is an ongoing problem across all media. At Packt, we take the protection of our copyright and licenses very seriously. If you come across any illegal copies of our works, in any form, on the Internet, please provide us with the location address or website name immediately so that we can pursue a remedy.

Please contact us at copyright@packtpub.com with a link to the suspected pirated material.

We appreciate your help in protecting our authors, and our ability to bring you valuable content.

Questions

You can contact us at questions@packtpub.com if you are having a problem with any aspect of the book, and we will do our best to address it.

1
What is DotNetNuke?

From company intranets to mom and pop shops, to local chapters of the 4-H club, most organizations are looking to have a presence on the World Wide Web. Open source web portals answer this demand by providing easy to install and use website frameworks that are not only extremely functional but are also freely available. Whether it is to sell services or to have a place to meet, web portals play an important role in communication on the Web.

In this chapter, we will discuss the following topics:

- What web portals are and what the successful web portals have in common
- Different types of open source web portals and why we selected DotNetNuke for our project over other available web portals
- The benefits gained by using an established framework and the benefits of using DotNetNuke specifically
- An introduction to Coffee Connections, our fictional client
- A brief overview of Coffee Connections, determining the specific requirements for its website and gathering the requirements using user stories

This will give you a general overview of what to expect from this book and how to make the most of it depending on your role and experience with web portals and .NET development.

Open source web portals

So what does it actually mean to have a web portal? We begin this chapter with an explanation of what a web portal is and then go on to the features of a web portal and the reasons for selecting open source web portals.

What is a web portal?

You have decided to start a web portal and first need to find out what makes a web portal. Does creating a few web pages with links to different topics make it a web portal? A **web portal**, in its most basic sense, aims to be an entry point to the World Wide Web. Portals will typically offer services, such as search engines, links to useful pages, news, forums, e-mails, and so on, depending on their targeted audience, all in an effort to draw users to their site. In most cases, portals provide these services for free, in hope that users will make the site their home page or at least come back often. A couple of successful examples include Yahoo! and MSN. These sites are **horizontal portals** because they typically attract a wide audience and primarily exist to produce advertising income for their owners. Other web portals may focus on a specific group of users or be part of a corporate intranet. Most often, they will concentrate on one particular subject like gardening or sports. These types of portals are **vertical portals** as they focus inward and cater to a selected group of people.

The type of portal you create depends on the target audience you are trying to attract. You may discover that the portal you create is a combination of both horizontal and vertical portals so as to address specific needs, while simultaneously giving a broader range of services to your visitors. Regardless of the type of portal you decide on, horizontal or vertical, they both share certain key characteristics and functionalities that will increase the probability of users returning to your site.

Common portal features

Let us first briefly discuss the difference between a portal and a standard or content-based website. The majority of the sites that you use on a daily basis are designed to provide information on a particular topic or similar topics. The standard sites usually do not provide a great deal of interactivity and have a limited number of services. For example, many sites contain a blog, but not a forum. Generally, a portal not only contains content, but also several interactive services or areas of the site.

Please keep in mind that these are generalizations and are not always clearly defined, and the differences cannot be easily identified. In fact, the difference between a portal and a standard site is pretty much a philosophical discussion, which can be debated from multiple positions. To get the most out of this book, it is important for us to know the concepts outlined in the previous paragraph. It is also important to know that the DotNetNuke framework is more than capable of supporting a portal-oriented or a more standard website. With that said, our example for this book is going to focus more on a portal.

So, what makes a great portal? Is it a free prize giveaway, local weather forecasts, or sports scores for the teams you watch? While this package of extras might attract some users, you will certainly miss a large group of people who have no interest in these offerings. You can choose from a large number of web portals that are as many in number as the programming languages they are written in. However, one thing is certain, that in order to make your web portal successful and attract a wide audience, there are particular services that it should incorporate. They are as follows:

- **A gateway to the World Wide Web**: Web portals are the way we start our day. Most of us have set up our home page to one web portal or another and whether you start at MSN, Yahoo!, or Apple, you will notice some common features. Local weather forecasts, movie reviews, or even maps of your community are a few features that make the web portal feel comfortable and tailored for you. It gives you a sense of home just like reading the morning newspaper with a cup of coffee. Web portals attempt to be the place where all of your browsing starts.

- **Content management**: Content management has come a long way from the days of paper memos and sticky notes. Computers have done away with the overflowing file cabinets holding copies of every document that crossed our desks. Little did we realize that even though we would be solving one problem, another one would arise in its place. How many times have you searched your computer wondering where you saved the document your boss needs right now? Then once you find it, you need to make sure that it is the correct version. Alternatively, if you run a soccer club, how do you ensure that all of your players can get a copy of the league rules? One of the most common uses for a web portal is content management. It allows users to have one place to upload, download, and search for a file that is important to them or their company. It also alleviates the problem of having more than one copy of a document. If the document is stored only in one location, then you will always have the current copy. Most web portals use a **WYSIWYG (What You See Is What You Get)** style editor that allows users to add and edit content without the need to know programming or HTML. It is as simple as adding content to a text file. This style of editing allows the administrators and/or members of the portal to manage the content easily.

- **Community interaction**: From the malt shop on main street to your local
  church, people like to find others who have similar interests. This is one
  of the main drawing powers of a web portal. Whether you are a Christian
  looking for other Christians (http://www.christianwebsite.com/)
  or someone who is interested in **personal digital assistants (PDAs)**
  (http://www.pdabuzz.com), there is a web portal out there for you. Web
  portals offer different ways for users to communicate. Among these are
  discussion forums that allow you to either post a question or comment to
  a message board or comment on others' posts. Chat rooms take this a step
  further with the ability to talk to one or more persons "live" and have your
  questions answered immediately.

  One of the most interesting ways to express your opinions or communicate
  your ideas to others on a web portal is to use a **blog**. A blog (also known as
  a web log) is sort of like a diary on the Web, except that you do not lock it
  when you have finished writing it. Instead, you make all your thoughts
  and observations available to the world. These blogs range in topic from
  personal and comical (http://entlib.codeplex.com/) to technical
  (http://weblogs.asp.net/scottgu) and, in recent years, have exploded
  on the scene as the de facto way to communicate on the Internet. Most web
  portals will offer at least one of these ways to communicate.

- **Security and administration**: Web portal security not only manages who can
  access particular sections of the site, but also enables administrators to access,
  add, and change content on the site. Having users authenticate with the
  portal allows you to tailor the site to individuals so that they can customize
  their experience.

Why DotNetNuke?

When the time comes to decide how you want to build your portal, you will have to
make many decisions: Do I create my portal from scratch? If not, which web portal
framework should I use? What type of hardware and software do I have available to
me? Moreover, what is my skill level on any particular platform? In this section, we
will discuss some of the better-known portals that are available.

For our portal, we have decided that it would be counterproductive to start from
scratch. So, we will be using an already-developed framework for designing our
portal. We will have many options to select from. We will discuss a few of our
options and determine why we believe DotNetNuke fits us best.

PHP-Nuke

The grandfather of DotNetNuke (in name at least) is most likely **PHP-Nuke** (`http://www.phpnuke.org`). PHP-Nuke is a web portal that uses PHP (a recursive acronym for **Hypertext Preprocessor**) pages to create dynamic web pages. You can use it in a Windows environment, but it is most flexible in a Linux/Unix environment. PHP is an open source HTML-embedded scripting language, which is an alternative to Microsoft's **Active Server Pages (ASP)** — the precursor to ASP.NET, which is the programming language used in DotNetNuke. PHP-Nuke, like DotNetNuke, is a modular system that comes with prebuilt standard modules and allows you to enhance the portal by creating custom modules. As we will be using a Windows platform and are more comfortable using ASP.NET, this choice would not fit our needs.

Joomla!

Joomla! is another open source content management system available to those looking to create a website. Joomla! also claims to be easy to use to create a website. However, like PHP-Nuke, Metadot runs primarily on the Linux operating system (although it supports Windows as well), Apache web server, and a MySQL database. For the same reasons as PHP-Nuke, this framework will not fit our needs.

DotNetNuke

Why did we select DotNetNuke as the web portal for this book? Well, here are a few reasons for selecting DotNetNuke:

- **Open source web portal written in VB.NET**: As we wanted to focus on building our web portal using the new VB.NET language, this was an obvious choice. DotNetNuke was born out of a "best-practice" application called **IBuySpy**. This application, developed for Microsoft by Scott Stanfield and his associates at Vertigo Software, was created to highlight the many things that .NET was able to accomplish. It was supposed to be an application for developers to use and learn the world of .NET. IBuySpy was an application by the original author of DotNetNuke (formerly IBuySpy Workshop), Shaun Walker of Perpetual Motion Interactive Systems Inc. He originally released DotNetNuke 1.0 as an open source project in December 2002. Since then, DotNetNuke has evolved to version 5.x and the code base has grown from 10,000 to over 120,000 lines of managed code and contains many feature enhancements over the original IBuySpy Starter Kit.

- **Utilizes the new ASP.NET 2.0 Provider Model**: With the release of ASP.NET version 2.0, Microsoft debuted a new provider pattern model. This pattern gives the developer the ability to separate the data tier from the presentation tier and provides the ability to specify your choice of databases. The DotNetNuke framework comes prepackaged with an SQL Data Provider (Microsoft's SQL Server, MSDE, or SQL Express). DotNetNuke introduces several of its own providers for tasks such as caching, authentication, and so on. For you to be able to easily switch between the choices in a plug-and-play fashion, you can also follow this model to create your own data provider or obtain one from a third-party vendor. In addition, the DotNetNuke framework also uses many of Microsoft's building block services like the **Data Access Application Block** for .NET (http://failblog.org/), introduced by Microsoft in its *Patterns* and *Practices* articles.

- **Contains key portal features expected from a web portal**: DotNetNuke comes prepackaged with modules that cover discussions, events, links, news feeds, contacts, FAQs, announcements, and more. This gives you the ability to spend your time working on specialized adaptations to your site. In addition to this, the DotNetNuke core team has created subteams to maintain and enhance these modules.

- **Separates page layout, page content, and the application logic**: It allows you to have a designer who can manage the look and feel of the site, an administrator with no programming experience who can manage and change the content of the site, and a developer who can create custom functionality for the site.

- **Ability to skin your site**: Separating the data tier from the presentation tier brings us to one of the most exciting advancements in recent versions of DotNetNuke, **skinning**. DotNetNuke employs an advanced skinning solution that allows you to change the look and feel of your site. The skinning framework allows you to build your own design for your site, but you will also find many custom skins for free on websites like core team member Nina Meiers' eXtra Dimensions Design Group (http://www.xd.com.au), and Snowcovered (http://www.snowcovered.com). These give you the ability to change the look and feel of your site without having to know anything about the design, HTML, or programming.

- **Supports multiple portals**: Another advantage of using DotNetNuke as your web portal is the fact that you can run multiple portals using one code base and one database. This means that you can have different portals for different groups on the same site, but can still have all of the information reside in one database. This gives you an advantage in the form of easy access to all portal information and a central place to manage your hosting environment. The framework comes with numerous tools for banner advertising, site promotion, hosting, and affiliate management. If you are still unclear about the portal functionality, then you can think of a **DotNetNuke** (**DNN**) portal as being a subsite for different departments of your organization, where each department can manage its site independently, but you, the organization lead, can centrally manage all subsites through what are called host accounts.

- **Designed with an extensible framework**: You can extend the framework in a number of ways. You can modify the core architecture of the framework to achieve your desired results (we will discuss the pitfalls of doing this in later chapters) and design custom modules that plug in to the existing framework. This would be in addition to the prebuilt modules that come with DotNetNuke. These basic modules give you a great starting point and allow you to get your site up and running quickly.

- **Mature portal framework**: At the time of writing this book, DotNetNuke is on version 5.2.x. It means that you will be using an application that has gone through its paces. It has been extensively tested and is widely used as a web portal application by thousands of existing users. What this offers you is stability. You can feel comfortable knowing that thousands of websites already use the DotNetNuke framework for their web portal needs.

- **Active and robust community**: Community involvement and continuing product evolution are very important parts of any open source project, and DotNetNuke has both of these. The DotNetNuke support forum is one of the most active and dynamic community forums on the ASP.NET website. There are currently over 740,000 users registered on the DotNetNuke website. At the time of writing, the much-anticipated DotNetNuke version 5.1 had just been released and brought about a significant improvement over its previous releases. The core team continues to move forward, always striving towards a better product for the community.

- **Recognized by the Microsoft team as a best-practice application**: In March 2004, at the VSLive! conference in San Francisco, the premiere conference for Visual Studio.NET Developers, DotNetNuke 2.0 was officially released and showcased to the public. This gave DotNetNuke a great leg up in the open source portal market and solidified its position as a leader in the field.

Benefits of using an established program

Whether you are building a website to gather information about your soccer club or putting up a department website on your company's intranet, one thing is certain — to write your web portal from scratch, you should plan on coding for a long time. Just deciding on the structure, design, and security of your site will take you months. After all this is complete, you will still need to test and debug. At this point, you still haven't begun to build the basic functionality of your web portal.

So why start from scratch when you have the ability to build on an existing structure? Just as you would not want to build your own operating system before building a program to run on it, using an existing architecture allows you to concentrate on enhancing and customizing the portal to your specific needs. If you are like me and use Visual Studio for developing your website, then you already adhere to this concept. There is no need for you to create the basic building blocks of your application (forms, buttons, textboxes, and so on); instead, you take the existing building blocks and assemble (and sometimes enhance) them to suit your needs.

The DotNetNuke community

The DotNetNuke community has one of the most active and dynamic support forums and over 740,000 users are registered on the DotNetNuke website.

Core team

The core team comprises individuals invited to join the team by Shaun Walker, whom they affectionately call the "Benevolent Dictator". Their invitations were based on their contributions and their never-ending support from others in the DotNetNuke forum. Each team member has a certain area of responsibility based on his or her abilities. From database functionality and module creation to skinning, they are the ones who are responsible for the continued advancement of the framework. However, not being a member of the core team does not mean that you cannot contribute to the project. There are many ways for you to provide help for the project. Many developers create custom modules that they make freely available to the DotNetNuke community. Other developers create skins that they freely distribute. Still others help answer the many questions in the DotNetNuke forum. You can also be a contributor to the core architecture. You're welcome to submit code improvements to extend and/or expand the capabilities of DotNetNuke. These submissions will be evaluated by the core team and could possibly be added to the next version.

The DotNetNuke discussion forum

When the DotNetNuke project started, one of the things that helped to propel its popularity forward was the fact that its forums were housed on the ASP.NET forums website. With over 200,000 individual posts in the main DotNetNuke forum alone, it was one of the most active and attentive forums on the ASP.NET forums website (`http://www.asp.net/forums/`). Beginning sometime after the version 3.x release, the DotNetNuke team puts its finishing touches to its own forum module. It now utilizes this module for DotNetNuke discussions (`http://www.dotnetnuke.com/tabid/795/Default.aspx`). The DotNetNuke forum is the best place to find help for any issue you may be having in DotNetNuke.

The main forum is where you will find most of the action, but there is also a subforum that covers topics such as core framework, resources, getting started, and custom modules. You can search and view posts in any of the forums but will need to register if you want to post your own questions or reply to other users' posts. The great thing about these forums is that you will find the core team hanging out there. Who could be better to answer questions about DotNetNuke other than those who created it? However, don't be shy, because if you know the answer to someone else's question, then feel free to post an answer. That is what the community is all about, helping people through challenging situations.

The bug tracker

Like any application, there are bound to be a few bugs that creep into the application now and then. To manage this occurrence, the DotNetNuke core team uses a third-party bug tracking system called *Gemini*, by CounterSoft. The bug tracker is not for general questions or setup and configuration errors; questions of that nature should be posted in the discussion forum. You can view the status of current bugs at the Gemini site (`http://support.dotnetnuke.com`), and you can also add new bugs to the system. Before submitting a bug to the tracker, please review the guidelines currently posted on the DotNetNuke website (`http://www.dotnetnuke.com/Support/ReportABug/tabid/645/Default.aspx`).

To summarize, you need to first search the bug tracker to make sure that it has not already been reported. If you cannot find it in the system, then you will need to supply the details including what you did, what you expected to happen, and what actually happened. Also, if you are going to include code to reproduce the bug, then be sure to limit the code to 10 lines or less. Verified bugs will be assigned to core team members to track down and repair.

The DotNetNuke project Roadmap team

If you want to find out what is in the works for future releases of DotNetNuke, then you should check out the DotNetNuke project **Roadmap** (http://www.dotnetnuke.com/Development/Roadmap/tabid/616/Default.aspx). The main purpose of this document is, as a communication vehicle, to inform users and stakeholders of the project's direction. The Roadmap accomplishes this by allowing users to submit enhancement requests. The priority of the enhancements depends on both the availability of resources (core team) and the perceived demand for the feature, based on the number of votes it receives.

The license agreement

The license type used by the DotNetNuke project is a modified version of the **Berkeley Software Distribution (BSD)** license. As opposed to the more restrictive **GNU General Public License (GPL)** used by many other open source projects, the BSD license is very permissive and imposes very few conditions on what a user can do with the software. These conditions include charging clients for binary distributions, with no obligation to include source code. If you have further questions on the specifics of the license agreement, then you can find information in the documents folder of the DotNetNuke application or on the DotNetNuke website.

Coffee Connections

Wherever your travels take you, from sunny Long Beach, California, to the cobblestone streets of Hamburg, Germany, chances are that there is a coffee shop nearby. Whether it is a Starbucks (located on just about every corner) or a local coffee shop tucked neatly in between all the antique stores on the main street, they all have one thing in common—coffee. Right? Well yes, they do have coffee in common, but more importantly, they are places for people with shared interests to gather, relax, and enjoy their coffee while taking in the environment around them. Coffee shops offer a wide variety of services in addition to coffee, from Wi-Fi to poetry readings to local bands. They keep people coming back by offering them more than just a cup o' Joe.

But how do you find the coffee shops that have the type of atmosphere you are looking for? In addition, how do you locate them in your surrounding area? That's where Coffee Connections comes in; its desire is to fill this void by creating a website where coffee lovers and coffee shop regulars can connect and search for coffee shops in their local area that cater to their specific needs. Coffee Connections has a vision to create a website that will bring this together and help promote coffee shops around the world. Users will be able to search for coffee shops by zip code, types of entertainment, amenities, or name. It will also allow its customers to purchase goods online and communicate with others through chat rooms and forums.

Determining client needs

In any project, it is important to determine the needs of the client before work begins on the project. When designing a business-driven solution for your client, your options range from an extensive **request for proposal** (**RFP**) and case modeling, to user stories and **Microsoft Solutions Framework** (**MSF**). To determine the needs and document the requirements of Coffee Connections, we will use user stories.

We selected user stories as our requirements collection method for two reasons. Firstly, the DotNetNuke core team uses this method when building enhancements and upgrading the DotNetNuke framework. Thus, using user stories will help to give you a better understanding of how the core team works, the processes the team members follow, and how they accomplish these tasks in a short period of time. Secondly, it is a very clear and concise way to determine the needs of your client. We will be able to determine the needs of Coffee Connections without the need for a large number of requirement documents.

What is a user story?

User stories were originally introduced as part of **Extreme Programming** (**XP**). Extreme Programming is a type of software development based on simplicity, communication, and customer feedback. It is primarily used within small teams when it is important to develop software quickly while the environment and requirements of the program rapidly change. This fits the DotNetNuke project and the DotNetNuke core team well.

User stories provide a framework for the completion of a project by giving a well-designed description of a system and its major processes.

The individual stories, written by customers, are features that they wish the program to possess. As the user stories are written by the customer, they are written in the customer's terminology and without much technical jargon. The user stories are usually written on index cards and are approximately three sentences long. The limited space for detail forces the writer to be concise and get to the heart of the requirement. When it is time to implement the user story, the developer will sit down with the customer—in what is referred to as an iteration meeting—to go over particular details of each user story. Thus, an overview of a project is quickly conceptualized without the developer or customer being bogged down in minor details.

User stories also help in the creation of acceptance tests. Acceptance tests are specified tests performed by the user of a system to determine if the system is functioning correctly according to specifications the user presented at the beginning of the development process. This assures that the product performs as expected.

Advantages of using user stories

There are many different methods of defining requirements when building an application, so why use user stories? User stories fit well into **Rapid Application Development (RAD)** programming. In general, the software and computer industry change on a daily basis. The environment is changing fast. In order to compete in the marketplace, it is important to have quick turnaround for your product. User stories help to accomplish this in the following ways:

- **Stressing the importance of communication**: One of the central ideas behind user stories is the ability to have the users write down what exactly is expected from the product. This helps to promote communication by keeping the client involved in the design process.

- **Being easily understandable**: As user stories are written by the customer and not by the developer, the developer will not have the problem of "talking over the head" of the customer. User stories help customers know exactly what they are getting because they personally write down what they want in the terms that they understand.

- **Allowing for deferred details**: User stories help the customer as well as the developer to understand the complete scope of a project without being bogged down by the details.

- **Focussing on project goals**: The success of your project depends less on creative coding strategies and more on whether you were able to meet the customer's goals. It is not what you think it should do but what the customer thinks it should do (although this does not mean that you should not follow established coding practices).

Coffee Connections user stories

In the following table, you will find the user stories for Coffee Connections. From these stories, we will use DotNetNuke to build the customer's website. The title of the card is followed by a short description of what is needed. Throughout the book, we will refer to these as we continue to accomplish the project goals for Coffee Connections.

Title	Description
Web Store	Users will be able to purchase coffee and coffee shop-related merchandise through the website.
Coffee Shop Search	Users will be able to find coffee shops in their area by searching a combination of zip codes, coffee shop names, amenities, or atmosphere and ratings.
Coffee Finder Additions	Users will be able to post coffee shops they find and give a description of the coffee shop for other users to see.
Coffee Shop Reviews	Users will have the ability to rate the coffee shops that are listed on the website.
Site Updates	Administrators will have the ability to modify the site content easily using a web-based interface.
Coffee Chat	Users will be able to chat with people from other coffee shops on the site.
Coffee Forum	Users will be able to post questions and replies in a coffee shop forum.

When referring to the user stories later in the book, we will use a card to compare and determine if we have met the customer's needs.

Summary

In this chapter, we have discussed the meaning and purpose of web portals, what successful web portals have in common, looked at different types of open source web portals, and discussed why we selected DotNetNuke. We then met our fictional client Coffee Connections, and using user stories, gathered the requirements to build a site for it. The next chapter will cover the always-enlightening task of installing the software. We will cover what we need to run DotNetNuke and describe the process of installing the framework.

2

Installing DotNetNuke

DotNetNuke version 5 can be downloaded in several different packages. The options that exist are the Source Code, New Install, Starter Kit, and Version Upgrade packages. The Starter Kit basically creates the same file structure as the New Install package, but requires Visual Web Developer or any version of Visual Studio, and it uses the Visual Studio web server to host the site. The Source Code package contains the install package plus all of the source code for the entire DotNetNuke framework. While the Install package can be used for building extensions, the Source Code package can be used to view additional details about the DNN core. The Version Upgrade package is used to upgrade a DotNetNuke site from a previous version. In this chapter, we will look at how to create a local DotNetNuke installation using the New Install package. This is a straightforward process that has the least number of software requirements and suits the needs of most scenarios.

In this chapter, we will also discuss the overall upgrade process in brief. However, we will not dive too deeply into this topic. Upgrading a DotNetNuke site can be challenging depending on how the site is configured. We will address a few of the things to consider before upgrading. There are also a few recommended steps to take to back up your site before the upgrading which we will discuss.

Installing DotNetNuke (local version)

We are using Windows 7, IIS 7.5, and SQL Express 2008 SP1 with the management tools in all of the examples in this chapter. If you are using different versions of this software, then there maybe some discrepancies between the screenshots provided and what you see on your computer. DotNetNuke also requires the .NET Framework version 2.0 or above to be installed on the computer. However, we strongly encourage that you install the .NET Framework version 3.5 SP1 or above, regardless of the version of Windows, IIS, or SQL you are using. If you are using Windows 7, . NET 3.5 SP1 is also installed by default. The module development examples in this book will be using features of the .NET Framework that are only available in version 3.5 SP1 and above. Now would be a good time to ensure that you have installed this version so that you can follow along with examples later.

If you are using Windows Vista with IIS 7, there should be little to no difference in the examples provided and the setup process on your PC. However, if you are using Windows XP or Windows Server 2003, you may want to review this page for detailed instructions on how to configure a **virtual directory** using IIS 5.1/6 at http://msdn. microsoft.com/en-us/library/zwk103ab.aspx.

Clean installation

This chapter will mainly be demonstrating how to install DotNetNuke 5 from scratch, as opposed to upgrading a 4.x installation. Creating a clean install is typically easier to accomplish than performing an upgrade from a previous version. With this in mind, we will provide the simplest set of instructions to get your site up and running. However, if you would like information on upgrading an existing DotNetNuke 4.x site to use version 5.x, then please refer to the *Upgrading* section later in this chapter.

Downloading the code

Beginning with DotNetNuke version 4.9.1 and 5.0.0, the download packages for DNN have been moved to Microsoft's CodePlex site. CodePlex is Microsoft's open source environment that allows developers to share their software and source code with the community. If you have not seen or heard about CodePlex, then it is well worth your time to browse the site and become familiar with what it has to offer. This is especially true if you are a developer who is involved with or would like to be involved with an open source project.

The partnership between DotNetNuke and CodePlex has provided many benefits to the DotNetNuke community and to the overall .NET open source community. The official press release concerning this partnership can be found under the news section of DotNetNuke's website and is titled "DotNetNuke Moves to CodePlex". If you would like to know more about the benefits and changes this partnership has made, then the article is a great place to start.

By now, you are probably wondering why I took the time to mention the move to CodePlex. The most important reason was to inform you that you can now download the install package directly from the DotNetNuke CodePlex site. Before the move to CodePlex, you were required to register an account on DotNetNuke's website to view the download packages. We still recommend registering an account on the DotNetNuke website in order to participate in the forums, comment on blog entries, and generally interact with the other DotNetNuke users and developers.

However, for this example, we will download the install package directly from the CodePlex site, in order to reduce the number of steps required to get your site up and running. To do this, open a browser and navigate to `http://dotnetnuke.codeplex.com` and click on the **Downloads** tab. On the **Downloads** page, click on the **New Install** link. You will be prompted to agree to the license agreement. Click the **I Agree** button to begin your download. You should then be prompted to open, save, or cancel the file download. Click **Save** and select a folder to save the file that you will be able to access easily. You should now have a file saved on your PC that looks similar to this.

Right-click on the file and choose **Extract All** to extract the package to the folder that you will use to host your DotNetNuke site. This folder can be anywhere on your computer. However, for this example we suggest a folder at the location `C:\Code\DotNetNuke`. We will refer to this location in later steps of the installation process.

Setting up an application

Please note that you must have administrative privileges to Windows in order to complete this task. If you are currently logged in with an account that does not have administrative access, then you must switch to a user that does before continuing.

To begin, please verify that the necessary Windows features are installed and ready to use. These features include the following:

To enable these features, navigate to the control panel, click on **Programs** and then on **Turn Windows features on or off.** Now, select the features shown and click the **OK** button. Once these features are installed, you may continue with the installation of DotNetNuke.

In order to register the folder you just created with the extracted DotNetNuke installation files with your local web server, you must configure an application using the **Internet Information Services (IIS) Manager**. To open this tool, click on **Start** and then choose **Control Panel**. Once you are in the **Control Panel**, click the **System and Maintenance** icon. In the **System and Maintenance** section, click on the **Administrative Tools** icon. Finally, click on the **Internet Information Services (IIS) Manager** icon to launch the web server configuration tool.

Inside the IIS Manager, expand the top-level icon that shows the name of your computer and the username you are currently logged in as.

 To expand the icons in this tool, click on the arrows next to the icons.

Then you will need to expand the `Sites` folder to display the **Default Web Site** icon. Right-click on this icon and choose **Add Application**.

The **Add Application** dialog window should now be displayed, which appears as shown in the next screenshot. Enter an alias into the **Alias** textbox. We will use **DotNetNuke** for our example; it is recommended that you also use the same alias, as we will reference this alias as we continue this example. If you extracted the DotNetNuke install files to the recommended folder, then you can type `C:\Code\DotNetNuke` into the **Physical path** textbox. Otherwise, enter the path to the folder to which the file was extracted to or you may click the ellipse positioned after the **Physical path** textbox. Browse to the folder to which you extracted the install file, in our case it is `C:\Code\DotNetNuke`. Select the folder and click the **OK** button. This should fill in the **Physical path** textbox with the location of the DotNetNuke installation files. Once the path to the DotNetNuke install files is entered into the textbox, click the **OK** button to close the **Add Application** dialog window.

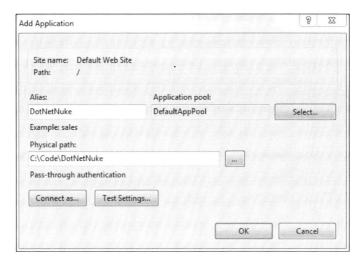

Now navigate to the `Application Pools` folder located above the `Sites` folder, which we expanded previously.

A list of the currently configured application pools should now be displayed. Right-click on **DefaultAppPool** and choose **Advanced Settings** to display the dialog window, which is shown in the next screenshot. Under the **Process Model** section of the dialog window, change the value of **Load User Profile** to **True** and click the **OK** button. This helps prevent a potential error message being displayed, later when we browse to the site.

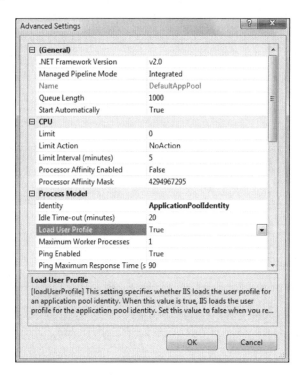

 The error we are preventing is a security exception, while requesting the `AspNetHostingPermission` when loading the site. For more information on the **Load User Profile** setting, please refer to the IIS website. For more information on `AspNetHostingPermission`, you may refer to the MSDN site.

Verifying default documents

Unlike previous version of IIS such as 5.1 and 6, IIS version 7.5 installed on Windows 7 typically includes the proper **Default Document** setting for DotNetNuke websites. This section will briefly walk you through verifying that the setting is properly applied and how to add the correct setting if it is not configured already.

To do this, you first need to select the newly-created application in the **Connections** panel. In our example, the application will be named **DotNetNuke** and should be listed below the **Default Web Site**.

In the middle section of the window you should now see various configuration tools, as shown in the following screenshot:

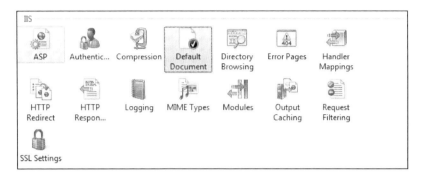

From here you will need to double-click the **Default Document** icon in the **IIS** section near the middle of the screen. You should now see a list of default documents listed; ensure that there is a document named `default.aspx` in the list.

> **Wrong view**
>
> If you are seeing what looks like the filesystem, then you may need to click on the **Features View** button located near the bottom of the window.

If `default.aspx` is not listed, then click the **Add** link located under the **Actions** section (shown in the next screenshot) located on the right-hand side of the screen.

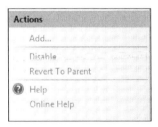

The **Add Default Document** dialog will be displayed. Type in `default.aspx` and click the **OK** button to add the document name to the list.

Setting security permissions

As we will see in the **Running the Install Wizard** section, DotNetNuke must have write access to the files and folders where the install files are located. This allows DotNetNuke to create new files, modify configuration, and other tasks needed for the features provided by the framework. The following are the steps needed to grant DotNetNuke the required access to the files and folders.

To begin, browse to the folder you extracted the install files to. In our example this would be `C:\Code\DotNetNuke`. Right-click on the folder and select **Properties**. On the **General** tab, you will see a **Read-only** checkbox located in the **Attributes** section. If this is checked, then uncheck the box and click the **Apply** button at the bottom of the **DotNetNuke Properties** dialog window.

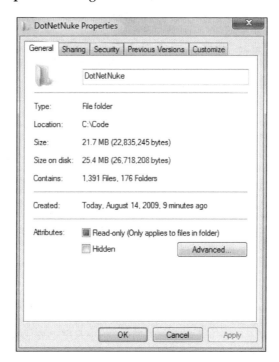

A confirmation dialog (shown in the next screenshot) will be displayed asking if you would like the setting to be applied to the folder, subfolder, and files. Verify that the **Apply changes to this folder, subfolders and files** radio button is selected and then click the **OK** button.

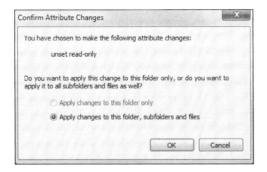

A progress indicator window will be displayed while the new setting is applied.

 You may also be prompted to continue or cancel if you are running as a low privileged user. Be sure to always choose to continue.

Once this is complete, click on the **Security** tab to view the users and groups that currently have permissions set on the folder. The tab should look as shown in the following screenshot:

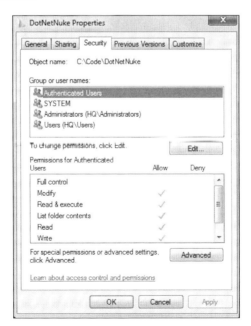

Click on the **Edit** button to modify the permissions for the folder. You will then need to click on the **Add** button to select the proper user account to grant access to the folder. You should now see the **Select Users or Groups** dialog window as shown in the next screenshot. Type **Network Service** into the textbox located under the **Enter the object names to select** label and click the **Check Names** button. **NETWORK SERVICE** will now be displayed in capital letters and underlined. Click the **OK** button to return to the **Permissions** dialog.

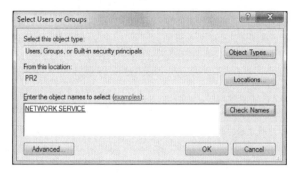

Make sure that **NETWORK SERVICE** is selected in the **Group or user names** list and check the **Allow** checkbox next to the **Full control** item in the **Permissions for NETWORK SERVICE** list. Verify that checking this box checked all of the checkboxes under **Allow** except the **Special permissions** checkbox. Now you may click the **OK** button to save your changes and return to the folder **Properties** dialog. You will then need to then click **OK** once more to complete the process of setting the permissions on the DotNetNuke install folder.

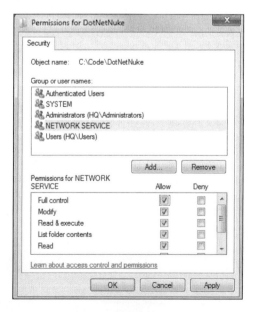

Setting up the database

If you are going to use SQL Server Express, then there are two options on how to set up the database for your website. If you would like to use the auto-attach feature of SQL Server Express, then there is no need to configure that database at all. The Database.mdf file, which is located in the App_Data directory of the DotNetNuke site will be automatically attached to SQL Express when the website is run.

However, in this section we will walk through how to manually configure the database using SQL Management Studio. In our experience, manually configuring the database has proven to be a more reliable solution and is our recommended practice.

 This requires that you be logged in to Windows with an account that has administrative rights to the SQL Server instance you will be configuring.

To begin, open **SQL Server Management Studio** located on your start menu under **All Programs** and then open the **Microsoft SQL Server 2008** folder. You will then be prompted to connect to the SQL Server instance. Enter localhost\sqlexpress in the **Server name** textbox, select **Windows Authentication** in the **Authentication** drop-down list, and click the **Connect** button.

To continue, please ensure that SQL Server's **Server Authentication mode** is set to **SQL Server and Windows Authentication mode**. This is done by right-clicking on the server in the **Object Explorer** pane and choosing **Properties** in the context menu, as shown in the next screenshot:

The **Server Properties** window will then be displayed. Click on **Security** under the **Select a page** list. The **Server authentication** section will now be displayed on the right-hand side of the window. Select the **SQL Server and Windows Authentication mode** radio button and then click the **OK** button located at the bottom of the window.

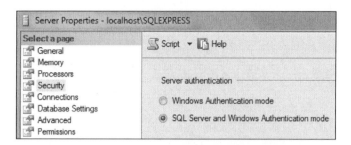

Once you are connected and the authentication mode is properly configured, expand the server icon in **Object Explorer** by clicking on the plus sign and right-click on the `Databases` folder. Choose **New Database** on the context menu that is shown.

The **New Database** dialog window will be displayed, as shown in the next screenshot. Enter **DotNetNuke** as the **Database name** and click the **OK** button. The progress section will display a message letting you know that the process of creating the database is executing. When it has completed, the new database will be listed in the **Object Explorer** pane.

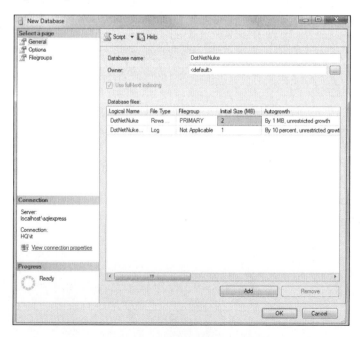

Now expand the `Security` folder shown in the **Object Explorer**. Right-click on the `Logins` folder and choose **New Login** to display the **Login - New** dialog window (shown in the next screenshot). Enter **DotNetNuke** as the login name and select the **SQL Server authentication** radio button. You should now be able to type a password into the **Password** and the **Confirm password** textboxes. Be sure to uncheck the **Enforce password policy** checkbox to prevent the password from expiring and therefore causing the login to fail for this user in future. Now select **DotNetNuke** in the **Default database** drop-down list and click the **OK** button.

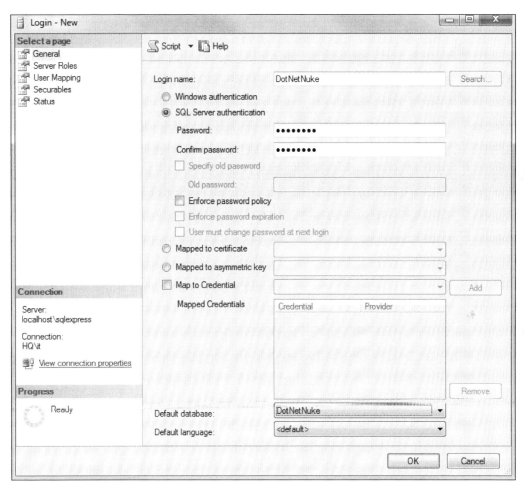

In the **Object Explorer**, expand the **DotNetNuke** database, then the Security folder, and finally select the Users folder. Right-click on the Users folder and choose **New User** to display the **Database User – New** dialog window. Type **DotNetNuke** into the **User name** and **Login name** textboxes as shown in the next screenshot. Check the **db_owner** checkbox in the **Database role membership** list. You may now click the **OK** button to complete the setup of your DotNetNuke database.

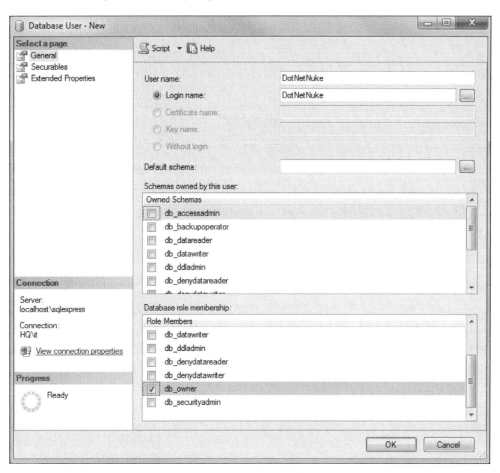

Running the install wizard

Once you have completed the database setup, you are now ready to launch the **DotNetNuke Installation Wizard**. To begin the wizard, open your browser and navigate to http://localhost/DotNetNuke (if you specified a different name when adding your application, then you would navigate to http://localhost/YouApplicationName). Once the browser has loaded the page, it should look similar to the following screenshot:

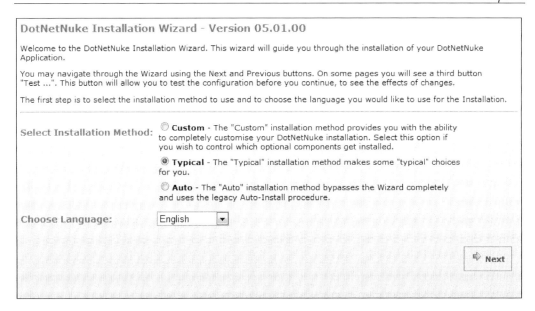

Leave the **Typical** radio button selected and click the **Next** button to continue. In the next screen, you should see the **Checking File Permissions** step (shown in the next screenshot). Go ahead and click the **Test Permissions** button. The installation wizard will now verify that the permissions on the folder configured in the application settings are set correctly. If you have completed the *Setting security permissions* section correctly, then you should receive a **Your site passed the permissions check** message as shown in the next screenshot. If you did receive this message, the wizard will instead show what failed during the check. If this is the case, please refer back to the *Setting security permissions* section and correct the failing items. Otherwise, click on the **Next** button to continue the wizard.

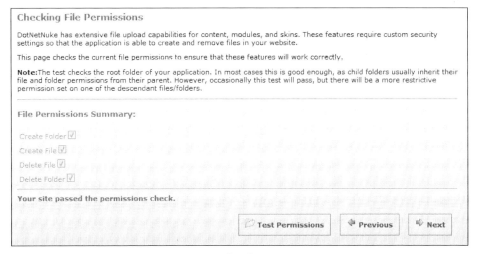

You should now see the **Configure Database Connection** screen as shown in the following screenshot:

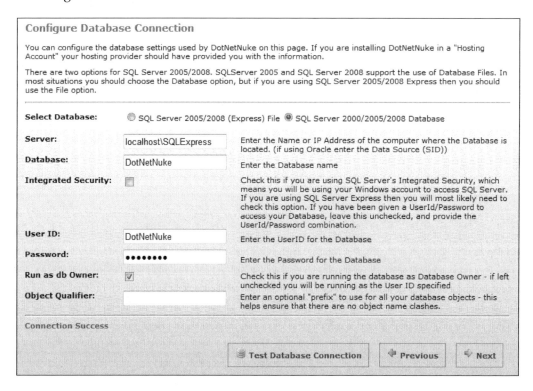

As you can see, this screen provides the ability to configure the connection to the database you would like to use for your DotNetNuke site.

 If you skipped the *Setting up the database* section in order to use the SQL Express setup, then leave the settings at their default and continue to the next step in the installation wizard.

Verify the SQL Server instance name, database name, and the credentials for the SQL user. These settings should appear as they do in the previous screenshot, if you have used the same values as shown in the *Setting up the database* section.

Once you have the proper values entered, click the **Test Database Connection** button. You should then see the **Connection Success** message displayed at the bottom of the screen. Once again, click the **Next** button to continue to the following step in the installation process. The installation wizard should now be executing the SQL scripts that set up the database for use with DotNetNuke.

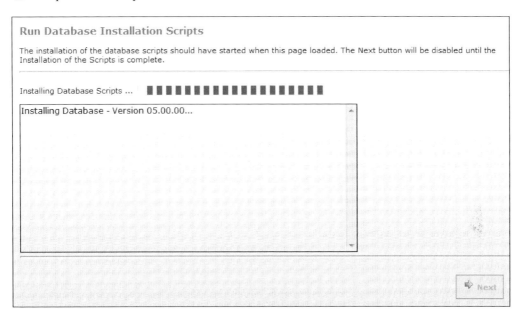

You should see additional status messages in the textbox as portions of the database scripts are completed. The **Next** button will be disabled until all of the scripts have completed.

When enabled, clicking on the **Next** button will display a screen that allows you to configure the host account and SMTP settings for this installation. In the previous versions of DotNetNuke, you were given a default host account with a well-known password, namely a username of host and a password of dnnhost. Obviously, this was not an ideal solution from a security or configuration standpoint. Thankfully, the ability to configure your own host account during installation is now included.

On a similar note, SMTP configuration was not provided during installation and you would have to wait until the portal was created, log in as the default host account, navigate to the **Host Settings** page, and finally configure and test your SMTP settings. As you can see, the new features in the installation wizard are a big improvement from a security perspective, as well as for ease of installation. However, it is still possible to leave the SMTP configuration blank when installing and modifying the settings after the portal is running. These settings can still be viewed or modified by accessing them on the **Host Settings** page.

For those that may need a little background information, **SMTP** stands for **Simple Mail Transfer Protocol** and is the technology used for sending e-mails. This is the same technology and settings that would be used for the "Outgoing Server" while configuring your e-mail client application.

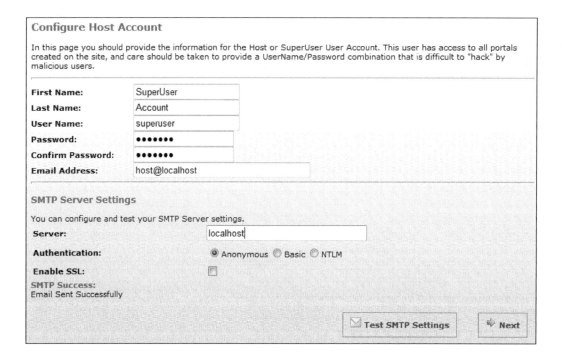

Go ahead and fill out the fields for the host account section with whatever information you like.

 Please note that it is very important that you use a username and password that you will remember. There is no easy way to reset the host account password, in case it is forgotten.

After the host account fields are completed, fill in the name of your SMTP server and select the authentication type you would like to use. A **Test SMTP Settings** button is provided to verify that the settings you have supplied are indeed correct. When you are satisfied with the information entered on this screen, click the **Next** button once again.

You are now viewing a form that allows you to configure the default or "Host" portal that the installation wizard will create to complete the installation. This form is similar to the previous screen; however, the account you are now configuring is the **Administrator** account on the default portal only. The previous screen was the **SuperUser** account that is an administrator on all portals on this installation.

The **Portal Administrator** section is yet another new feature added to the installation wizard that improves the security and configuration of the initial DotNetNuke installation. Similar to the host account, in previous versions of DotNetNuke, there was a default administrator account created with a well-known username (admin) and password (dnnadmin). This would then need to be changed once the portal was created.

It is important to use an easy to remember, yet secure, username and password combination for the **Portal Administrator** account. With that said, in case you forget the password for the administrator account, it can be reset using a **SuperUser** account.

Fill out the form to set up the **Portal Administrator** account; the username and preferably the password should be different from the host account created on the previous screen.

The next section of this screen is the **Portal Properties** (shown in the next screenshot) that is used to configure the title for the default portal. There is also a **Template** drop-down list that will have **Default Website** selected by default. This represents the default template for a DotNetNuke portal and will create one page named **Home** and place the standard content on the page.

DotNetNuke provides the ability to create portal templates to control the pages and content that is created during the portal setup. However, the creation and use of these templates is outside the scope of this discussion.

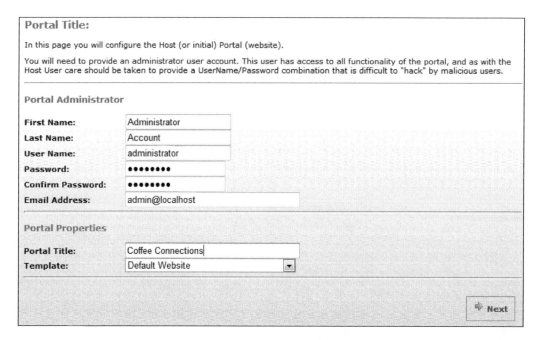

Portal Title:

In this page you will configure the Host (or initial) Portal (website).

You will need to provide an administrator user account. This user has access to all functionality of the portal, and as with the Host User care should be taken to provide a UserName/Password combination that is difficult to "hack" by malicious users.

Portal Administrator

First Name:	Administrator
Last Name:	Account
User Name:	administrator
Password:	••••••••
Confirm Password:	••••••••
Email Address:	admin@localhost

Portal Properties

Portal Title:	Coffee Connections
Template:	Default Website

➪ Next

When satisfied with the information provided on this form, click the **Next** button to be taken to the final screen in the installation wizard.

You will now see the **Congratulations** screen that simply informs you that you have successfully installed DotNetNuke. Click the **Finished (Goto Site)** button to be taken to your newly-created DotNetNuke portal.

You will now be presented with the default page and content created by the **Default Website** template that was selected in the installation wizard. Well done, you have completed the installation of your DotNetNuke web site!

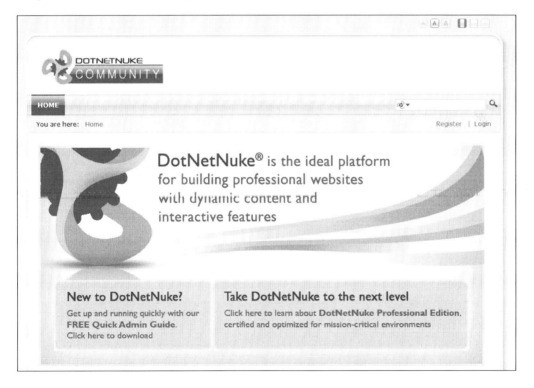

Notice that you are not logged in to the site, and would need to click the **Login** button to access the administration section of the site. You could use either the host or portal administrator account that you set up during installation. In later chapters, we will discuss what options are available depending on which account you use to log in to the site.

Upgrading

The DotNetNuke team has put a vast amount of effort into providing an easy way to keep your site up-to-date with the latest release of the software. Overall they have done an excellent job in doing so; however, there are some inherent challenges with any software upgrades. These challenges are further complicated by the fact that third-party software can be integrated into DotNetNuke. So, it is very important that you take the necessary steps to prepare your site to be upgraded. In this section, we will outline a general process for upgrading your site to a new version of DNN.

In addition to the information in this section, you are strongly urged to check the DotNetNuke website for the most current information on the recommended process to perform an upgrade. Additionally, you can find an *Installation Guide* in the 05.00.00 downloads on the CodePlex site that may contain some helpful information regarding the upgrade.

Upgrading the checklist

The following is a list of a few items to keep in mind while you prepare your site for the upgrade process:

- **Any modifications you have made to the core DotNetNuke files will be overwritten during the upgrade process**. You would then need to redo any changes you had made to any of the files. This is the main reason why making any changes to the files provided by DotNetNuke is strongly discouraged. Maintaining changes to the core can become extremely challenging as new versions are released.

- **Compatibility of installed modules needs to be verified before you upgrade your site.** While most commercial module vendors generally release updates to their modules to maintain compatibility with the latest versions of DotNetNuke, it may take them some time to do so after a new version is released. The delay can be drastically increased for free or open source modules, and sometimes the developer(s) may not update the module at all. This makes it very important to check with the vendor or developer of any third-party modules you use to verify compatibility, before you proceed with the upgrade process.

- **Always, and I mean ALWAYS ensure you make usable backups of your site files and database before you upgrade!** It is vitally important that you make a complete backup of your site and database before you upgrade your site. In this way, no matter what happens, you can always restore your site to the exact state it was before attempting the upgrade. One of the most important files to back up in this process is the `web.config` file. In previous versions of DotNetNuke, you were required to migrate certain settings contained in this file to the new version of the file provided with the upgrade. Thanks to a new feature, these settings will be automatically merged with the new version of `web.config` for you during the upgrade. However, this feature does not diminish the need to make a complete backup of the site. Being diligent in this particular process can be a saving grace, if something goes wrong during an upgrade.

If you are upgrading a site other than a local development or testing site, then you will want to modify a setting before performing the upgrade. The **AutoUpgrade** option located in the **appSettings** section of `web.config` should be set to `false` for any site that may be accessed by anyone other than the individual performing the upgrade. This will prevent the next user browsing the site from being automatically redirected to the upgrade wizard. Instead, you will need to manually navigate to the install page. The path to the page is `/Install/Install.aspx`. If the URL of your site is `http://localhost/DotNetNuke`, the full path to the install page would be `http://localhost/DotNetNuke/Install/Install.aspx`.

Backing up your database

SQL Management Studio makes it fairly straightforward to back up and restore databases that are attached to the server.

 If you have decided to use the SQL Express feature of attaching a database file located in the App_Data folder of your site, then following the steps to back up your site will also create a backup of your database.

We will provide an overview of the process to create a backup of a manually attached database. However, for information on restoring the database or more detailed information on the backup process, please refer to the SQL Server documentation.

 Considering the critical nature of the backup and restore process we do suggest that you are comfortable with your understanding of how SQL Server handles the backup and restore process before you perform an upgrade.

To begin the process of backing up your database, first launch the SQL Management Studio. You will then be prompted to connect to a database engine. You can enter localhost\sqlexpress for the server address, verify that **Windows Authentication** is selected in the **Authentication** drop-down list and click the **Connect** button.

Expand the **localhost\sqlexpress** node in **Object Explorer**, then expand the **Databases** node, and finally select your database. In the screenshot, our database name is **DotNetNuke**.

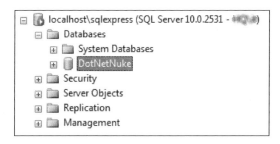

Right-click on your database and choose **Tasks | Backup** to display the **Back Up Database** dialog window.

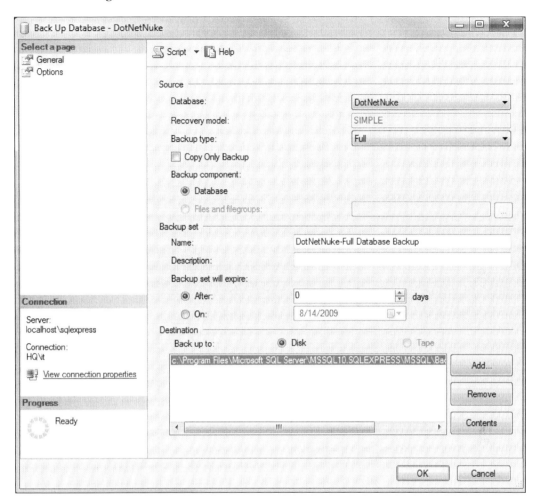

Verify the **Destination** of the backup file and be sure it is in a memorable location in case you need to restore from the file. Then click the **OK** button to begin the backup. You will then see the **Progress** area display an **executing** animation. Once the backup is complete, a dialog will be displayed informing you that the backup has been created successfully.

Backing up your DotNetNuke files

It is a common practice and you are strongly encouraged to make a copy of the folder that contains your DotNetNuke site before installing a new version of DNN or even a module. In this way if you encounter issues with the installation, you can always rollback to the copy of the folder that you made. This can be done by creating a zip file of the folder or even simply copying the folder to a different location. I typically find it easier to simply right-click on the folder and choose **Send To | Compressed (zipped) Folder**. Once you have tested the site and are satisfied that the install was successful, you can delete the copy.

Performing the upgrade

Perform the following steps for upgrading:

1. Once you have completed the backup steps mentioned in the previous sections and verified the latest information regarding upgrading, you may begin the actual upgrade process. As mentioned at the beginning of this chapter, there are several download packages available for DotNetNuke. To simplify the process of upgrading DNN, ensure that you have downloaded the Version Upgrade package. Using this package allows the site to be upgraded in a few simple steps. Extract the package to a temporary location (that is, C:\Temp\DNN Upgrade).

2. Select all of the files and folders in the folder that was created while extracting the upgrade package. This can be done easily by holding the *Ctrl* key and pressing the *A* key on your keyboard.

3. Copy the files to your clipboard by holding down the *Ctrl* key and pressing the *C* key on your keyboard.

4. Navigate to the folder where DotNetNuke is installed.

5. Paste the files into the folder by holding down the *Ctrl* key and pressing the *V* key on your keyboard.

6. During this process of pasting these files and folders, you will be prompted to confirm the replacement of several folders. Check the **Do this for all current items** checkbox and click **Yes**.

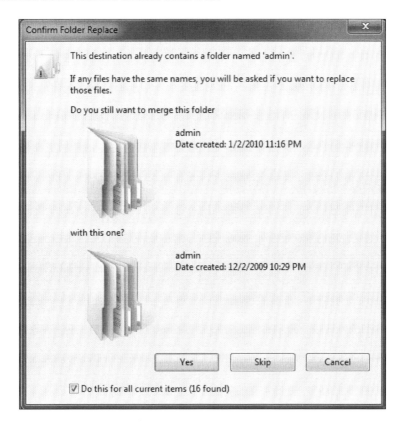

7. You will also be prompted to replace several files located in these folders. Similar to the prompt regarding the replacement of folders, be sure and click the **Do this for the next** *(number of)* **conflicts** checkbox. Then click the **Copy and Replace** option.

8. Once the files and folders have been successfully copied to the DotNetNuke installation folder, simply navigate to the site to begin the upgrade wizard.

 Note that if you have turned off the **AutoUpgrade** feature, you will need to navigate directly to the install page as stated in the *Upgrading the checklist* section of this chapter.

9. Once the upgrade has been completed, you will be presented with a link to navigate back to your portal.

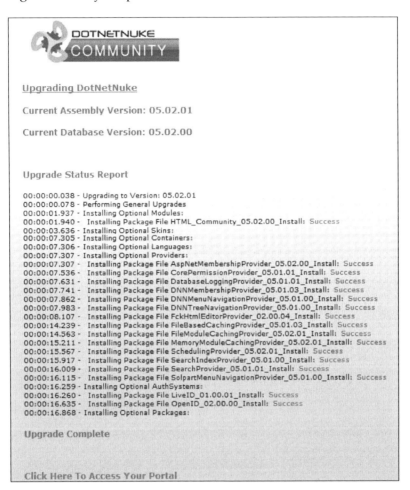

The DotNetNuke installation should now be successfully upgraded. After completing the upgrade, we recommend that you take some time to browse through the site to verify that all of the pages are functioning as expected.

Summary

In this chapter, we have seen how easy it is to set up a DotNetNuke site on your local workstation. This process has become much easier with each release of DNN, and we expect to continue to see improvements in this area as new versions are released. Some of the new features included in the installation wizard allow you to get your site up and running without needing to modify additional settings once the portal is installed. The ability to configure the host account, admin user account, and the SMTP settings during the installation are excellent examples of some of the advances of the installation wizard that are very helpful.

3
Users, Roles, and Pages

One of the most important aspects of running a DotNetNuke portal is trying to figure out how to administer the portal. From adding modules to working with users, it may take a while before you have mastered all the administration tasks associated with running a portal. The next few chapters are designed to give you a general understanding of how things work, and also to act as a reference for the tasks you have to perform only on an occasional basis. This chapter will familiarize you with managing users and pages within your portal.

DotNetNuke uses a few terms that may be unfamiliar at first. For example, the term "portal" can be used interchangeably with the more common term "site". Similarly, the terms "tab" and "page" may be used interchangeably within the context of DotNetNuke. Further explanation of these terms will be provided later in this book. However, for now, knowing that they are interchangeable will help to understand the topics that we will discuss.

When you are done with this chapter, you will possess a better understanding of the following areas:

- Creating and modifying user accounts
- How user accounts tie into the security of your site
- What DotNetNuke pages are and how to create and administer them
- How to structure your site using pages
- The new Membership Provider Model

User accounts

If you are used to working within a network environment, or have worked with different portals in the past, then you are probably comfortable with the term "users". For those of us who may not be very familiar with this term, can think of a website that you have registered with in the past. When the registration had been completed, a user account was provided to you. This account lets you return to the site and log in as a recognized user.

Everything that takes place on your portal revolves around users and user accounts. Whether users are required to register in order to use your services (such as a member site) or only a few user accounts are required to manage the content, functionality, and layout of your site, you will need to understand how to create and manage user accounts. Let's start with a general description of a user, and then you will see how to create and manage your users. In order to work through the examples, you will need to bring up your portal and sign in as an administrator account, such as the one created during the initial portal installation described in the previous chapter.

Who is a user?

The simplest definition of a **user** is an individual who consumes the services that your portal provides. However, a user can take on many different roles, from a visitor who is just browsing (unregistered user) or a person who registers to gain access to your services (registered user), to a specialized member of the site such as a content editor, to the facilitator (administrator or host) who is responsible for the content, functionality, and design of your portal. The difference between an administrator account and a host (or super user) account will be explained later in detail. For now, we will focus on the administrator account that is associated with a single portal. Everything in DotNetNuke revolves around the user, so before we can do anything else, we need to learn a little about user accounts.

Creating user accounts

Before you create user accounts, you should decide and configure how users will be able to register on the site. You can choose from the following four different types of registrations:

- None
- Private
- Public (default)
- Verified

To set the registration type for your portal, go to the **Site Settings** link found in the **ADMIN** menu, as shown in the following screenshot:

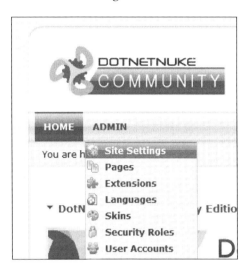

The **User Registration** section can be found under **Advanced Settings | Security Settings**, as shown in the next screenshot:

Many sections within DotNetNuke may be collapsed or hidden by default. To view these sections, you will need to expand them by clicking the '+' in front of them.

The type of registration you use depends on how you will be using your portal. The following table gives a brief explanation of the different **User Registration** types:

Registration setting	Description
None	Setting the user registration as **None** will remove the **Register** link from your portal. In this mode, users can only be added by the administrator or host users. Thanks to the new features in DotNetNuke 5, users who have been given the proper permissions can also manage user accounts. This allows the administrator or host users to delegate account management to other individuals with the proper access. If you plan to have all sections of your site available to everyone (including unregistered users), then selecting **None** as your registration option is a good choice.
Private	If you select **Private**, then the **Register** link will reappear. After users fill out the registration form, they will be informed that their request for registration will be reviewed by the administrator. The administrator will decide whom to give access to the site. Unless an administrator approves (authorizes in DNN terms) a user, they will not be able to log in.
Public	**Public** is the default registration for a DotNetNuke portal. When this is selected, the users will be able to register for your site by entering the required information. Once the registration form is filled out, they will be given access to the site and can log in without requiring any action on the part of an administrator.
Verified	If you select **Verified** as your registration option, then the users will be sent an e-mail with a verification code, once they fill out the required information. This ensures that the e-mail address they enter in the registration process is valid. The first time they sign in, they will be prompted for the verification code. Alternatively, they can click on the **Verification** link in the e-mail sent to them. After they have been verified, they will need to type in only their login name and password to gain access to the site. Please note that proper SMTP configuration is required to ensure delivery of the verification e-mails.

Setting required registration fields

The administrator has the ability to decide what information the user will be required to enter when registering. If you are logged in as an administrator, then you can accomplish this through a combination of **User Settings** and **Profile Properties**.

 A user who is given the appropriate permissions can also modify these settings; however, this requires a few additional configuration steps that we will not cover in this section.

To manage the **Profile Properties** for your site, select the **ADMIN | User Accounts** link. The **User Accounts** section appears as shown in the following screenshot:

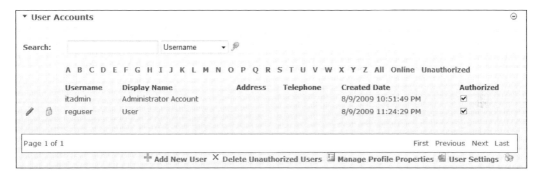

In the preceding screen, select **Manage Profile Properties**, either by selecting the link at the bottom of the module container or by selecting the link in the **Action** menu — the menu that pops up when you point on the drop-down button adjacent to the module title, **User Accounts** (more information on **Action** menu is provided later). When you select this link, you will be redirected to a screen (see the next screenshot) that displays a list of the currently configured **Profile Properties**.

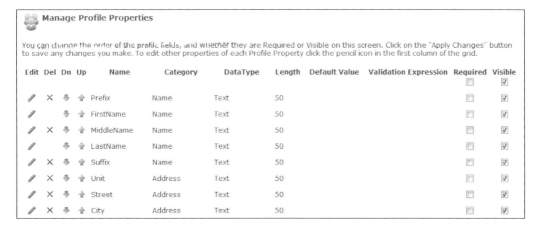

You can manage some attributes of the **Profile Properties** from within this screen. For instance, you can delete a property by clicking on the 'X' icon in the second column. Alternatively, you can change the display order of the properties by clicking on one of the **Dn** or **Up** icons in the third and fourth columns. If you change the order this way, make sure you click the **Apply Changes** button at the bottom of the page to save any changes. Your changes will be lost if you leave this screen without clicking the **Apply Changes** button.

If you want even more control, then you can edit a single property by clicking on the pencil icon in the first column.

 You will see this icon extensively in the DNN user interface. It allows you to **Edit/Modify** the item it is associated with.

You can also add a new property by selecting the **Add New Profile Property** action from the **Action** menu. In either case, you will be redirected to another page, where you can enter information about the property. You will be redirected to the **Add New Property Details** page, as shown in the following screenshot:

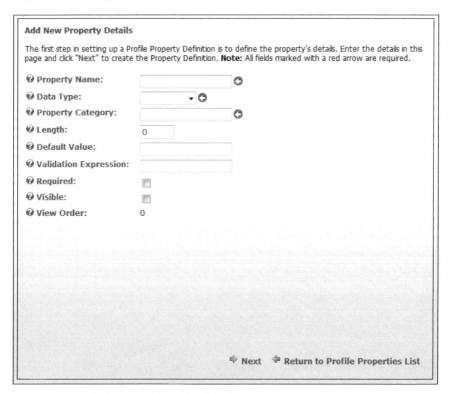

Note that if you are editing an existing property, the **Property Name** field cannot be changed, so make sure you get it right the first time. If you need to change the **Property Name**, then you will need to delete and recreate the property. Most of these fields are self explanatory, but we will describe a few of these fields.

The **Visible** checkbox controls whether the user can see the property. You can hide a property from the user by making sure that this checkbox is left unchecked—the important thing to remember is that the administrator can still see this property. This feature allows an administrative account to record private confidential information about a user.

The **Required** checkbox controls whether the user is required to enter information for this property. If it is set, the user will not be able to proceed without entering anything, although there are some settings that affect how this works in practice.

After completing this form, you will need to click the **Next** link to be taken to the **Manage Localization** screen (shown in the next screenshot). It is recommended that this feature is used; however, if you plan to support only the default language, you are able to click the **Return to Profile Properties List** link instead to skip this screen.

These fields allow you to modify the text displayed to users based on the language settings of the portal. The information entered into these fields will be displayed to the user when managing their profile. It is recommended that values are provided for the default language at a minimum.

Manage Localization

The next step is to manage the localization of this property. Select the language you wish to update, add text or modify the existing text and click "Save Localized Text"

- Choose Language: English (United States)
- Property Name:
- Property Help:

- Required Error Message:
- Validation Error Message:
- Category Name:

          Save Localized Text

In addition to configuring the **Profile Properties** for the site, there are also some **User Settings** that control the registration process. On the **User Accounts** screen, you can access the **User Settings** by clicking on the link at the bottom of the pane, or the link in the **Action** menu. This will redirect you to the **User Settings** page that appears as shown in the following screenshot:

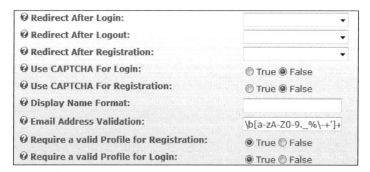

There are a lot of settings on this page. We will be focusing on this discussion in the settings that relate to registration, towards the bottom of the page. In our discussion of the **Profile Properties**, we indicated that you can set some properties to 'required', by checking the **Required** checkbox. In the normal registration, only the information required for validating the user's credentials is collected. The **User Registration** page appears as shown in the following screenshot:

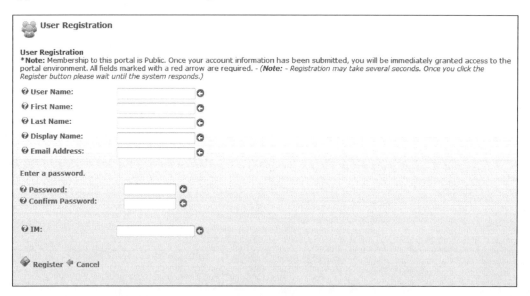

If the **Require a valid Profile for Registration** radio button is marked as **True**, then the registration page also contains the list of **Profile Properties** and the registration will not be complete unless all the required properties have valid values.

Furthermore, if the **Require a valid Profile for Login** radio button is marked as **True**, then a user will be required to update his or her profile on login if it is no longer valid. This can happen if an administrator decides to make a profile property required after users have already registered, or if the administrator decides to add a new required property.

Managing your own profile

When you log in to the portal, you will see the **Display Name** entered during registration, located just below the search bar of the current page (if you are using the default skin). Click this link to bring you to the **Manage Profile** page that allows any registered and logged-in user to manage his/her own profile. The **Manage Profile** page appears as shown:

All users can access this screen in a similar way. There are four tabs (hyperlinks) at the top of this screen. A user can manage his/her own profile properties by clicking on the **Manage Profile** link. You will be directed to a page similar to the following screenshot:

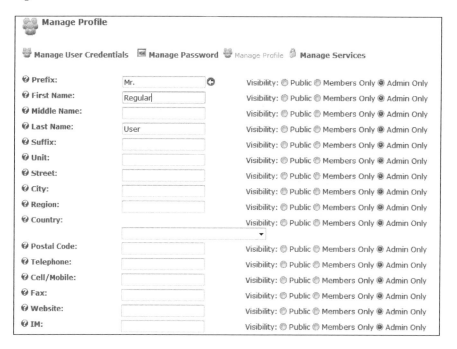

Here, the red arrow icon indicates that a property is required, while the **Visibility** radio buttons indicate who can view this profile property. By default, this is set to **Admin Only**, but users can allow their profile information to be available to other users (**Members Only**) or all users, including unauthorized users (**Public**).

Registering a user manually

As we discussed earlier, you can set your portal registration to **None**. This will remove the **Register** link from your site. So, the only way to add users to your portal is to register them manually. An administrator can also add users manually even if the portal registration is set to **Public** or any other allowed value.

To do this, go to **ADMIN | User Accounts** on the main menu or you can click the **Users** link in the **Common Tasks** section of the control panel. This will bring you to the **User Accounts** screen. There are actually two ways to add a new user from this screen. You can select **Add New User** from the drop-down menu on the left-hand side of the module or click on the **Add New User** link at the bottom of the module, as shown in the following screenshot:

We will be setting up a user to help us administer the Coffee Connections site. We fill in the required information and click on the **Add New User** link.

If the **Notify** checkbox is selected, an e-mail will be sent to the specified e-mail address upon creation of the account. Also, note that if the **Random Password** checkbox is selected, DotNetNuke will generate a password for the account. When using the **Random Password** feature, make sure to select the **Notify** checkbox to ensure that the password will be sent to the user during account creation. This is very useful when creating user accounts manually. Otherwise, you must enter a password for each account you create. This, again, shows the importance of properly configuring the SMTP settings, which we discussed earlier.

When we are done, we will test the account we just created. To do this, we need to log off from our administrator account by clicking on the **Logout** link in the upper right-hand portion of the current page. Then click on the **Login** link. Enter the **Username** and **Password** of the user we just created. You will notice that while you are logged in as this user, you lose access to all the updating functionality that the administrator account possesses. Your screen will now appear as shown in the following screenshot:

The ability to update the portal is not available to our new user because he/she does not have the authority to make the changes. We certainly wouldn't want any user updating the content or the settings on the site. In other words, they do not belong to the right security role.

Understanding DotNetNuke roles and role groups

We just discussed how to add a user to your site. But are all users created equal? To understand how users are allowed to interact with the portal, we will need to take a look at what a **role** is and how it factors into the portal. There are plenty of real-world examples of roles we can look at. A police station, for example, can have sergeants, patrol cops, and detectives, and with each position come different responsibilities and privileges. In a police station, there are multiple people filling those positions (roles) with each of those belonging to the same position (role) sharing the same set of responsibilities and privileges.

Roles in our portal work the same way. Roles are set up to divide the responsibilities needed to run your portal, as well as to provide different content to different groups of users of your portal. If we refer to the user stories we created in *Chapter 1, What is DotNetNuke*, we will see that one of them falls into the area of users and roles.

We want our portal to be easy for the administrators to manage. To do this, we will need to settle on the different user roles needed for our site. To determine this, we first need to decide on the different types of users who will access the portal. We will detail these user types in the following list:

- **Administrator**: The administrators will have very high security. They will be able to modify, delete, or move anything on the site. They will be able to add and delete users and control all security settings. (This role comes built-in with DotNetNuke.) The default administrator account is created during the creation of the portal.

- **Home Page Admin**: The home page admins will have the ability to modify only the information on the home page. They will be responsible for changing what users see when they first access your site. (We will be adding this role.)

- **Forum Admin**: The forum moderators will have the ability to monitor and modify posts in your forum. They will have the ability to approve or disapprove messages posted. (We will be adding this role.)

- **Registered User**: The registered users will be able to post messages in the forum and be able to access sections of the site set aside for registered users only. (This role comes built into DotNetNuke; however, we would need to provide the proper permissions to this role to perform the mentioned tasks.)

- **Unauthenticated User**: The unauthenticated user is the most basic of all the user types. Any person browsing your site will fall under this category, until they have successfully logged in to the site. This user type will be able to browse certain sections of your portal, but will be restricted from posting in the forum and will not be allowed in the **Registered Users Only** section. (This role comes built into DotNetNuke; however, we would need to provide the proper permissions to this role to perform the mentioned tasks.)

Once you formulate the different user roles that will access the site, you will need to restrict users' access. For example, we only want the **Home Page Admin** to be able to edit items on the home page. To accomplish this, DotNetNuke uses role-based security. Role-based security allows you to give access to portions of your website based on what role the user belongs to. User-based security is also available per page or content section of the portal. However, the benefit of using a role-based security method is that you only have to define the access privileges for a role once. Then you just need to add users to that role and they will possess the privileges that the role defines. The following diagram gives you an idea of how this works:

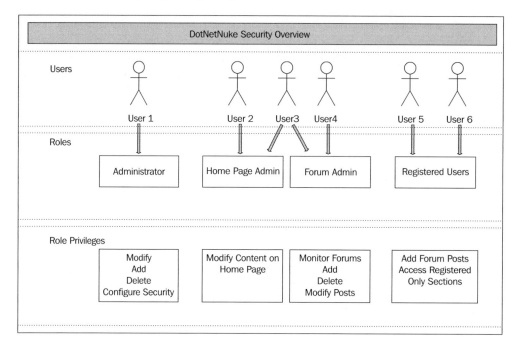

Looking at the diagram, we notice two things:

- Users can be assigned to more than one role
- More than one user can be assigned to a single role

This gives us great flexibility when deciding on the authorization that users will possess in our portal.

To create the roles we have detailed, sign in with an administrator account, and select **ADMIN | Security Roles** on the main menu or click the **Roles** link in the **Common Tasks** section of the control panel. This is available on the top of every DNN page for authorized users. You might need to click the double down arrows on the top-right of the page to maximize the panel. The **Security Roles** page appears as shown in the following screenshot:

Notice that DotNetNuke comes with three roles already built into the system: the **Administrators** role (which we have been using), the **Registered Users** role, and the **Subscribers** role. Before we jump right into creating the role, let us first discuss the role group feature of DotNetNuke, as we will be using this feature when we create our roles.

A **role group** is a collection of roles used, mainly, in large sites with a large number of roles, as a way of managing the roles more effectively. For the site we are building, the benefit of using role groups will be minimal. However, in order to demonstrate how to use them, we will create one for our administrative roles.

While on the **Security Roles** page, click the **Add New Role Group** link located below the list of roles. This will present us with the **Edit Role Group** page containing two form fields.

- **Group Name**: Simply enter a name for the group of roles. In our case, we will enter **Administrative Roles** in this field.

- **Description**: Use this field to provide more information about the roles that are contained in this group. Let's enter **Roles used to administer portions of the site**.

Once these fields are filled out, click the **Update** link at the bottom of this page. A **Filer By Role Group** drop-down list should now be displayed above the list of roles on the **Security Roles** page. If you select the **Administrative Roles** group that we just created, two noticeable things happen on this page. Firstly, the list of roles become empty as no roles are currently assigned to this role group. Secondly, an edit (pencil) icon and a delete (red cross **X**) icon now appear next to the drop-down list. These icons can be used to update or remove any custom role groups that exist on the site. These red '**X**' icons are standard icons used throughout DotNetNuke to represent the ability to delete/remove items.

Now that we have created our role group, we want to create the role for **Home Page Admin**. To do this, you again have two choices. Either select **Add New Role** from the dropdown in the upper left, or click on the **Add New Role** link. This will bring up the **Edit Security Roles** page, as shown in the next screenshot. We will use this page to create the **Home Page Admin** role that we need.

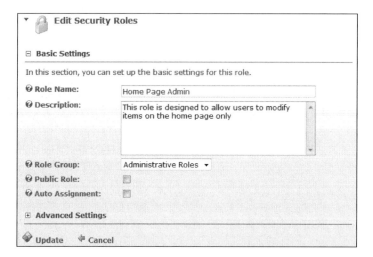

The **Basic Settings** shown in the screenshot are as follows:

- **Role Name**: Make the name of your role short, but descriptive. The name should attempt to convey its purpose.

- **Description**: Here you may detail the responsibilities of the role.

- **Role Group**: Set this field to the **Administrative Roles** group that we created earlier.

- **Public Role**: Checking this will give registered users of your site the ability to sign up for this role themselves. We will be creating a **Newsletter** role and will demonstrate how this works when it is created.

- **Auto Assignment**: If this is checked, users will automatically be assigned to this role as soon as they register for your portal.

CAUTION

Do not check the **Public Role** and **Auto Assignment** checkboxes, unless you are sure. Checking these options would allow all users of the site to become members of the associated role, which would grant them the privileges assigned to the role.

As we want to decide who will be able to modify our home page, we will leave both of these unchecked. To save the settings, click on the **Update** link.

The **Advanced Settings** section allows you to set up a fee for certain security roles. We will not be configuring any of these settings for this particular exercise. However, we will briefly discuss how these settings can be used in *Assigning security roles to users* section.

Now to complete the roles that we will require for Coffee Connections, we will add two more security roles.

The first role will be called **Newsletter**. We will be using this role to allow users to sign up for the newsletter we will be hosting at the Coffee Connections site. Set up the security role with the following information:

- **Role Name**: Newsletter
- **Description**: **Allows users to register for the Coffee Connections Newsletter**
- **Role Group**: Leave this as the default **<Global Roles>** as it is not going to be used to grant administrative rights to its members
- **Public Role**: Yes (checked)
- **Auto Assignment**: No (unchecked)

Click on the **Update** link to save this role.

The second role will be called **Forum Admin**. We will be using this role to administer the forums at the Coffee Connections site. Set up the security role with the following information:

- **Role Name**: **Forum Admin**
- **Description**: **Allows user to administer Coffee Connections Forum**
- **Role Group**: **Administrative Roles**
- **Public Role**: No (unchecked)
- **Auto Assignment**: No (unchecked)

Click on the **Update** link to save this role.

The security roles, by themselves, do not determine the security on your portal; you would need to assign the appropriate privileges to each role. As the diagram showed, users and roles work together to form the basis of the security in your site, based on the privileges assigned to the roles.

Assigning security roles to users

Security roles can be assigned to users by an administrator or any user given edit access to the **User Accounts** management section. Additionally, if **Public Role** is checked for any role, it can be assigned by the users themselves. To show you how users can sign up for security roles, log out as administrator and log in as our sample user, **JonnyA**.

When signed in as **JonnyA**, in order to modify your user information, click on the user name in the upper right-hand corner of the portal. This will bring you to the **Manage Profile** screen shown in the next screenshot. This is the same as the screen we looked at, when signed in as the administrator previously; however, this time it is displaying information associated with **JonnyA**, the currently logged-in user.

Note that when logged in as a regular user, there is no information on the right-hand side of the page. Only an administrator can see this information. A user can change his/her password by clicking on the **Manage Password** tab. They can manage their profile by clicking on the **Manage Profile** tab (refer to the following screenshot), or they can unregister from the site by clicking on the **UnRegister** link.

The **Manage Services** tab allows the user to manage the public security roles available to them. These are the roles for which we checked the **Public Role** checkbox. To subscribe to the role, click on the **Subscribe** link, as shown in the next screenshot:

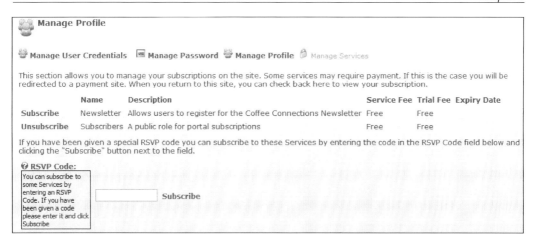

After you have subscribed to a service, you can unsubscribe by clicking on the **Unsubscribe** link. As security roles, like **Home Page Admin**, allow the user to modify the portal, they should not be assigned in this manner. As the administrator of the site, we want the ability to decide who is assigned to this role. To do this, we will again need to sign off as **JonnyA** and sign in back as an administrator.

Once logged in, select **ADMIN | Security Roles** on the main menu or you may use the **Roles** link in the **Common Tasks** section of the control panel at the top of the page. Once there, click the pencil icon next to the **Home Page Admin** security role. Click on the **Manage Users in this Role** link that is located near the bottom of this screen. You will then be presented with the **User Roles** administration page, which is shown in the following screenshot:

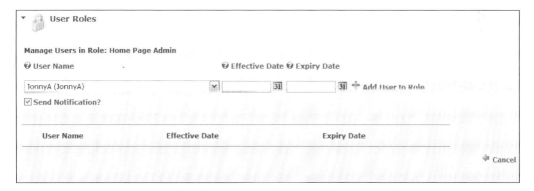

To add a user to a role, select them from the **User Name** drop-down list. If you would like the role to expire after a specific date, you may enter a date in the **Expiry Date** textbox or click on the **Calendar** link to select a date from a calendar. In addition to expiring a user's membership to a role, you can also use the **Effective Date** to specify when to begin the user's membership in the role. For example, this feature may be useful for creating an employee's account before their hire date. When you are done, click on the **Add User to Role** link to add the role to the user.

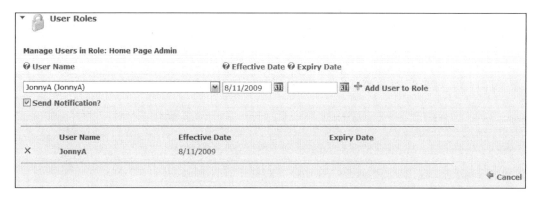

You can add as many users to the role as you wish. To remove a role from a user, click on the delete icon '**X**' (see the preceding screenshot) next to the user's name. Note that the delete icon may not be visible if a user cannot be removed from a particular role. For example, the portal admin account cannot be removed from the administrator's role.

If the **Send Notification** checkbox is checked, then the portal will send an e-mail notification to the users when they are added or removed from the role.

Up to this point, we have added security roles, and added users to roles, both as an administrator and by allowing users to add themselves through membership services. However, the security role privileges (or authorizations) still need to be set. To do this, we will introduce you to the page (also referred to as a tab) architecture of DotNetNuke. In the process, we will show you how to add security roles to sections of our portal.

Role advanced settings

Depending on what you are offering on your portal, you can ask for a fee for a user to register for your portal or just to access particular sections. To enable this feature, the **Payment Processor** section of the **Site Settings** page must be configured. To do this, make sure you are logged in as an administrator, and click on the **Site Settings** item under the **ADMIN** menu.

On the **Site Settings** page, expand **the Advanced Settings** section and then expand the **Payment Settings** section. Here you will find the following fields:

- **Currency**: This will determine the currency used when users make payments through the site.

- **Payment Processor**: This is the merchant gateway used to process payments. By default the only choice is PayPal.

- **Processor UserId**: The username, user ID, or e-mail address used to log in to the payment processor. PayPal currently uses an e-mail address.

- **Processor Password**: The password associated with the user ID specified in the previous field.

Once this is configured, navigate back to the **Security Roles** page we used earlier to create our custom roles. One way to do this is to click on the **Roles** link in the **Common Tasks** section of the control panel. Choose a role to modify to require a fee, and click on the edit (pencil) icon next to that role. Now on the **Edit Security Roles** page, expand the **Advanced Settings** section. The following fields will be displayed:

- **Service Fee**: The fee charged to users in this role.

- **Billing Period**: Two fields are associated with this setting. The drop-down list allows you to select from a list of time periods, such as month or year. The textbox is used to specify the number of such periods, for example, 2 months.

- **Trial Fee**: This field works like the **Service Fee**, but can be used to offer a trial at a different rate, allowing for a free trial.

- **Trial Period**: This field works like the **Billing Period**, but can be used to offer a shorter trial period.

- **RSVP Code**: This code can be shared among roles to allow users to subscribe to multiple roles using a single code.

- **RSVP Link**: The link provided here can be sent to users to automatically add them to the associated role(s).

- **Icon**: A specific icon can be provided for each role.

These features allow for several useful scenarios for membership-based sites. Allowing a trial period can be especially helpful when trying to promote the site. When using the **RSVP Link**, be aware that the user using the link must already be logged in to the site or log in to the site from the link. This can be problematic, due to the fact that the page does not inform the user that they need to log in if they have not.

To work around this limitation, you can create a page that shows a message to unauthenticated users informing them to log in to activate their membership. Then modify the link to the new page to include `?rsvp=[RSVPCODE]` where `[RSVPCODE]` is replaced with the code entered in the **RSVP Code** field. This work around is not necessary, but it does make the experience a little more user friendly.

Understanding DotNetNuke pages and tabIDs

As we have been navigating through different pages, you may have noticed that the page address changed; however, this is a bit of an illusion. While browsing through the pages, the page name displayed in the address bar closely resembles the title of the page. For example, while on the home page, the page name in the address bar is `Home.aspx`. This is because DotNetNuke uses dynamic page generation to render the correct information for each page. In a nutshell, the DotNetNuke framework uses the page name displayed in the address bar to determine which information to display.

 You will see that some of the screenshots in this book, as well as other pages on your DotNetNuke portal refer to something called a **tab**. In previous versions of DotNetNuke the word "tab" was used instead of the word "page".

I am sure that in time, all of these references will be changed inside the portal. Until then be aware that the words "tab" and "page" are interchangeable; for instance, the host pages still use the word "tab".

In traditional web applications, pages are created in an application such as FrontPage, Dreamweaver, or Visual Studio.NET. The designer decides where to place the text, inserts images, saves the page, and then posts it on the website. Navigating the traditional web application takes you from one "physical" page to another "physical" page. The following diagram is an example of how a traditional web application would be constructed:

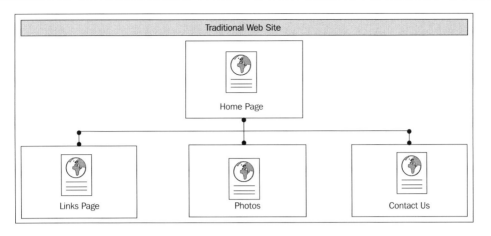

In the DotNetNuke web portal, there is only one "physical" page used in the application. Instead of placing the information directly on the page, DotNetNuke holds the information for each page in the database. When a page is requested on a DNN portal, the application looks in the database to determine what information should be on the page and displays it on `Default.aspx`. The database knows what information to pull from the database by looking at the page name in the URL (for example, `http://localhost/DotNetNuke/Home.aspx`). I can hear you saying "incredible" and I completely agree. This is one of the great features provided by DotNetNuke. The process of determining what page to display based on the page name is handled by the human friendly URL provider. The following image shows an example of how the DotNetNuke web application is constructed, in relation to the traditional web application:

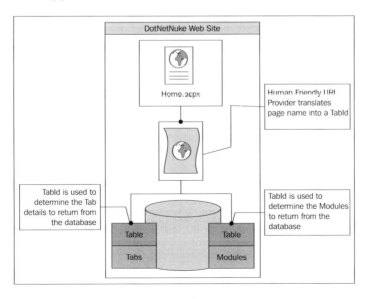

When users navigate to different items on the menu, they will see different information and will be presented with the illusion of multiple physical pages.

When you create new pages in DotNetNuke, you are not only creating the page information for the database, but also building the navigation menu for your site.

To understand the pages and menu structure better, we will create some new pages. To create a new page, we first need to log in as an administrator. When you do so, you will see the **Page Functions** pane at the top of your portal, as shown in the following screenshot:

 In DotNetNuke 5.2 and later versions, you can grant access to security roles other than administrators to manage the pages on the portal, by placing the **Tabs** module on a page and grant users or roles access to it.

To add a page, click on the **Add** link on the left-hand side of the pane. We will be adding a page that will hold our Coffee House search engine, as well as a page that will eventually hold our forums. This **Edit Page** screen is broken up into three different sections, **Basic Settings**, **Copy Page**, and **Advanced Settings**.

We will start with the **Basic Settings**, which appears as shown in the following screenshot:

This is where we enter the following information to set up our page:

- **Page Name**: This is the name that will show up on the menu. You should keep this name short, in order to save space on the menu.

- **Page Title**: This is used to display the name of the page on the Internet Explorer title bar. This can be more descriptive than the page name. If this field is left blank, it will automatically be filled in with the value entered into the **Page Name** field.

- **Description**: Enter a short description of what the page will be used for. The values in this field are used to populate the meta description tag that is used by search engines.

- **Keywords**: This section is used to enter keywords that will be picked up by search engines.

- **Parent Page**: As we discussed earlier, this information not only creates a page dynamically, but is also used to create your site menu. If you would like this page to be positioned under another page in the menu, then select the parent page from the drop-down list.

- **Insert Page**: This selection determines where the page will be placed in the site navigation menu. The page can be inserted **Before** or **After** the **Parent Page** selected. The **Add to End** selection inserts the page as the last page in the menu.

- **Template Folder**: This drop-down list lets you specify a folder to look for page templates.

- **Page Template**: Page templates allow you to save the configuration of a page as a template. Then it can be used to create copies of the saved page by selecting the template when you create a new page. The **Default** template is provided by DotNetNuke and creates a page with a single **HTML** module already added to the page.

- **Include In Menu?**: Uncheck this option to prevent the page from being displayed in the site navigation menu. Administrators, or users granted access to the **Tabs** module, will be able to see and modify hidden pages using the **Tabs** module or the **Pages** administration page. This can be useful if you would like to navigate to a page in a non-traditional way. For example, you can add a link to specific page using the **Links** module that we will discuss in *Chapter 4, Standard DotNetNuke Modules*.

- **Permissions/View Page**: Roles or users that are selected in this column will have the ability to view the page. This means that only those roles or users who have been checked will be able to see this page. If you are not in one of these roles, or your account is not specified, then you will not see the page. This can be used to restrict portions of your portal to certain groups or people. Clicking the permission a second time will display a red circle with a '**X**' to explicitly deny the permission for the associated role or user.

- **Permissions/Edit Page**: Roles or users that are selected in this column will have the ability to administer this page. This means that a user who belongs to any of the roles or users checked will have the ability to edit, modify, and delete information on this page. Remember these privileges apply to this page only. Clicking the permission a second time will display a red circle with a '**X**' to explicitly deny the permission for the associated role or user.

Under the **Copy Page** section (refer to the next screenshot), you can select whether you would like to copy information from an existing page to create a new page.

To copy a page, select the page you would like to copy from the drop-down list. This results in a list of the modules on that page. You can select whether to copy each module by checking the checkbox on the left-hand side of the list. You also have the ability to rename the module, or change its title, by changing the text in the textbox. Finally, there are three options that relate to how the module is copied.

- **New**: An empty module of the same type is created on the new page
- **Copy**: An exact duplicate of the module is created on the new page (with a new ID)
- **Reference**: A new instance of the module is created on the new page (with the same ID)

Initially, there appears to be no difference between the last two options as the resulting modules look the same. However, a copied module is not related in any way to the original module, so modifying the contents of a copied module does not change the original module. On the other hand, a referenced module is the *same* content displayed on a *different* page. Changing the content in a referenced module will affect both pages. DotNetNuke's module structure is very flexible, as we will see later.

The **Advanced Settings** section, as shown in the next screenshot, is divided into three subsections, **Appearance**, **Cache Settings**, and **Other Settings**.

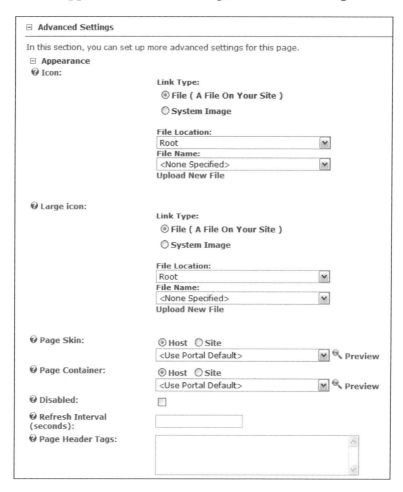

The **Icon** drop-down menu allows you to add an icon next to the page name on the menu. You can see an example of this in the **ADMIN** menu as shown:

In the **ADMIN** menu, the admin page is the parent for **Security Roles**, as well as the others in the list. As you can see, if you use an icon, it will be placed on the left of the page name.

The **Large icon** drop-down list works similar to the **Icon** selection; however, instead of being displayed in the menu, it will be displayed in the container, as long as the container supports an icon.

The next portion of the **Page Functions** pane (see the next screenshot) deals with skinning. For now, we will leave **<User Portal Default>** selected. A full discussion on skinning is beyond the scope of this section; however, a brief description is definitely in order.

The terms **skin** and **container** are used throughout the DotNetNuke platform to describe portions of the "look and feel" of a site. Specifically, skin refers to the overall design (that is, layout, color palette, and so on.) of the site. A **container** is the portion of the design that contains or surrounds a module. The settings in this section allow the skin for the particular page to be set, as well as the default container for each module on the page.

Checking the **Disabled** checkbox (shown in the next screenshot) will allow a page to show up on the menu, but will not allow the page to be shown. A disabled page is used only as a parent page to allow you to navigate to the other pages beneath it. If you click on the menu item that is disabled, nothing will happen and you will remain on the current page.

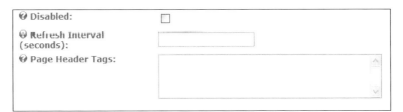

Finally, at the end of this section, you have the ability to add a **Refresh Interval** and **Page Header Tags**. The **Refresh Interval** will automatically refresh this page after the specified time (in seconds). The **Page Header Tags** section allows you to interject meta tags into the header of this page. This is helpful; as DNN builds pages dynamicity, and you can use this to modify the header. We will be leaving these sections blank.

In the **Others Settings** section (shown in the preceding screenshot), you can administer when your page appears and how its menu item is utilized.

- **Secure?**: This determines if the page should be forced to use SSL and will only be available if the **SSL Enabled** checkbox has been checked in the **Site Settings** for the portal.

- **Site Map Priority**: The number entered here ranges from 0.0 to 1.0 and helps the search engine crawlers determine the importance of the given page compared to other pages on the site.

- **Start Date**: This will determine the start date that your page will become visible to your users.

- **End Date**: This will determine the end date that your page will no longer be visible to your users.

- **Link Url**: If you would like a menu item to link to information that already exists on your site, then you can fill in the **Link Url** information. You can link to an external resource (a page or file on another site), a page on your site (an existing "physical" page on your website), or a file on your site. This can be used to incorporate existing ASP or HTML files that you may already have.

To save your settings for this page, click on the **Update** link. When it is complete, you will see your new page on the menu bar. Therefore, when you build a page you are creating both a page to add content to and also an item for your menu.

Administering pages

You have now seen how you can create a page using the **Page Functions** pane. Next you will see how to work with all of your pages to build your menus in a straightforward manner. To get to the **Pages** administration section, select **ADMIN | Pages** on the main menu. Your screen will appear similar to the following screenshot:

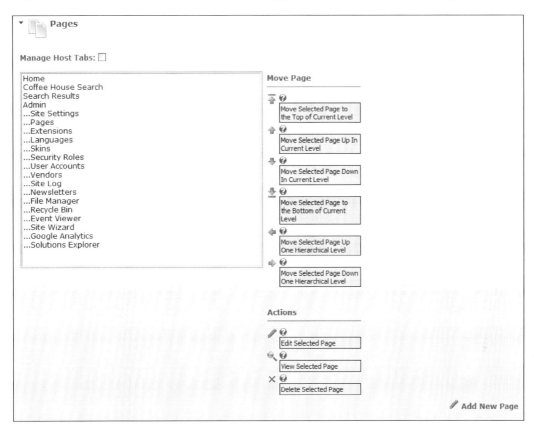

By using the icons on the module displayed here, you will be able to create a new page, edit or view an existing page, or modify where the link to the page appears on your menu. To test this, highlight the **Coffee House Search** menu item and click on the **View Selected Page** icon (magnifying glass). This will bring us back to the page that we just created. Notice that the page is separated into five distinct panes. The **TopPane**, **LeftPane**, **ContentPane**, **RightPane**, and **BottomPane** (you may need to click on the **Layout** radio button above the **Page Functions** pane if the panes are not visible).

Take some time to try out the functionality on this page and get comfortable with how you can edit, move, and modify your pages.

You will notice that the **ADMIN** menu items appear on this page with the other pages on your site. You are able to modify those menu items as you would on any other page. The **Manage Host Tabs** checkbox will change the module to allow you to manage the **HOST** menu items. Please be cautious when modifying the **ADMIN** and **HOST** menu items. If you remove items from these menus, then you will have to recreate these pages yourself. This may prove to be a challenge is some cases.

Summary

In this chapter, we covered the concepts of users, roles, and pages. This should lay a foundation for the rest of the information we will be covering in this book. Most of the concepts we will cover will deal with one or all of these items. In the next chapter, we will introduce you to the concept of modules and discuss the core modules that are prepackaged, as well as all of the other available modules from the DotNetNuke team.

4
Standard DotNetNuke Modules

As we discovered in the last chapter, DotNetNuke dynamically builds its pages using the human friendly URL provider and a tabID to retrieve the information for each page from the database. This includes the modules that are located on each page as well as the content in those modules.

In this chapter, we will cover the following:

- The basic concepts of the module
- How to add modules to a page and how to remove them
- The standard modules that come prepackaged with DNN
- Additional modules provided by the DotNetNuke core team
- An overview of third-party module options

In previous versions of DotNetNuke, the install came preloaded with many different modules available from the DNN team. However, in recent versions, they have decided to install only the core modules that all DNN sites will use. We will outline what modules come preloaded with version 5.2, as well as the other modules available for download from the DNN team. However, some modules (for example, **Blog**, **Forum**, **Gallery**, and so on) are robust enough to justify dedicating an entire chapter, or even book, to the module. Due to this fact, this chapter is best used as a quick reference guide to the modules and will provide an introduction to each module. For detailed information on a particular module, we suggest you consult the corresponding documentation.

DotNetNuke modules

Adding content to DotNetNuke is done using modules. Modules are used as building blocks for your portal. Each module is designed to perform a given task. From providing links, to storing contacts, to adding a simple welcome message for your users, modules are what make your portal buzz. We will first discuss modules in general, discussing the features that all modules have in common. Then we will discuss how to add, delete, and set properties on modules. Finally, we will cover all the standard modules that come prepackaged with DotNetNuke. We will discuss their practical purposes and any administration or modification needed to work with each module.

Adding a module

To begin, make sure you are logged in as administrator and navigate to the Coffee Connections **Search** tab we created earlier. We will then turn our attention to **Control Panel** at the top of the page. We will be using this pane to work with the modules on our page. To demonstrate the common module features, we will be using the **HTML** module. Select **HTML** in the **Module** drop-down list.

The **Pane** dropdown allows you to decide in which pane (or section) of the page you would like to place the module. Our choices for a default skin are **Left**, **Right**, **Content**, **Top**, or **Bottom**. These choices will vary depending on the skin (which, again, defines the overall layout of the page) you are using on your portal. We will be placing the **HTML** module in the **ContentPane**, that all skins must provide. The **Title** box allows you to create a title for the module. The **Visibility** dropdown allows you to decide who is allowed to see the module (same as page or page editors only), and the **Insert** dropdown allows you to tell it where to insert the module into the page (for example, on top or below other modules in the same **Pane**).

To add the module to the tab, just click on the **Add Module To Page** link located below the options we just mentioned. This will place the **HTML** module into the content pane of the current page.

Module Settings

To access a module's settings, you need to access the **Action** menu. To do this, use the drop-down icon in the left-hand corner of the module, as shown in the following screenshot:

From this menu, you will be able to do the following:

- Access the **Edit** pages for the module
- **Import** or **Export** content
- **Syndicate** the information in the module using RSS
  - This option must be enabled in the module settings
- Access local and online **Help** and documentation
- **Print** the contents of the module
- Change module **Settings**
- **Delete** the module
- **Refresh** the module content if it is cached
- **Move** the module in relation to other modules in the same pane, or to an entirely different pane

Editing a module

The first item on the menu allows you to modify the content of the module. The **Edit** page, as well as the name of the link, may be different for each module depending on its functionality. The module developer can decide what shows up on the menu. We will cover how to use this option on each of the standard modules.

Importing and exporting content

Beginning in version 4.0, DotNetNuke allows you to export the content from one module and import it into another module. You can test this by going to the home page and using the export function on the DotNetNuke® Community Edition **HTML** box. To export the content of a module, you will need to select the **Folder** to export the content to. The module title is entered in the **File** textbox by default; however, you may also specify a filename. After these fields are filled, click the **Export** link.

If you then go to the **HTML** box we placed on our **Coffee House Search** page, you can use the import function to import the information into this page. To import the content, you will need to select the **Folder** you previously specified during the export. Then a file will be available to be selected, with a name that matches the filename of the title of the module you exported the content from. Simply select this file and click the **Import** link.

Syndicate information

You can also syndicate the information contained in your module, allowing others to pull your information using RSS Readers. (We will discuss this further when we look at the **News Feeds** module.)

 This option must be enabled using the **Module Settings**, before it is available for use by visitors of the site.

Help and Online Help documentation

The **Help** link takes you to the **Help** page on your own installation, if provided by the module. The **Online Help** link will typically take you to the module developer's website, where they may post additional help content for the module.

Editing module functionality

The **Settings** menu item allows you to edit the basic functionality of each module. This will be the same for all modules. Let's take a look at this section. On the **HTML** module, select **Settings** from the **Action** menu.

This will open the **Module Settings** page. This section is divided into two sections: **Module Settings** and **Page Settings**. Each of these sections has subsections that contain additional settings.

When creating a module, you have the choice of adding custom settings to the settings section. We will cover this when we learn how to develop custom modules later in this book.

Basic Settings

The first item on this page allows you to set a title to show at the top of your module. The title will default to the name of the module. This is followed by the permissions for the module, which work in the same way as the role and user privileges on the page. Note that these permissions override the ones set on the page. So, you can, for example, keep a tab available to the **All Users** role, but allow only users in the **Registered Users** role to see the modules on that tab. Keep in mind that the overriding works only one way. If you restrict the page to **Registered Users** and then try to give **All Users** access to the modules on the tab, they won't see the module because they will never see the page. Users must be granted access to a page, in order to view the modules on it. Additionally, individual modules can be selectively hidden from users even if the page is available to them. The default permissions for a module will be inherited from the page. However, this inheritance can be overridden on an individual module basis.

 Some modules will include additional permissions that can be assigned and correspond to functions of that particular module. For example, the **Forum** module includes two additional permissions for **Forum Admin** and **Global Moderator**. These permissions allow you to specify a user or role that can perform the actions associated with these permissions.

⊟ **Module Settings**

In this section, you can define the settings that relate to the Module content and permissions (ie. those settings that will be the same on all pages that the Module appears).

   ⊟ **Basic Settings**

   ❷ **Module:**   HTML

   ❷ **Module Title:**   Text/HTML

   ❷ **Permissions:**

	View Module	Edit Module
Administrators	🔒	🔒
All Users	🔒	☐
Registered Users	🔒	☐
Subscribers	🔒	☐
Unauthenticated Users	🔒	☐

Username: [_____] ➕ Add

☑ Inherit **View** permissions from **Page**

Advanced Settings

The **Header** and **Footer** sections allow you to enter information that will appear at the top and bottom of your module. Just as you did with the page, you can also decide on showing this module during a specific date range. In addition, you can also make a module show up on all the tabs (pages) that you create. You might want to do this if you have a set of links that you want on every tab (page). If this option is selected, an additional option **Add to new pages only is displayed** is also shown. There is also an **Added to Pages** section below **Advanced Settings** that displays a list of all of the pages the current module has been added to.

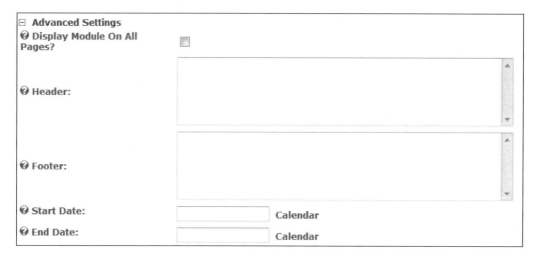

Page Settings

This final section deals mostly with the appearance of the module.

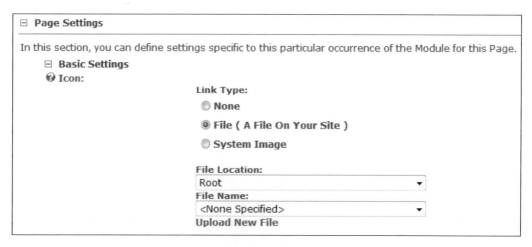

If you would like a custom icon to appear before the title, select the **File** radio button and choose one from the **File Name** dropdown or upload a new icon by clicking on the **Upload New File** link. You can also use the **System Image** option to select a standard DotNetNuke image for the icon. The default setting for this option is **None**.

The next section allows you to modify the look and feel of your module. Although any formatting to the module should be done in the module's skin, you can change the alignment of the text by selecting **Left**, **Right**, or **Center** from the list. Change the background color by entering a color code into the **Color** box, or add a border by entering a thickness in the **Border** box.

When you looked at the **HTML** module, you may have noticed a small minus '-' sign in the upper right-hand corner across from the title. This gives the users of your site the ability to show or hide the content of each module. This acts similar to a minimize/maximize functionality for each module.

You can set the default setting to **Minimized**, **Maximized**, or **None** that will allow users to hide the content.

The next section allows you to determine whether you would like the title to be displayed on your module (the **Display Container?** option), whether you will allow users to print the contents (**Allow Print?**), and if RSS syndication (**Allow Syndicate?**) is allowed. An interesting feature that has been added is the ability to turn a module into a Web Slice for Internet Explorer 8. Check the boxes to enable these features.

In addition, you may select a **Module Container** to skin your individual modules. Module containers are discussed in *Chapter 9, Silverlight Coffee Shop Viewer*.

The **Cache Time** is used to speed up the rendering of your page. Caching stores a representation of the data contained in your module for the number of seconds that you place in this box. This means that subsequent attempts to access this page (even by other users) will show the same data. If the text in this module does not change very often, then set this to a high number like 360. If this data is dynamic, or changes frequently, then set it to a low number or leave it at zero. For dynamic modules, like **Forum**, where the content can change according to the user viewing the module, make sure you disable caching by setting the **Cache Time** property to **0**.

❷ Cache Time (secs):	1200

You can set the settings for this module as the default settings and/or apply the settings to all modules in your site. The final option is to move your module to another page by selecting the page name from the dropdown. When you are finished with your modifications, click the **Update** link to save your settings.

⊟ **Advanced Settings**	
❷ **Set As Default Settings?**	☐
❷ **Apply To All Modules?**	☐
❷ **Move To Page:**	Coffee House Search ▾

Changes to the organization of modules

The previous versions of DotNetNuke came prepackaged with 19 standard modules for you to use on your portal. To further help the DotNetNuke core team focus on the core architecture, it was decided that the standard modules were to be broken into separate subprojects. Each of these subprojects is managed by a different team member. A list of the projects can be found on the DotNetNuke site by clicking on the **FORGE** icon and filtering the list by **Core DotNetNuke Projects**.

In addition to separating the individual modules into subprojects in DotNetNuke 5.0, the team decided to change the way the administration portions of DotNetNuke were designed. This change allowed the administration functionality to be packaged as modules as well. With this new design, an administrator can easily delegate certain administrative tasks to other users. In previous versions, only members of the administrator's role were able to use these tools. We will be discussing these modules and their functionality in *Chapter 5, Host and Admin Tools*.

However, the following sections will briefly describe each of the subproject modules. We will begin with the standard modules that are preloaded with a fresh DotNetNuke installation. We will then cover the additional modules that are made available by members of the DotNetNuke team.

As we cover each module, we will first give you an official description for the module as stated on the DotNetNuke website. We will then discuss the modules in the following context:

- Practical purposes
- Administration and modifications
- Special features

Standard modules

Modules that come prepackaged with DotNetNuke are considered here to be standard modules. In the following sections, we will review each of the standard modules in order to become familiar with them.

Account Login module

Modules that come prepackaged with DotNetNuke are considered here to be standard modules. In the following sections, we will review each of the standard modules in order to become familiar with them.

The **Account Login** module permits users to log in to your portal after providing their credentials (username and password). It features a **Register** button that a user can use to become a registered user of your portal, and a **Forgot Password?** link.

Practical purposes

The **Account Login** module is a unique standard module. It is used to allow user login for your site. The site will come preloaded with this module already working on the site.

The page that is preloaded with the **Account Login** module contains no other modules. You may find that you want to add other modules or images to the page that a user sees when they are logging into the portal. To accomplish this, you will need to create a new page and place the **Account Login** module on the page. Then you may add other modules to the page just as with any other page.

Administration and modification

To show you how this works, we will need to add a new page to the site. Create a page with the following attributes:

- **Name**: Login
- **Title**: Login Tab

- **Include In Menu?**: Unchecked
- **View Tab Roles**: **Administrators, Unauthenticated Users**

We do not want users to be able to navigate here so we do not include it in the menu. We also want to make it available to unauthenticated and administrator roles. As we are not able to navigate to this page, we will need to access it from the **ADMIN | Pages** menu if modifications are needed in the future. However, we will be redirected to this tab automatically when we first create it. Once the **Login** tab is created, select **Account Login** in the **Module** dropdown section of the **Control Panel** and add it to the **ContentPane** by clicking on the **Add Module To Page** link.

Next, we want to modify some settings in the **Account Login** module. Hover your mouse cursor over the **Edit** icon and select **Settings**. Modify the following properties:

- **Collapse/Expand**: **None**
- **Permissions (View)**: **Administrators, Unauthenticated Users**

We change the **Collapse/Expand** to **None** to avoid users inadvertently minimizing the module and not seeing it when they attempt to log in.

 Make sure you click the **Update** link after changing the settings.

To use this tab for logging in instead of the default login, we will need to go to the **ADMIN | Site Settings** tab. We will need to change the **Login Page** property:

- **Login Page** (under **Advanced Settings | Page Management**): Setting this property to our **Login** tab will tell DotNetNuke to use our new tab instead of the default tab. Just select our tab from the dropdown.

Once you have set these properties, click on the **Update** link to save your settings. We now have the ability to add further content to the **Login** tab. We will show how this is done as we talk about other standard modules.

Special features

Registration is built into the login control. Clicking on the **Register** button will bring the user to a registration page to create an account.

The login control gives users the ability to have the portal remember their login name and password. If the **Remember Login** checkbox is selected, it will save the users' information in a cookie on their machine. The next time they navigate to the site they will automatically be authenticated.

If the users forget their password, they will be able to enter their username and click on the **Password Reminder** button. This will send a mail with their login information to the e-mail account they used when they registered.

Banner module

For a discussion on how to use the **Banner** module in conjunction with vendor advertising, see the *Vendors* subsection under the *Host tools* section in *Chapter 5, Host and Admin Tools*.

Console module

The **Console** module displays children pages of a particular page as links to allow for easy navigation. Examples of this module in use can be seen on the **ADMIN** and **HOST** pages. To view these pages, click the **ADMIN** or **HOST** menu items (links) on the menu bar.

Administration and modification

Viewing the **Module Settings** screen allows you to modify the following options:

- **Show children of**: Select a parent page to display the pages below the parent in the navigation menu.
- **Default icon size**: This option can be set to **Large Icons (32px)** or **Small Icons (16px)**.
- **Allow icon resize**: If checked, the viewer will be presented with a drop-down list to choose the icon size they prefer.
- **Default View**: This option can be set to **Detailed View** or **Simple View**. **Detailed View** will include the descriptions of each item in the list shown.
- **Allow view change**: If checked, the viewer will be presented with a drop-down list to choose the view they prefer.
- **Show tooltip**: If checked, the detailed description will be shown when hovering over an icon while the list is in **Simple View**.
- **Width**: If blank, the icons will expand horizontally. Otherwise, a specific size can be entered to limit the number of columns of icons.

Feed Explorer module

By default, the **Feed Explorer** module displays listing from the DotNetNuke marketplace directory. This is designed to allow the administrators of the portal to find third-party modules for their site. However, this module can be customized to display content from other sources that expose an OPML feed.

> **OPML (Outline Processor Markup Language)** is an XML format for outlines (often blogrolls). Originally developed by Radio UserL and as a native file format for an outline application, it has been adopted for other uses, the most common being to exchange lists of web feeds between web feed aggregators. For more information on OPML, check out http://en.wikipedia.org/wiki/OPML.

Administration and modification

On the **Module Settings** screen, you are presented with the following options:

- **Content Source**: This option allows you to modify the source of the OPML feed that the module uses to retrieve the content displayed. The default setting is **DotNetNuke Solutions Explorer**. However, you can select either **Custom OPML URL/File** or **Custom OPML Text** to provide the module with your own OPML configuration for content.

- **Custom OPML URL/File**: Use this setting to provide the absolute URL or file path for the custom OPML document.

- **Custom OPML Text**: This setting can be used to provide a small OPML document direct to the module without the need to create a file.

- **Theme**: There are two themes provided with the current version of the module. These two themes are **Platinum** and **Graphite**; you may select the one that works best for your site.

> At the time of writing this, the file path for the News.opml file used by the **News Explorer** option is not valid in DotNetNuke version 5.2.x.

HTML module

The **HTML** module provides for the input of simple or HTML-formatted text. Simple text is input in a standard textbox and a filter converts carriage returns (paragraph breaks) to HTML breaks. HTML-formatted text can be input directly or generated by an alternative rich-text input utility that provides a number of advanced WYSIWYG features as well as a gallery of all uploaded images. CKeditor (http://ckeditor.com) is the default WYSIWYG editor installed with DNN. However, you can freely choose between other popular alternatives such as TinyMCE. However, you would need to install an appropriate provider for your editor.

Practical purposes

- Adding welcome information to your home page
- Creating short tutorials with bolding, highlighting, and images
- Building professional-looking advertisements to place on your site
- Displaying general information on your site
- Migrating content from older static HTML websites or any static content that does not vary with the user

Administration and modification

To edit the **HTML** module, sign in as administrator and select the module's **Action** menu. When adding content, you have two options: you can add text to the module using the basic textbox, or you can use the rich text editor.

You are able to edit the text in many different ways. You can use tables to organize data, insert images, and modify the color, type, and size of the font. To accomplish this, DotNetNuke uses CKEditor as its default HTML editor. CKEditor is a freely available control that can be used with ASP.NET or any other server-side web framework. To save your data, click on the **Update** link.

Special features and additional information

Because of its versatility, the **HTML** module is probably the most widely used module on a DotNetNuke site. Most tabs are filled with static data and this module fits the bill.

Search Input and Search Results module

The **Search Input** and **Search Results** modules are similar to the **Account Login** module in the fact that they come preconfigured with each new portal. However, unlike any module we have looked at so far, these two modules work together to provide their functionality. The **Search Input** module displays a textbox to enter the search criteria and a button to execute the search. After clicking the button, the **Search Results** module displays a list of the pages containing the terms entered into the **Search Input** module.

This enables you to drop the **Search Input** module to any or each page of your portal, enabling users to initiate search from anywhere, and still take them to a common page to display the search results. Additionally, DotNetNuke provides a **Search SkinObject** that can be used in custom skins. The search box you see on the right of the menu bar on a default DNN skin is not the **Search Input** module, but the **Search** SkinObject.

A **SkinObject** is a control that can be added to a custom skin to provide a particular piece of functionality. The **Search** SkinObject is just one example. Others examples include, but are not limited to, Language Selection, Copyright Display, and Breadcrumb.

Practical purposes

- Adding the ability to search from a particular page on the site
- Creating a custom search results page that displays additional content

Administration and modification

After adding these modules to the desired pages, navigating to the **Module Settings** screen will display a few configurable options. The **Search Input Settings** has the following three available options.

- **Search Results Module**: This option lets you select the **Search Results Module** you would like to use to display the results of searches executed from this module.

- **Show Go Image**: If this option is checked, an image will be displayed after the search textbox, instead of the default **HTML** button. You can replace this image by overwriting the `images/search.gif` inside your DNN installation directory. Be warned that this will affect every portal in the installation.

- **Show Search Image**: If this option is checked, an image of the word *search* will be displayed before the search textbox. You can replace this image by overwriting the `images/search_go.gif` inside your DNN installation directory. Be warned that this will affect every portal in the installation.

The **Search Results Module** provides the following options:

- **Maximum Search Results**: Determines the number of results displayed for each search
- **Results per Page**: Number of results displayed at a time
- **Maximum Title Length**: If the title of the result is longer than the value entered, then it will be truncated to the specified number of characters
- **Maximum Description Length**: If the description of the result is longer than the value entered, then it will be truncated to the specified number of characters
- **Show Description?**: If checked, shows the description of each of the results

Additional Modules

Modules developed by members of the DotNetNuke core team are also available to be installed as additional modules. The following sections will help us to become familiar with these modules. Later in this chapter we will also look at modules provided by third parties.

Announcements module

The **Announcements** module produces a list of simple or HTML-formatted text announcements consisting of a title and a brief description. Options include a **Read More** link to a file, tab on your site, a user of the site or other site, the ability to associate an image, ability to order the items, announcement publish date, and expiration date.

Practical purposes

- **What's New Section**: This is of great use for the **Announcements** module. It is usually put on the home page of your site. It gives a headline with a short description of the content. It allows you to show a lot of information in a less amount of space by giving the users a **Read More** link for the items they want to read about more.
- **Article Listing**: The **Announcements** module allows you to link to pages internally and externally. This allows you to link to either articles you write or those that you have found on the Internet.

Administration and modification

To create an announcement, click on the **Add New Announcement** link. This will bring up the **Edit Announcements** page. The properties of an announcement are as follows:

- **Title**: Type in a short title for the announcement; this will be displayed in bold at the top of the announcement.

- **Image**: Enter a URL to any image hosted on any site or select a file that resides on your site. This image will be displayed next to the announcement. Be careful in choosing image dimensions. They should fit in the size of the module pane, or you could have formatting issues on your page.

- **Description**: The description is what allows you to give a short teaser of the full announcement. You can also use this to give a short announcement without giving a link to a larger article.

- **Link**: You have three choices as to where to link your announcement; you can link to any Internet URL, link to a tab on your site, or link to a file located in your folders. The last option allows you to link to a PDF, HTML, Word document, or any other file located on your portal.

- **Track**: If this is checked, the module will track the number of times the link has been clicked. Link tracking is an integral feature of DNN, and allows you to track the number of clicks of any URL on your portal, together with some additional logging as described below.

- **Log**: If this is checked, the module will track who clicks on the **Read More** link and when.

- **Open Link in a New Browser Window?**: As the title explains, this will cause a new browser window to open when a user clicks on the **Read More** link.

- **Publish Date**: You can choose the publish date by clicking on the **Calendar** option; the date will be added to the title of the announcement and the announcement would automatically become visible on this date, if it is a future date.

- **Expire Date**: You can choose the expire date by clicking on the **Calendar** option. You can also select the time for the publish date using the dropdowns. Depending on this date and time, the announcement will no longer be displayed under the current announcements.

- **View Order**: By default, announcements are ordered by the date that they are added or updated to the module. You can override this by placing a number in the **View Order** box. The announcements will then be ordered numerically by the view order. If no number is entered, the order will be zero.

Special features and additional information

Once you save your announcement, you will have the ability to track which announcements have the greatest interest to your users. To see this information, click on the pencil icon next to a particular announcement. (This option will be available only if the **Preview** option is unchecked.) At the bottom of the **Edit Announcement** page, you can see how many times this announcement has been clicked and a log of who has clicked on it (if the **Log** option is checked).

The layout of the announcements are completely template driven and can be altered by editing the individual templates located on the **Module Settings** page.

Blog module

The **Blog** module is actually a collection of related modules, which comprise all the working parts of a blog. When you add the **Blog** module to a page, you actually add all the working parts (which you can choose to delete or move). These presently include:

- **New_Blog**: List of blog-related actions that a user can take, based on permissions (for example, changing settings, adding a post, and so on)
- **Search_Blog**: Utility for searching blog content
- **Blog_List**: List of blogs on the site (or in some logical grouping)
- **Blog_Archive**: Calendar indicating dates when blogs have been posted
- **View_Blog**: Display of the lists and content of the blogs

If the current user does not have a blog, and the user has been granted permission, then the **New_Blog** module indicates this displaying only one option—**Create My Blog**.

When the module is added to a page, all the individual modules are added automatically to the pane chosen by the user adding the module. Once the modules have been added, they can be moved to provide the traditional blog view.

Administration and modification

The Blog **module** is one of the modules available from the DotNetNuke website that has many advanced settings. These can be split into three categories:

- Settings that affect the **Blog** module as a whole
- Settings that relate to a single blog
- Settings that relate to a single blog post

A full description of all the administrative settings for this module is beyond the scope of this book. Let's look at the settings that relate to a single blog. To create a new blog, click on the **Create My Blog** link in the blog menu.

This screen provides a number of properties that affect the new blog, some of these include:

- **Title**: This is the title of the new blog. This will display in the blogroll.
- **Description**: It provides a description of the blog. It will display at the top of the **Posts** module when a user is viewing the new blog, and is a good place to provide information about your intentions for the blog.
- **Make this blog public**: It allows anonymous users to view the blog posts.
- **Comment Options**: This group of settings allows comments to be added to individual blog posts and how they are handled.
- **Syndication Options**: These options control how you can syndicate your blog.
- **Date and Time Options**: The date and time options control how dates and times appear in your blog.
- **Child Blogs**: This area allows you to split up your blog into different categories, by creating sub-blogs of your blog.

Once the blog is created, it will be displayed in the **Blog_List** module. Additionally, the **New_Blog** module now provides a number of options, including the ability to modify the settings for this blog, and add a new blog entry.

To add a new blog entry, click on the **Add Blog Entry** link. The following fields are available on the edit screen:

- **Entry Date**: The date for this blog entry.
- **Parent Blog**: Select the blog that this entry belongs to.
- **Title**: The title for this blog post.
- **Summary**: A summary (or abstract) of the blog this will be displayed with a **Read More** link to view the entire post.
- **Blog**: The blog text itself.
- **Entry Options**: At the bottom of the page is a group of options that apply to this blog entry. They are fairly self-explanatory.

Click on **Update** to create your blog. Clicking on **Cancel** would cancel the current entry.

Special features

One of the most useful features of this module is the ability to add blog entries from applications that support the Metaweblog API, such as Windows Live Writer. Under the **Blog Settings** screen, there is a **MetaWeblog Options** section. Here you will see a URL that can be used to connect the application to the blog. Please consult the documentation for your favorite editor on setting up a connection to a blog.

Chat module

The **Chat** module is a straightforward module that, as the name suggests, allows users to chat while on the portal. This can be a very helpful module if you want to provide real-time support to the users of your site.

Administration and modification

The **Module Settings** screen provides options to control how often the chat window refreshes, how much content to display, how much history to maintain, and the option to turn on or off the ability to use formatting in the chat window. Other options include the height of the window; CSS classes for the sender and messages, as well as how to format the chat event text. Chat events include, users entering the chat, leaving the chat, and contributing a message to the chat.

Special features

If formatting is enabled in the **Module Settings**, users can format their messages with basic styling options. This includes bold, italics, underline, font size, and color. Users can also include emotion icons and hyperlinks in their messages.

Contacts module

The **Contacts** module renders contact information for a particular group of people. For example, you could use it for a project team or a certain department. A contact includes an **Edit** page that allows authorized users to edit the contacts data stored in the SQL database.

Practical purposes

- Storing a list of contacts on your portal for all users
- Storing internal company phonebook information protected by security roles

Administration and modification

To add a new contact, sign in as administrator, hover the mouse cursor over the drop-down arrow by the **Contacts** title, and click on the **Add New Contact** link.

The following fields are available on the edit screen:

- **Name**: Enter a name for the contact
- **Role**: Enter the role for this contact; this is not a security role, this should be the title of the contact (Manager, Owner, Partner, and so on)
- **Email**: Enter the e-mail address for this contact
- **Telephone 1**: Enter a primary phone number for this contact
- **Telephone 2**: Enter a secondary phone number for this contact

Click **Update** to save your settings.

Special features

- **Mailto** hyperlink created by contacts' e-mail address is cloaked by creating a JavaScript function utilizing `String.fromCharCode` to keep spambots from harvesting e-mail addresses
- **Call** link is available if the page is browsed by a wireless telephone

Documents module

The **Documents** module produces a list of documents with links to view (depending on users' file associations) or download the document.

Practical purposes

- Can be used as a document repository for Word, Excel, PDF, and so on
- Can be used to give access to programs, modules, presentations, and so on contained inside a ZIP file
- Can be used as a resource section by adding links to downloads on other sites

Administration and modification

To add a new document, sign in as administrator and click on the **Add New Document** link.

The following fields are available on the edit screen:

- **Title:** Fill in the title of the document.

- **Link**: Select a URL or file. Use a URL for content located on another site. Specify the file location for content located on this site. Either select the file from the dropdown or enter the URL for the download. You can use the upload link to upload new content to the portal.

- **Track** and **Log**: Check the **Track** and **Log** checkboxes if you would like this module to track downloads for this content. It will give you a detailed list at the bottom of the **Edit** screen showing you the date and time when each user downloads this item. As mentioned earlier, tracking is widely available across DNN and can be used to monitor activity on your portal.

- **Category**: Enter a category for this download. The category is used to help organize the downloads.

Click on **Update** to save your settings.

Special features and additional information

The owner of the download, as listed in the module, will be the user who adds the download to the module. Users with appropriate permissions can also switch the owner of the download to another user. This can be useful, for example, where a backend support engineer wants to upload files in the name of frontend contact personnel of an organization. Also, several features are available on the **Module Settings** screen. These include selecting fields to display, creating a category list, and configuring sorting options for the documents.

Events module

The **Events** module produces a display of upcoming events as a list in chronological order, in a weekly view or in a monthly calendar view. Each event can be set to automatically expire on a particular date or to reoccur after a specified number of days, weeks, months, or years.

The **Events** module has changed drastically from its original design and now includes many features in addition to the great new layout options already mentioned. For example, the module has the ability to allow viewers to register for events, and pay for the registration through PayPal, as well as the ability to merge multiple calendars into a single display. At present, there so many features included in this module that they go beyond our ability to discuss them in this chapter.

Practical purposes

- Listing upcoming events for an organization
- Keeping track of upcoming deadlines in a calendar format
- Listing recurring appointments or reminders
- Providing concert information for a band or other performer

Administration and modification

The **Events** module uses the **Module Settings** screen heavily for configuring the options of this module. To see the custom options for this module, hover the cursor over the **Action** menu and click on the **Settings** menu item.

Each of the sections shown in this image has a number of settings that can control the behavior or layout of the module.

For example, as just mentioned, you have the option to have the events displayed as a list, a weekly view, or inside a monthly calendar. All of these views can be customized by editing the associated template under the **Template Settings** section of this screen.

To add a new event, sign in as administrator, and click on the **Add Events** button that appears as a green plus sign.

The following fields are available on the edit screen:

- **Title**: Enter a title for the event. This will be displayed in bold on the first line of the event for the list view or inside the cell for the calendar view.
- **All Day Event**: Determines if this event be shown as lasting an entire day.
- **Start Date/Time**: This is the date and time when the pattern will start if this is a recurring event. For a one-time event, this is the date and time of the event.
- **End Date/Time**: This is the date and time that the event will stop showing up on the calendar, if this is a recurring event.
- **Importance**: This controls if an importance icon should be shown for the event.
- **Category**: Allows events to be filtered by category.
- **Location**: Allows location information to be associated with the event.
- **Owner**: The creator or manager of the event can be set to a user account on the site.
- **Notes**: Enter a description for the event. This will be displayed in regular text under the title in list view. If you are using calendar view, then this field will be displayed in a floating window when the mouse is hovering over the event title.

In addition to these basic settings, the edit screen allows options to be set for a reminder to be sent, an image to be displayed for the event, and options for recurring events.

Special features and additional information

The new **Events** module provides many extra features and flexibility. These include, but are certainly not limited to:

- The ability to merge individual calendar modules into a single display
- The ability to enroll for events, including the ability to use PayPal to collect any necessary payments
- The ability to export events as calendar items to import into your favorite calendar application
- An extensive set of options for recurring events

FAQs module

The **FAQs** module produces a list of linked frequently asked questions. The corresponding answer is displayed when a question is clicked.

Practical purposes

- List product FAQs
- Display special contact information
- FAQs regarding usage of the site
- General information for members of a club

Administration and modification

To add a new FAQ, sign in as administrator and click on the **Add New FAQ** link. The following fields are available on the edit screen:

- **Category:** Select a category for the FAQ. Categories are managed through the **Manage Categories** screen found on the **Action** menu for the module.
- **Question**: Enter the FAQ question.
- **Answer**: Enter the FAQ answer.

Click on **Update** to save your changes.

Special features and additional information

The question is presented as a hyperlink. When the question is clicked, the answer will be shown. The **Module Settings** screen contains an option to **Enable AJAX** for the module to prevent a screen refresh, when the question is clicked. The **Module Settings** screen also allows the question, answer, and loading templates to be modified. This allows the layout of the FAQ to be customized to fit your needs. The sorting of the questions is controlled by the **Default Sorting** option located on the settings screen.

Feedback module

The **Feedback** module produces a form for visitors to provide feedback for your site, which can be automatically mailed to a specific e-mail address, if you desire. If users are already logged in, then their name and e-mail address will be automatically placed into the form.

As with the **Blog** module, this module is also comprised of more than one module. In this case, they are the **Main Feedback** module that is used to collect the feedback from the user, and the **Feedback Comments** module that provides a listing of all the comments. In most scenarios, this second module would be visible only to administrators.

Practical purposes

- Have users request content or changes on your portal
- Can be used as a **Contact Us** section
- Allow users to give general feedback about your portal

Administration and modification

By default, all **Feedback** modules send the e-mail to the administrator of the site. If you would like to send the feedback to a specific e-mail address, log in as **administrator**, go to **Module Settings** on the module's **Action** menu, and add the e-mail address into the **Send To** box found in the **Feedback Settings** section. Click on the **Update** link when finished.

Special features and additional information

When we discussed the general features of modules earlier in this chapter, we looked at an option that would put a module on every tab. The **Feedback** module would be a good candidate for this action. It fits nicely on either the left or the right pane and allows your users to contact you with questions without having to go to any particular tab to use the module. The **Search Input** module was another such candidate.

Form and List module

This module was originally named as the **User Defined Table** module and allows you to create a custom data table for managing tabular information.

Practical purposes

- This module can be used to store and display lists of custom information
- Create sorted and paged lists of information for users of the site

Administration and modification

When using the **Form and List** module, the first thing you must do is to decide what columns you would like in your table. To do this, sign in as administrator, hover over the down arrow next to the **Form and List** title, and click on **Form and List Configuration**.

Click on **Add New Column**. This will present you with the fields necessary to create a new column for your table. The fields presented are as follows:

- **Title**: Enter a title for the column.
- **Type**: Enter a type for the data. You can choose from many types including **Text, Integer, True/False, Date, Decimal**, and **Download** to name a few. Select the appropriate type from the dropdown. **Advanced Column Options** will change based on the **Type** you select.
- **Required**: Requires the user to enter a value into this field when submitting the form.
- **Display on List**: If you want the column to be visible only to administrators and other specified roles, uncheck the **Display on List** checkbox.
- **Restricted Form Field**: If you want to specify the roles that are allowed to edit the data in this field, check the **Restricted Form Field** checkbox.

Click on the **Save** icon to save the current column to the database. Repeat the previous steps for each of the columns you require. Use the arrows to determine the order of the columns. When you are finished adding columns, click **Save Configuration and Return**.

After you have created your columns, you can add rows of data. To do this, make sure you are signed in as a user with **Create Record / Submit Form** permission, hover the cursor over the pencil icon next to the **Form and List** module, and click on **Add New Record**. The fields presented are as follows:

- Enter the data for the row. The data you enter will be validated from the type you selected when setting up the columns. If the data you enter is not valid, you will be shown an error message at the top of the page.

- Click on **Update** to save your row.

- Repeat these steps for additional rows.

Special features and additional information

As it is impossible to predict the different types of data that portal administrators may want on their site, the **Form and List** module gives you the ability to customize your site with data that is pertinent to you and your users. There are several features that make this a very powerful and flexible module.

Forums module

The **Forums** module is one of the largest and most complicated module provided by the DotNetNuke team. A full description of this module is way beyond the scope of this book; in fact, this module is large enough to warrant its own book. Along with its size and complexity, its popularity is another factor that makes this module stand out. In fact, to see this module being used in a very high capacity, simply visit the forums on DotNetNuke.com.

Practical purposes

- Provide product support for an online store

- Provide a discussion for members of a club

- Provide a highly utilized forum to discuss an open source application development platform

Administration and modification

The **Forums** module has a complex set of administration pages that are accessed through the **Forum Administration** menu item. It is also worth noting that users and roles can be assigned **Forum Admin** or **Global Moderator** permissions via the **Module Settings** page. Please note that these permissions are only available for the **Forums** module. This is another powerful feature of DNN, where a module can add permissions specifically for itself.

The **Forums** module is different from most of the other modules we have described so far, for the fact that it can be considered as an interactive module. Most other modules provide a fairly static content that can be created and updated by a user with administrative rights to the site.

Typically, the **Forums** module is interactive for all users. We will therefore describe the interface that most users will use for creating a new thread, or for replying to an existing thread. Here are the fields available when posting a comment in the **Forums** module:

- **Forum**: This is a drop-down list of the forums on the site, which are available to the user. This option is disabled and simply displays the forum the thread will be posted in.
- **Subject**: This is the subject of the post. In a reply, the subject defaults to the same subject as the previous post preceded by **Re:**.
- **Message**: Next is the message itself (the body of the post).
- **Attachments**: This allows a user to upload multiple files and attach them to a thread or reply. Note that this is displayed only if attachments are enabled in the **Forum Administration** options.
- **Pinned**: Some roles can pin the thread, make sure it remains at the top of a list of threads. This is useful for common questions or general forum guidelines for example.
- **Notification**: If selected, and provided this is configured correctly in the **Administration** settings, a user can opt to receive an e-mail whenever anybody replies to this post.
- **Locked**: A user who has been granted permission can lock a thread (disable the ability to reply to the message).

Gallery module

The **Gallery** module provides central repository for media files. These files can be grouped into albums. This module has been around for several major versions of DotNetNuke and has become quite complex over time. We will address only a small portion of the features available in this module.

At the time of writing, this version 4.3.0 of the **Gallery** module is still considered a beta version and is not approved for production use. However, previous versions of this module will not work with DotNetNuke 5.2.x. We anticipate that the 4.3.0 version will be approved for production use in the very near future. Please check the project page on the DotNetNuke website for the latest information on this module.

Practical purposes

- Provide an album of pictures from a vacation on a personal site
- Provide an album of pictures from a club meeting on a club site

Administration and modification

The **Gallery** module has several administration sections that are accessed through the **Gallery Configuration** menu item. However, most of the activities in this module are about uploading new media content to the module. This is accomplished through a separate action menu that is part of the module. To access this menu, simply move the mouse over the icon next to the **Gallery** title located at the top of the module.

Clicking on the **Add Files** menu item brings up the **Add File(s)** screen that allows you to edit and delete existing media and albums in the gallery, as well as add new content. The fields presented are as follows:

- **Add File**: An upload file textbox that allows the user to browse for the media file on their local computer
- **Title**: A title/name for the new media item
- **Author**: The author of the media item
- **Client/Location/Description**: These are extra fields that allow the user to categorize the media items being stored in the gallery
- **Categories**: The type of the media item (currently image, movie, music, and flash are supported types)

Once these fields are filled in with the desired information, clicking on the **Add Files** link will place the file selected into an upload queue. It will then be displayed in the **Pending Uploads** list below these fields. This allows the user to select multiple files and upload them all together. When you are ready to upload the file(s), click the **Upload Pending Files** link to begin the upload process.

Also, note that at the bottom of this screen is a list of the current media files and albums in this gallery and these items can be edited or removed from this screen as well.

Help module

The **Help** module provides a list of articles or tutorials that can be assigned to one or more categories. This is another module that is made up of more than one individual module. The two modules that compose the **Help** module are a **Category Tree** and the **Tutorial List**.

Practical purposes

- Provide an online help guide for a software product
- Provide a knowledge base of articles for a society

Administration and modification

Each of the two modules that compose the **Help** module has its own administration. Clicking **Manage Categories** on the **Category Tree** module will bring up a screen to edit the available categories.

The **Manage Categories** edit page works somewhat similarly to the **Lists Editor** on the **HOST** menu. First you need to select an existing category in the tree. You can then edit that category by modifying the fields on the right-hand side of the screen, add a new category at the same depth in the hierarchy (**Add Sibling**), or you can add a child category of the current category (**Add Child**).

Adding a new category of either type immediately creates the new category and populates the fields on the right with default values, which you can then edit and update. The following fields are available on the edit screen:

- **Name**: The name of the category
- **Description**: A description of the category
- **Keywords**: These keywords help in search for tutorials in a large collection
- **Visible**: Is this category visible to the user?
- **Parent**: This dropdown allows you to change the parent category of the current category in the category hierarchy
- **View Order**: Allows you to arrange the categories within the hierarchy

Clicking the **Add Tutorial** menu option in the **Tutorial List** module brings up the **Edit Tutorials** page that allows users that have been granted permission to create new tutorials. The following fields are available on the edit screen:

- **Title**: The name of the tutorial.
- **Short Description**: A short description of the tutorial (or abstract). This will be displayed in the **Tutorial List** followed by a **Read More** link that will take the reader to the complete tutorial.
- **Tutorial**: The complete text of the tutorial.

At the bottom of the edit page (after the **Tutorial Editor**), are two options that allow you to categorize the tutorial:

- **Keywords**: You can provide a list of keywords that assist in searching the list of tutorials for a specific tutorial
- **Categories**: The tutorial can be assigned to one or more of the categories created in the **Manage Categories** module

IFrame module

IFrame is an Internet Explorer browser feature that allows you to display content from another website within a frame on your portal. Although this was originally a feature for Internet Explorer, the major browsers typically support this feature as well.

Practical purposes

- Display dynamic content from another website
- Keep users up-to-date on information on other sites
- Include information from older site while migrating content to a new DotNetNuke site

Administration and modification

To modify the **IFrame** module, sign in as **administrator** and click on **Edit IFrame Options**. The fields presented are as follows:

- **Source**: Enter a source for the **IFrame** (the source is the web page you would like to be displayed in the IFrame). The **IFrame** captures a web page from another site like a mini browser.
- **Width**: Enter the width for the IFrame in pixels. This is how much of the page will be shown in your module.

- **Height**: Enter the height of the IFrame in pixels. This is how much of the page will be shown in your module.

- **Auto Height**: If checked, the height of the IFrame will be stretched to the content inside the IFrame. However, this option only works if the source for the IFrame belongs to the same domain as the portal.

- **Scrolling**: Select a scrolling option. As you are showing only a portion of the web page as determined in the **Width** and **Height** options, you will determine whether you would like to allow users to scroll the page for more information. Your options are **Auto** (scrollbars will appear when needed), **Yes** (scrollbars will be shown at all times), and **No** (scrollbars will not be available).

- **Border**: Select whether you would like a border. **Yes** will display a border around your IFrame, **No** will not.

Click **Update** to save your settings.

Special features and additional information

In addition to the basic options discussed above, this module allows you to specify **QueryString Parameters** and a few more options for advanced use of the IFrame. As the IFrame allows you to show content from other websites, you must make sure that you have permission to do this before setting up the IFrame. Contact the webmaster of the site to find out if this is allowed.

Links module

The **Links** module produces a list of hyperlinks to any tab, image, or file on the portal or to a web page, image, or file on the Web. The links can be set to display as a vertical or horizontal list or as a drop-down box. The links appear alphabetically by default. An indexing field facilitates custom sorting. A supplemental description can be set to appear either on mouse rollover or on the click of a dynamically generated link.

Practical purposes

- Link to resources connected to your portal
- Link to pages on your site
- Link to internal site documents

Administration and modification

To add a new link to the **Links** module, sign in as administrator and click **Add Link**. The following fields are available on the edit screen:

- **Title**: Enter the title for the link. The title is what the users see in the module and it is what they click on to open the link.

- **Link Type**: The **Links** module allows you to link in the following different ways:

    ◦ **URL**: Allows you to link to an external web page (such as Yahoo or MSN).

    ◦ **Page**: Allows you to link to a page on your site. With this option you can create a **Quick Links** menu that allows users to quickly navigate to particular pages without having to navigate the main menu.

    ◦ **File**: Acts as an option to the **Documents** module and allows you to give your users access to documents on your site.

    ◦ **User**: Allows links to be created for view profile information for users registered on the site.

- **Link**: Enter the destination of the link. Your options here will depend on what type of link you are using. If you are using **URL**, you can enter the address into the textbox. If you are using **Page**, you will be presented with a dropdown of all your pages. If you are using **File**, you will be shown a dropdown displaying the files on your portal.

- **Log** and **Track** boxes: Check these options. This will allow you to see how many users have used the links you provided.

- **Open Link In New Browser Window**: Check this box if you want your link to open in a new window (for example, when you link to another website or file).

- **Description**: This section describes what the link is used for. You will be able to see this depending on the options you select.

- **View Order**: It will be used to sort your links numerically. If nothing is entered, this will default to zero and the links will be sorted by when they were added.

Special features and additional information

The **Links** module gives you a choice of how you would like to view the content. To edit these options, sign in as administrator and go to **Settings** on the module's **Action** menu. You will find the following settings under **Link Settings**:

- **Control Type**: Select the control type you would like to use for your links. The default view for the **Links** module is to display them in a **List**, but you can choose to have them displayed in a **Dropdown**.

- **List Display Format**: Select the format in which you want to display your links, vertically or horizontally.

- **Display Info Link**: If **Yes** is selected, an ellipsis will be placed next to the link. When it is clicked it will show the description of the link that you entered when you created the link.

- **Wrap Links**: If set to **No Wrap** the width of the module will stretch to fit the links. Otherwise the module will be of a fixed width.

- **Display Icon**: Allows an icon to be selected to display in front of each link.

Map module

Google maps have become a very popular and powerful tool and have been utilized to provide very detailed information by some sites. In an effort to allow users to make use of this tool, the DotNetNuke team has created the **Map** module. This is a very powerful module that allows you to customize information at particular points on a map.

Practical purposes

- Displaying information on locations for businesses
- Providing information about points of interest
- Using a map to show the location of real estate listings

Administration and modification

The administration of this module is quite complex and is far beyond the scope of this chapter. We will briefly address how to get started using this module. However, you will need to consult the documentation for the details of configuring and using this module.

The first step to using the **Map** module is defining both a **Map Configuration** and data **Source Configuration** for the maps on your site. To do this, sign in as administrator, hover over the down arrow next to the **Map** title, and click on **Edit Map.** Then, click on the **General** icon to be presented with the form to create the **Map Configuration** and **Source**. Enter a **Name** for the configuration and one for the source. Then, click the **Save** link at the bottom of the screen.

Once you have your configurations created, you will need to click on the **Interface** icon and provide a **Google License Key**. This key allows you to retrieve data from Google's map service for display on your site. Click the **Add License Key** link and enter the **Domain** and **Key** and then click the **Save License Key** link.

 If you do not already have a key, there is a **Get One** link provided by the module to direct you to the proper page to request a key.

Now that the configurations and key have been saved, you can begin to **Add Markers**, or locations to the map. These markers allow you to show "push pins" on the map that will display a **Description** when clicked on by a user.

Special features and additional information

There are numerous features in this module that we have not touched. However, the ability to store Map and Source configurations and use them in multiple instances of the module is both powerful and necessary. Other features include a built-in Geocoder to automate the process of assigning global positions to addresses.

At the time of writing, there is currently an issue with installing this module under some versions of DotNetNuke 5.x. You may also want to check the DotNetNuke forums for the latest information regarding this issue before attempting to install this module.

Media module

The **Media** module displays a single item of media, such as an image, audio, or video file.

Practical purposes

- Display a video for users to view on the site
- Provide sample music for a band website

Administration and modification

To edit the options, sign in as a user who has been given edit permission to the module. Then click the **Edit Media Options** link to view the following settings:

- **Media Alignment**: Allows for more control over the alignment of the media displayed in the module.

- **Media**: Selects the source of the media. This can be a URL on an external site or a file on your own site. Note that the allowable file extensions may need to be updated in the **Host Settings** of the portal before some files can be uploaded.

- **Alternate Text**: The alternate text is displayed if the browser cannot display the media. This is a required field.

- **Width / Height**: You can specify the width and height in pixels. If the image or video is of a different size, then the browser will scale the media accordingly. Obviously, this has no effect on audio media.

- **Link**: You can turn the media into a hyperlink by providing a link here. (This feature does not work with audio or video media types.)

News Feed (RSS) module

The **News Feed** module provides visitors with up-to-date, topical information from any RSS publisher (see `http://w.moreover.com/categories/category_list_rss.html` for one of the more comprehensive selections). Information includes a title linked to the source document, source, and publication date.

Practical purposes

- Supply users with information updates on other sites
- View favorite blogs directly on your portal
- Provide a new aggregation site

Administration and modification

RSS (Rich Site Summary or **Really Simple Syndication)** is an XML-based format for syndicated content. It is designed to allow individuals to distribute news or articles in a format that is easy for programs to read (XML). RSS feeds are a great way for you to add important and relevant information to your site with very little effort. This allows you to gather relevant content from other sites without needing to rewrite the content or update articles on your site. There are many places to get RSS-syndicated content. One of the better known is `http://www.moreover.com`.

To add an RSS feed to your site, sign in as administrator and click on the **Edit Newsfeed** link and then click **Add Feed**. The following fields are available on the edit screen:

- **Feed URL**: You can select a news feed generated from your portal or from an external source. Type in the URL location for the news feed.
- **Cache Time Sheet**: The number of minutes to wait between refreshing the items from the specified **Feed URL**. By default this is set to **-1** to tell the module to always pull the latest information.
- **User and Password (optional)**: Some news feeds are not free and will require you to give a username and password to use them.

Click **Update** to add the feed and then click **Update** to save all of your changes.

Special features

The **Module Settings** screen provides options to configure the **Default Cache Time**, a custom **XSL Transformation**, and the ability to specify if the item date is shown along with a few others.

Reports module

The **Reports** module can be used to run custom queries against tables in the DotNetNuke database, other SQL databases, or ADO.NET data sources such as an ODBC connection.

The output of the results of these queries can be displayed in several different views. These views include a **Grid** that can be sorted and paged, a standard HTML view, and as a styled XML document.

Administration and modification

The configuration for this module is done on the **Module Settings** screen. This screen contains many options to allow for a great deal of customization of the data shown via this module. The options change based on which **Active Data Source** and **Active Visualizer** are selected.

The common options include:

- **Title**: Specifies a title to give to the report
- **Description**: Allows for a short description to be entered for the report
- **HTML Decode/HTML Encode**: Allows a comma-separated list of columns to be specified to decode or encode respectively

- **Caching**: If checked, the number of minutes to display cached data can be edited
- **Show Info Pane**: If checked, the **Title** and **Description** will be displayed above the report
- **Show Controls**: If checked, this will display **Run Report** and **Hide Report Results** buttons to users
- **Auto Run Report**: If selected, the report will run automatically when the module is displayed on the page

Special features and additional information

Custom data sources and visualizers can be developed for this module. Custom data sources allow the module to be configured to execute queries against other data stores, such as MySQL or XML documents. Custom visualizers allow the results of the query to be displayed in different formats.

The custom extensions are configured using the **Manage Add-Ins** screen available on the **Action** menu of the module. Please refer to the documentation for this module for information on developing data sources and visualizers.

Repository module

The **Repository** module provides a centrally-categorized resource library. It can be used to store any kind of file, categorize it, and provide a description. The module's view control is templatable, enabling the module to provide a flexible look and feel.

In addition, the module provides "moderation." This feature allows moderated users to upload new files and create new entries in the repository, but these new files do not become "active" until approved by a moderator.

This module is another complex module and we will be able to provide only an overview of the functionality provided by the module.

A separate **Repository Dashboard** module is also available. This module can be configured to provide multiple ways to access the resources. For example, two dashboard modules can be added to a page. One can be configured to provide a list of categories, while the other can be configured to provide a list of the most recent additions.

Practical purposes

- A membership directory: Each entry provides a link to a member's personal site
- A catalog of downloadable tutorials in a knowledge base
- A list of software packages for download by site members

Administration and modification

As mentioned, a full description of the configuration of this module is beyond the scope of this chapter. We will focus on the process of adding a new entry (or editing an existing entry).

When logged in as a user with edit rights, an **Upload** button will appear at the top of the module's display area. (The actual location of the **Upload** button will depend on the template being used to display the module's content.) Click this button to add a new entry to the repository.

Note that at the top of the edit page is a **Moderation Notice**. This indicates to the user whether their upload will require approval. In this case, as the user is a moderator, the upload will be automatically approved. The fields presented are as follows:

- **Title**: A title (or name) for the repository entry.
- **File**: Here you select the file (on your local hard drive) that you wish to add to the repository.
- **Image**: Here you can select an image to associate with the repository entry.
- **Categories**: You can identify the entry as belonging to one or more categories by checking the checkboxes in this row. (The categories are defined in the **Module Settings** for the module.)
- **Your Name**: You name is entered here.
- **Your Email Address**: Your e-mail address is displayed here, together with a checkbox that allows you to control whether your e-mail address is displayed in the repository listing. (Not all templates support the display of the e-mail address, so this only affects those that do.)
- **Description**: A description of the item being uploaded.

Store module

The **Store** module makes it possible to provide an e-commerce solution via a DotNetNuke portal. While the **Store** module is not as robust as some e-commerce solutions available, it does offer some great features for a basic online store. Similar to other modules discussed in this chapter, the **Store** module is made up of several modules. These include the **Store Account**, **Store Admin**, **Store Catalog**, **Store Menu**, and **Store Mini Cart**. Together these modules offer a complete e-commerce solution. The size of this module allows us to provide only an overview in this chapter. However, we do suggest further research on this module if you need e-commerce capabilities for your DotNetNuke site.

Practical purposes

- Selling items online using a traditional catalog approach

Administration and modification

Unlike most modules, it is recommended that the multiple pages are created to host the modules that make up the store. For example, a **Store Admin** page, a **Store Cart** page, and a **Store** page. The **Store Admin** page will host the corresponding **Store Admin** module and be accessible only to site administrators. The **Store Cart** page will host the **Store Account** module and be displayed to users during the checkout process. The **Store** page will host the **Store Catalog**, **Store Menu**, and **Store Mini Cart** modules to allow users to browse the items in the store and link to the cart page.

The majority of the administration for the store is done through the **Store Admin** module. The **Store Info** section of this module must be configured before other modules are available. The settings in the **Store Info** section include basic setup information such as **Store Name**, **Store Email**, **Store Page**, and **Shopping Cart Page**. Additionally, the payment **Gateway** must be selected and configured in this section before the store will run. Other sections of the **Store Admin** module are **Orders**, **Categories**, **Products**, and **Reviews**.

The **Store Menu** and **Store Catalog** modules allow you to manage the categories and products for the store respectively. The **Store Mini Cart** displays a list of the items a user has added to his/her cart and a link to the **Store Cart** module. The **Store Cart** module provides a detailed list of the items in the user's cart and a **Checkout** button.

Together these modules make up a fairly robust e-commerce package that provides features. Keep in mind that this module is provided for free, so some of the more advanced features may be missing. With that said, before spending money on a third-party e-commerce solution, the **Store** module is worth a look.

Special features and additional information

By default, the **Store** module provides three payment **Gateway** providers. These are PayPal, Authorize.Net, and Email. However, if additional **Gateway** providers are needed, they can be developed and installed for use with the store. Along with payment **Gateway** providers, custom providers for shipping and tax calculations can also be developed and installed. The provider-based design of this module makes it a serious competitor with some of the more expensive third-party e-commerce modules.

Survey module

The **Survey** module provides a way to solicit information from the visitors to a site. The module provides two primary types of survey questions—questions that can have multiple answers, indicated by the use of checkboxes, and questions that can only have one answer, indicated by the use of radio buttons.

When a user has answered all the questions, they can view the results of the survey, unless the survey results are marked as private in the **Module Settings** screen.

Administration and modification

When logged in as a user with **Edit** rights, a new survey question can be added by selecting the **Add Question** link. The following fields are available when adding a question:

- **Question**: The survey question to display to the user.
- **Type**: The type of survey question (single selection versus multiple selection).
- **View Order**: The order of the question in the list of questions.
- **New Option**: This field is used to add new options to the **Options** list. Add some text to this field and select **Add Option** to add a new option to display.
- **Option Is Correct Answer?**: Check this box if the option is considered to be the correct answer to the question.

The **Module Settings** screen provides configuration options that will affect the overall use of the module. These include:

- **Survey Closing Date**: The date the survey should no longer be available to the users.
- **Maximum Bar Graph Width**: This controls how wide the bar graph will be while viewing the results of the survey.

- **Vote Tracking**: This option can be set to **Vote tracking via cookie** (to allow anonymous users to vote only once) or **1 Vote / Registered User**. Note that tracking via a cookie cannot guarantee that a user votes only once. In order to ensure a user votes only once, you will require them to be logged in to complete the survey.

- **Survey Results**: If set to **Private**, only members of the administrator's role will be able to view the results of the survey.

- **Survey Result Template**: The template used to display the results of the survey.

- **Survey Results Data**: Provides an **Export Data** link to download the results of the survey. Note that only surveys completed by registered users will be included in the download.

- **Clear Results Data**: The **Clear** link effectively resets the survey by clearing all of the surveys completed by users.

Users Online module

The **Users Online** module displays information about site membership and activity. This includes the number of registered members, new registrations today, new registrations yesterday, and the username of the last registered user. Additionally, it can display the number of visitors and members currently online.

The **Users Online** module can put some pressure on computing resources of your web and database server. So, if you are not using this module, remember to uncheck the option **Enable Users Online** in HOST | **Host Settings | Advanced Settings | Other Settings**.

If you are using this module, you might also want to configure the **Users Online Time option** again available on the same path: HOST | **Host Settings | Advanced Settings | Other Settings**.

Administration and modification

The following options for this module are located on the **Module Settings** screen:

- **Module Status**: This item informs you if the host level settings to enable current site activity status are configured properly. (See the following information on configuring these options.)

- **Name Display Mode**: Determines how users are listed in the module.

- **Online User Prefix**: Changes the online users who appear in the module.

- **Show Super Users**: If checked, super user accounts will be included in the statistics.

- **Show Membership**: If checked, the membership statistics will be displayed in the module.

- **Show People Online**: If checked, the number of currently active users will be displayed in the module.

- **Show Users Online**: If checked, a list of currently logged in users will be displayed in the module.

To display the information regarding current site activity, host level settings must be configured. First, the **Enable Users Online** option needs to be checked. It is located in the **Advanced Settings** section on the **Host Settings** page. Also, the **DotNetNuke. Entities.Users.PurgeUsersOnline** item must be enabled on the **Schedule** screen located on the **HOST** menu. Once these options have been configured the statistics regarding current site activity will be available.

Wiki module

The **Wiki** module provides the ability to create linked pages of information easily. This module also allows you to override the standard DotNetNuke permissions for the module and allows users to edit the pages inside wiki without granting them full edit access to the module. This can be helpful if you have staff that would be in charge of keeping the content of the wiki updated, but do not need to administer the module.

Practical purposes

- Knowledge base for a software project

- Documentation on related research topics

- Collective and collaborative editing of site content between users

Administration and modification

A new instance of the **Wiki** module begins with a single page (**Home**). To modify this page, and create links to other pages inside wiki, click the **Edit** link located at the bottom of the module. Each page that is created has the following fields:

- **Page Name**: This is the page name that will be used in the URL.

- **Title**: This is the text that will be displayed in the title bar of the user's browser window.

- **Description**: The meta description used by search engines.

- **Keywords**: The meta keywords used by search engines.
- **Content**: A rich text editor used to modify the content of the page.
- **Wiki Text Directions**: There are no editable fields in this section; however, it explains how to create links to other pages in the wiki using double brackets. Reading this section will provide a solid understanding of how the wiki pages work.
- **Enable Page Comments/Enable Page Ranking**: These fields will be disabled unless they have been turned on in the **Administration** screen for the **Wiki** module.

On the module's **Action** menu, you will find an **Administration** link. This screen provides the ability to enable or disable page comments and rankings for all pages in the wiki. It also allows you to modify which roles can edit pages in the wiki. This will override the **Permissions** configured on the **Module Settings** screen.

Special features and additional information

The **Wiki** module provides a collapsible menu on the left side of the module. This menu contains the following links:

- **Home**: Returns to the original page in the wiki
- **Search**: Provides a search screen to locate article in the wiki
- **Recent Changes**: Provides a list of the most recently added or edited pages
- **Index**: A collapsible list of all of the pages in the wiki

XML/XSL module

The **XML/XSL** module renders the result of an XML/XSL transform. The XML and XSL files are identified by their UNC paths in the `xmlsrc` and `xslsrc` properties of the module. The **XML/XSL** module includes an **Edit** page, which is used to persist these settings to the SQL database.

Practical purposes

- Presenting XML data in a readable format
- Displaying data from external sources, such as web services or other XML feeds, as content on your site

Administration and modification

News feeds are not the only application to use XML to deliver data. Whether you have a program on your local intranet or you are trying to access a web service, the **XML/XSL** module allows you to translate the XML data to a readable format fit for your web page.

Special features and additional information

Like the **Form and List** module, the **XML/XSL** module gives you tremendous flexibility on the type of information you can present to your users. Using standard XML data, you can create different XSL stylesheets to present the data differently for different users.

Third-party modules

Along with the many modules provided by the DotNetNuke team, there is also a large ecosystem of third-party module developers. If you find that the modules provided by the core team do not suit your needs, a quick search of third-party module vendors usually returns what you are looking for. Module developer or vendors can be broken down into two general groups, commercial and open source. Each group has its own advantages and drawbacks. While we examine what the pros and cons are, keep in mind that these are generalizations and will not hold true in all scenarios.

We will also highlight a few developers or vendors for each group. These lists are meant to simply provide examples of the different types of module providers. The vendors listed were chosen because one or more authors of this book have had personal experience with these vendors or the sites are extremely popular with the overall community.

Commercial modules

These modules are created and sold by companies or individual developers through various channels. The most common places where modules are sold are on a vendor's own website or through a marketplace site. DotNetNuke's website provides a link to the most popular marketplace that just happens to be owned by the DotNetNuke corporation. Here you can find literally thousands of different modules to choose from.

Prices for these modules vary greatly depending on the type or complexity of the module and the vendor selling the module. Prices can range from as low as a few dollars to hundreds, or even thousands, of dollars. Another thing to be aware about pricing of modules is the license type. Some module's license allow you to use the module on a single portal, all portals in a single DotNetNuke installation, or on any portal you manage.

Obviously, if you need to use the module on several portals across multiple installations, you would want to look for a license that allows you to do so. Usually you will pay significantly more for this type of license, as the typical license allows the module to be used only on a single installation.

You may also want to research the vendor's policy on providing patches and upgrades for the module. Some vendors provide patches for bug fixes only, some provide updates only for a year, and others provide a subscription-based model. The subscription vendors typically allow you to download all of their modules, as long as you maintain an active subscription.

Commercial module vendors tend to provide a high level of support for their products and are interested in having satisfied customers. This is a huge advantage when something goes wrong. With that said, not all vendors are as dedicated to supporting their products as others. So, it cannot be assumed that just because you paid a lot of money for a module, the vendor will provide the level of support you are looking for.

Developers and vendors

- www.activemodules.com: Some of the products available through this vendor are a forum module, social networking module, and customer relations module. Each module is available for purchase directly on this site and most provide multiple licensing levels.

- www.itlackey.net: A subscription-based site that allows access to all of their modules and unlimited usage of the modules on the portal you manage. Examples of modules provided by this site are a customizable **Google Analytics** module, a PayPal **BuyNow** button module, and a **Page Last Updated** module. Subscriptions can be purchased directly through the site.

- www.opendnn.net: Provides some unique modules such as **Open-SmartModule**, **Open-ViewState**, and **Open-KeepAlive**. The purchase links on this site direct you to listing on the Snowcovered website. They provide multiple licensing options and allow the purchasing on the source code for some of their modules.

- `www.snowcovered.com`: The most widely used market place for purchasing modules and skins. Snowcovered works somewhat like `Amazon.com` and allows independent developers and companies to list the products for sale. The **Marketplace** link on DotNetNuke's website links to this site.

- `www.ventrian.com`: A subscription-based module vendor that provides all of their modules to users with an active subscription. Some of the more popular modules are their **News Articles**, **Simple Gallery**, and **Property Agent** modules. Source code is provided for all their modules and the license provided with these modules allows unlimited usage on portals you manage. Subscriptions can be purchased directly from the vendor's site.

Open source modules

Typically open source projects are available for free and are created and maintained by a single individual or small group of developers. These developers usually have a full-time job in the field of development and work on the open source project in their spare time. This can be a disadvantage when it comes to getting support for the module or waiting for features to be added. As the developers generally cannot spend much time working on these projects, when compared to commercial modules, things tend to move a bit slower. Again, this is not always the case, there are many open source projects that have better support and quicker turnaround on new features than commercial counterparts.

A benefit that works to offset this disadvantage is the fact that you have full access to the source code for the module. If you are a developer, you can modify the source code to include the features you are waiting for, fix the bug that is requiring support, and even contribute your efforts back to the community to assist other users. This also becomes a huge advantage if you are learning to develop your own modules. Having a working example of how others have developed modules usually helps overcome the initial learning curve.

The most obvious advantage to open source modules is the fact that they are typically available free of charge. Hobbyists, small businesses, and non-profit organizations probably benefit the most from this. However, regardless of the type of site, there are many open source modules that are worth evaluating before spending money to purchase a commercial counterpart. Keep in mind that all of the modules provided by the DotNetNuke team and the DotNetNuke platform itself are all open source and serve many large companies very well.

In the past, open source was usually viewed as not providing the same quality and reliability as commercial software. This mindset has been changing in the recent past and this has worked to further strengthen the position and products of the open source community. The growing number of interested consumers and successful products lends credibility to the concept of open source software.

Developers and vendors

- www.codeplex.com: As mentioned in *Chapter 2, Installing DotNetNuke*, CodePlex is a site provided by Microsoft to host open source applications. Searching for DotNetNuke on this site returns many modules and other projects that can be used with DotNetNuke.

- www.dotnetnuke.com: In addition to the modules discussed earlier in this chapter, the DotNetNuke website now provides a feature called the **Forge**. The **Forge** is a list of open source modules run by members of the DotNetNuke community. Each item in the **Forge** provides general information for the module and links to a project on the CodePlex website.

- www.openlightgroup.net: The group of developers includes two of the authors of this book and offers several modules. Modules provided by this group range from a popular **Help Desk** module to the most widely used web services module and several modules that integrate Silverlight applications with DotNetNuke.

- www.smart-thinker.com: This vendor was originally a commercial module provider. However, as of January 2009, all of their modules are now provided for free with the source code. These modules include an events module, user profile and user groups modules, a referrals module, and a social networking wall module.

Summary

In this chapter, we initially discussed the administration, common features, and settings of modules in a DotNetNuke portal. This included how to add modules to a page, how to adjust layout options, and permission modules.

We then covered the standard modules that come prepackaged with DotNetNuke. We covered their basic uses, as well as situations they may be used in. We also gave a brief overview of all of the modules developed by the DotNetNuke team of developers. These modules ranged from simple content display to fully interactive forums and e-commerce solutions.

After discussing the modules available from the DotNetNuke team, we discussed third-party commercial and open source modules. After covering the pros and cons of using commercial and open source modules, we reviewed a brief list of vendors from both of these groups.

Regardless of whom the modules are provided by, the DotNetNuke team, a commercial or open source vendor, you will use these modules to build the content of your portal.

In the next chapter, we will cover the administration options that are available to you, as well as the differences between the administrator and host login.

5
Host and Admin Tools

Running a DotNetNuke site requires someone to administer the site. There are two built-in roles for accomplishing the tasks associated with this. The host and admin roles are very similar in nature and ability, but possess some important differences.

In this chapter, we will learn the following:

- The difference between host and admin
- How to access and use the admin modules
- How to access and use the host modules

The difference between host and admin

There has always been a bit of confusion about what differentiates the admin and host roles. To understand the difference, you first have to look at how DotNetNuke works. An implementation of DotNetNuke is not restricted to one portal. DotNetNuke has the ability to run multiple portals (that is, websites) from one database. This is where the difference between the roles comes in.

The host has the responsibility of, for lack of a better word, hosting the portals. The host will have access to any parent and/or child portals that are created, as well as all the administrative functions across all portals. This user is sometimes called a **superuser**. In previous versions of DotNetNuke, you were allowed only one superuser per installation. Starting with DotNetNuke 3.0, and continuing, you can add additional users with superuser abilities. This helps to divide the tasks needed to run multiple portals.

On the other hand, the admin role is responsible for only one portal. There can be more than one admin for every portal, but unlike the superusers, they have the ability to access only one portal. While the superuser has access to both host tools and the admin tools on all portals, the admin will see only the admin tools on the portal to which they belong.

Admin tools

When you sign in to your DotNetNuke portal using an admin login, you will see an **ADMIN** menu item appear on the menu bar. In this section, we will cover these menu items in detail.

As mentioned in *Chapter 4, Standard DotNetNuke Modules*, one of the new and exciting features of DotNetNuke 5.0 was the ability to allow non-administrative users to have access to some of the admin modules. These modules include the following:

- **Banners**
- **File Manager**
- **Google Analytics**
- **Languages**
- **Log Viewer**
- **Newsletters**
- **Recycle Bin**
- **Site Log**
- **Site Wizard**
- **Skins**
- **Solutions**
- **Pages** (or **Tabs**)
- **Users And Roles**
- **Vendors**

These modules are listed on the **ADMIN** menu by default. However, they can also be added to pages, and the permissions to these items can be configured like any other module. Though, before doing so, you may want to consider this carefully. Granting users access to some of these modules may allow them privileges you may not want them to have. For example, you may not want a regular user to have the ability to add or remove pages or users.

In some cases, this may be helpful, but again be sure and take the time to analyze the consequences before granting access to these modules to non-administrative users. We will talk about each of these modules in detail in the coming sections. The information presented will help you decide when it is appropriate to allow users to access these modules.

 The **Pages**, and **Users And Roles** modules were discussed in *Chapter 3, Users, Roles, and Pages*. Please refer to the corresponding sections of that chapter for more information on these modules.

The first admin menu item is **Site Settings**. The **Site Settings** cover a wide range of services for a site. Because of this, we cannot cover this in one section of the book. We will walk through each item on the **Site Settings** page and either describe its functionality or point you to where you can find the information in this book.

Site Settings

Like the other admin screens we have seen, the **Site Settings** page lays out several options that allow the administrator to customize the portal experience. These settings are divided into three sections: **Basic Settings**, **Advanced Settings**, and **StyleSheet Editor**. We will begin with the **Basic Settings** section.

Basic Settings

The **Basic Settings** section appears as shown in the next screenshot. Here, the **Site Details** are used to tailor your portal with the information that describes what your site is used for:

- **Title**: The title or name for your website. This will be displayed in the top bar of your browser along with the current tab information.

- **Description** and **Keywords**: Used by search engines when indexing your site. The keywords should be entered in a comma-separated format.

- **Copyright**: The copyright notice that appears on the footer of each page on the portal. Change this to reflect your portal name.

The **Site Marketing** section provides the ability to manage how search engines interact with the portal and how banner marketing is handled on the portal. The various fields under the **Site Marketing** section are as follows:

- **Search Engine**: Allows you to submit your site to the selected search engine to request that the site be indexed.

- **Site Map URL**: Used to submit the sitemap for the site to Google Sitemaps. Using this feature requires a Google Webmaster Tools account. Information on this process can be found in the Webmaster Tools section of Google's site. Additional configuration options are available in the settings of each page that allow for customization of each entry. These options are discussed in *Chapter 3, Users, Roles, and Pages*.

- **Verification**: Creates the verification file required by Google Webmaster Tools. Google will provide a filename when signing up for an account. Once you have the filename, simply enter the name and click the **Create** button.

- **Banners**: Configure the type of banner advertising displayed on the portal.

The **Appearance** section, as shown in the following screenshot controls the basic look and feel of your site.

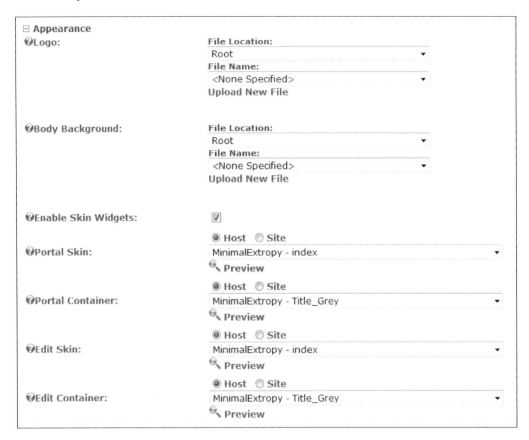

The various fields in the **Appearance** section are as follows:

- **Logo**: If you are using the default look of DotNetNuke, you can change the logo from the DotNetNuke `logo.gif` to one of your choice.

- **Body Background**: As an alternative to skinning your site, you can choose to change the background of your site to any image you would like. To do this, select the image from the dropdown. You will need to upload the image to your site first. The ease of using skins makes this option almost obsolete. Please note that the background image would be tiled both horizontally as well as vertically.

- **Enable Skin Widgets**: Skin Widgets are new to DotNetNuke and allow for several useful features. Some examples of these widgets can be seen in the default skin. These are the controls in the upper right-hand side of the skin used to control the text size and page width.

- **Portal Skin**, **Portal Container**, **Edit Skin**, and **Edit Container**: This section allows you to select a skin for your portal. There are different sections for edit and portal skins because edit sections of the site usually use only one pane, and portal sections use three or more.

Advanced Settings

The **Advanced Settings** are divided into several different sections—**Security Settings**, **Page Management**, **Payment Settings**, **Usability Settings**, and **Other Settings**. The options available in the **Security Settings** section are discussed in *Chapter 3*, *Users, Roles, and Pages*; so, we will first look at **Page Management**.

The **Advanced Settings** section is as shown in the following screenshot:

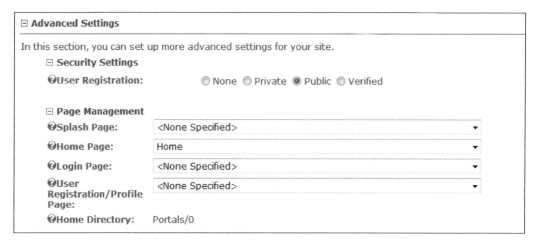

The various fields of the **Page Management** section are discussed in detail in the following list:

- **Splash Page**: Lets you choose from a drop-down a splash page that will load before your site is shown (if you want your site to begin with a splash page). Splash pages are commonly used to present an attractive Silverlight or Flash animation highlighting the major sections of your portal, and to provide links to them.

- **Home Page**: Determines where users are redirected to when they first navigate to, register, or log in to your portal. The default is the **Home** page; however, you may select any page on your portal from the drop-down. This is also the page where the user will be redirected when they enter the site's domain name into their browser, once they have completed the registration or the login process.

- **Login Page**: This is the page the user will be directed to when they attempt to log in to the portal.

- **User Page**: By default, administrators can't edit the user account information page, but can place the **User Accounts** module on a separate page along with other modules of their choice. To change the default user accounts page to a different tab, you can select the page from the drop-down box. The user will be redirected to this page, if he or she is registering on the site. This is useful if you use third-party modules for user management on your portal, or otherwise want to configure the page your users use to manage their account, in some way.

- **Home Directory**: The physical path of your portal's location.

The **Payment Settings** section, as the name implies, allows you to add payment processing to your portal. The **Payment Settings** section is as shown in the following screenshot:

- **Currency, Payment Processor, Processor UserId**, and **Processor Password**: DotNetNuke gives you the ability to charge users for subscribing to a service on your site (see the *Understanding DotNetNuke roles and role groups* section in *Chapter 3, Users, Roles, and Pages*). The only payment processor fully integrated into DotNetNuke at this time is PayPal.

The **Usability Settings** section provides options to control the administration experience for the portal. It appears as shown in the following screenshot:

The various fields of the **Usability Settings** section are discussed in detail in the following list:

- **Inline Editor Enabled?**: If checked, allows portions of the site to be edited directly without navigating to the corresponding editing area (for example, the **HTML** module allows inline editing without needing to navigate to the corresponding edit control).

- **Control Panel Mode**: Customize the default mode for the control panel.

- **Control Panel Visibility**: Specify whether the control panel should be expanded or collapsed by default.

- **Control Panel Security**: Determines whether the control panel is visible to page editors only or if it should be displayed to users authorized to edit modules.

The **Other Settings** section helps you customize your portal to fit the company's identity. It appears as shown in the following screenshot:

The various fields of the **Other Settings** section are discussed in detail in the following list:

- **Administrator**: The default administrator for this site. You can select anyone who has been added to the administrator role.

- **Default Language**: Beginning with DotNetNuke 3.0, localization has been integrated into the DotNetNuke portal. At the time of writing, only English and German were available, but many more are on the way. You can set the default language of your portal by selecting it from the dropdown.

- **Portal TimeZone**: Allows you to localize your portal's time zone.

Stylesheet Editor

The **Stylesheet Editor** section is the final portion of the **Site Settings**.

- **Edit Style Sheet**: This will allow you to edit the CSS stylesheet for the DotNetNuke site. You can change the look and feel of the site by modifying the styles located in the stylesheet.

Pages

You will find a discussion on pages under the *Understanding DotNetNuke pages and tabIDs* section in *Chapter 3, Users, Roles, and Pages*.

Extensions

The **Extension** page (see the next screenshot) provides a way to view or configure settings for the authentication systems, containers, modules, and skins available to the portal. All of the items listed allow you to view information regarding the installed item. This includes its name, description, version, and license among other information.

Items listed under authentication systems allow you to configure the options for the item. Each authentication system provides a unique set of options. For example, the default authentication system allows you to enable a **CAPTCHA** feature to be used during the login process for the portal. For detailed information on what options are available for a given authentication system, please refer to the documentation for that system.

 Module entries allow you to configure deployment permissions for each module that is currently installed. If you would like to prevent users from adding a particular module to a page, you can set the permission for that module to 'Deny'. The default permission is to allow users with permission to edit a page to add any installed module. The deployment permission can be used to limit what modules non-administrative users can use.

⊟ **Extension Settings**

In this section you can set deploy permissions for this module. Clicking a checkbox twice will make sure users in that role cannot put this module on a page (Deny Permission).

Desktop Module Permissions:

	Deploy Module
Administrators	✔
All Users	☐
Registered Users	☐
Subscribers	☐
Unauthenticated Users	☐

Username: [＿＿＿＿＿＿] ✚ Add

◈ Update Desktop Module

Languages

Starting with DotNetNuke version 3.x, you have the ability to localize your portal to the language of your choice. A superuser can install language packs that contain the default translations of DNN content (for example, help text, titles, and so on) for the corresponding language. This screen allows you to modify the localized values for each entry in the selected language. All changes made on this screen apply only to the current portal and will not affect the translations used by other portals. Using the tree view control located on the left side of the screen, you can navigate to resource files and modify the translations used by different portions of the portal. For instance, by navigating to **Local Resources | Admin | Control Panel**, you can modify the values used for the text in the **Control Panel** area.

Skins

This section allows you to browse through all of the skins and containers that have been uploaded to your portal. You may also select the default skin and container to be used by your portal here.

Security Roles

You will find a discussion on security roles under the *Understanding DotNetNuke roles and role groups* section in *Chapter 3, Users, Roles, and Pages.*

User Accounts

You will find a discussion of user accounts under the *User accounts* in *Chapter 3, Users, Roles, and Pages.*

Vendors

You will find a discussion of vendors under the *Host Tools* section in this chapter.

Site Log

The **Site Log** gives you access to log files that keep track of most things that happen on your portal.

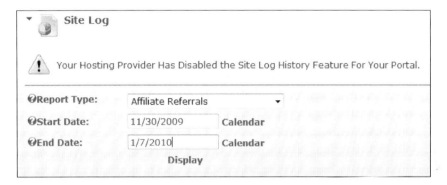

This feature must be enabled for your portal by a superuser or the logs will be empty. A warning will be displayed if this feature is currently not active.

To use the site report, select one of the following options from the drop-down, select a **Start Date** and **End Date**, and click on the **Display** link.

- **Affiliate Referrals**: You can track when users enter your site from sites that are affiliated with you. To make this work, the link coming from the affiliate site must add a query string to the URL. For example, instead of pointing the link to `http://www.CoffeeConnections.net`, you would point it to `http://www.CoffeeConnections.net?AffiliateID=108`. You would need to give different IDs to different affiliates. When someone logs in using one of those links, it is recorded into the database and you then have the ability to view reports of this data.

- **Detailed Site Log**: This report gives you the name of the user, the date and time they entered your site, the website they came from (referrer), the type of browser they are using (user agent), their IP address (**UserHostAddress**), and the name of the tab they entered on.

- **Page Popularity**: This report gives you the page name, number of times the page has been visited, and when the tab was last visited.

- **Page Views By Day**, **Day Of Week**, **Hour**, **Month**: The report gives you summarized views of how many visitors have been on your site.

- **Site Referrals**: This report gives you the website that referred users to the site (referrer), the number of times users came from the site, and the last time a user was referred by the site. Unlike the **Affiliate Referrals**, this tracks users from any website, and not just those with which you have a relationship.

- **User Agents**: This report gives the types of browsers (user agents) used to browse your site as well as the number of times each browser was used.

- **User Frequency**: This report gives you the number of times each user has logged onto your site. It also displays the last time users logged in.

- **User Registration By Country**: This report details what country your users come from. The report depends entirely on the country the users select when registering on your portal.

- **User Registrations By Date**: This report sorts the registrations on your site by the date the users registered. It provides you with the date and the number that registered on each date.

Newsletters

As an administrator, you can send out bulk e-mails to your users. The **Newsletters** section contains all that you need to send newsletters to your users.

 Be aware that sending out a large number of unsolicited mails might make the major mail providers flag your from e-mail address as a spammer. So, use this feature judiciously, and ask your users to add your **From** e-mail address to their contact list to avoid being accidently flagged as spam.

The **Basic Settings** of the **Newsletters** section appears as shown in the following screenshot:

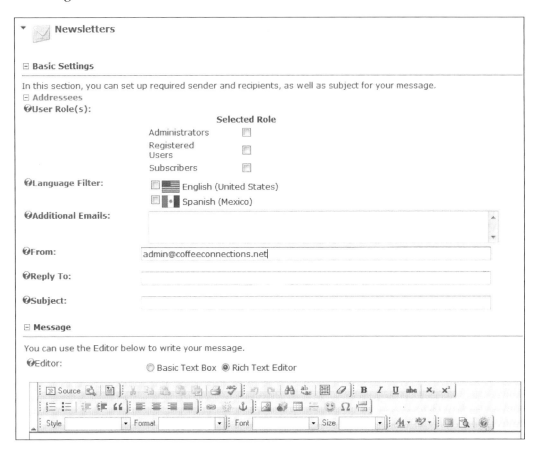

The various fields are as described in the following list:

- **User Role(s)**: You can send an e-mail to a select group of users based on the user roles you set up for your portal. (For more information on user roles, see the *Understanding DotNetNuke roles and role groups* section in *Chapter 3, Users, Roles, and Pages*.)

- **Language Filter**: If multiple languages are installed, you can filter users based on the languages specified in their profiles.

- **Additional Emails**: Optionally, you can send e-mails to e-mail addresses in this e-mail list. You will need to make sure that you separate each e-mail address with a semicolon.

- **From**: Here you may enter a from address for the e-mail. This will default to the e-mail address of the portal administrator.

- **Reply To**: Allows you to specify a reply-to e-mail address for the e-mail.

- **Subject**: This will appear on the subject line when the e-mail is received.

- **Message**: The body of the message that you want to send. You may use either a **Basic Text Box** or the **Rich Text Editor** (CKEditor).

The **Advanced Settings** section of the **Newsletters** section is as shown in the following screenshot:

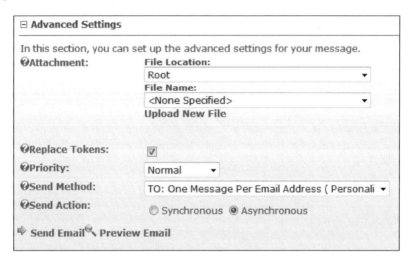

The various fields are as described in the following list:

- **Attachment**: You can add an attachment to be sent out in the e-mail. Select the attachment from the drop-down box or upload a new file. For more information on uploading files, see the *File Manager* section in this chapter.

- **Replace Tokens**: If checked, tokens will be replaced using the values of the current environment. Please note that tokens will not be replaced if the BCC **Send Method** is used.

- **Priority**: You can set the priority of your e-mail to **Low**, **Normal**, or **High**.

- **Send Method**: You have two choices on how to send your message. The first method will send a separate e-mail to each user that will be personalized with their username. The second method will send one e-mail with all the users entered into the BCC (Blind Carbon Copy) section of the e-mail. The e-mail will not be personalized, and all users will see the same message. The **Relay** option allows for personalized e-mail messages to be sent through an SMS relay provider. If this option is selected, a relay address textbox will appear to allow you to specify the provider.

- **Send Action**: Selecting **Synchronous** will have your web page wait while the e-mails are sent. Selecting **Asynchronous** will send the e-mails on a new thread behind the scenes. It is preferable to use the **Asynchronous** option, if sending out a large number of mails. Any exceptions in e-mail delivery would be available in the **Event Log**.

- Click **Send Email** when your message is complete.

File Manager

The **File Manager** allows the users to manage files and folders on the portal. As stated before, this is one of the modules that you are now able to add to other pages and allow users to access. This feature can be very helpful when the need to delegate file and folder management arises.

The **File Manager** appears as shown in the following screenshot:

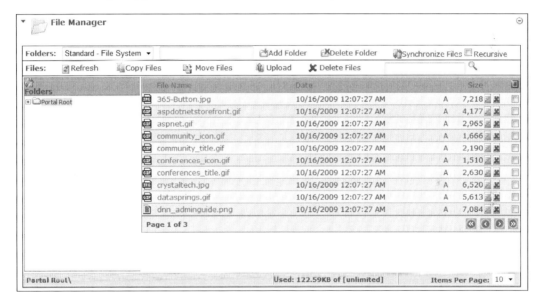

Version 4.3 of DotNetNuke introduced the concept of secure folders. Thus, there are now three types of folder that you can create, which are described as follows:

- **Standard-File System**: This is the normal folder type. Files in this folder are accessible to anybody who knows the correct URL of the file.

- **Secure-File System**: This folder type also exists on the server's filesystem but adds a level of security. This is achieved by renaming files that are uploaded to the folder, by adding a protected file extension. This file extension stops the server from serving the file to anybody who happens to know the correct URL. The file can still be processed through the DotNetNuke **File Handler**, thus achieving a level of security; in that only users with permissions to the file can access it. This works by appending a `.resources` extension to the names of the files in the folder. By default, ASP.NET will not serve files with this extension to a request. However, if the server administrator changes this setting, the files will no longer be secured by this method.

- **Secure-Database**: This option creates a database folder. Files in a database folder are actually stored in the database itself. This is the most secure type of storage, as it requires the file to be processed through the DotNetNuke **File Handler**.

To create a new folder, select the folder type from the drop-down list, type a name into the folder box, and click on the **Add Folder** icon (the folder icon with a down arrow in the corner). This will then allow you to upload files to this folder. To upload a new file to the portal from within the **File Manager**, click on the **Upload** icon and perform the following steps:

- Click on the **Browse** button to select the file to upload. This will open the **Choose File** dialog box. Navigate to the location of the file you would like to upload and select it. This will place the location of the file in the browse textbox.

- Select the folder where you would like to upload the file.

- Click on the **Upload File** link to add the file to the list of files to be uploaded.

- **Decompress ZIP Files?**: If you have selected a ZIP file to be uploaded to your portal, you can either have the files inside the ZIP file extracted (box is checked) or upload the ZIP file in its entirety (box is unchecked).

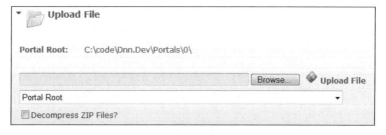

On the right side of the **Folders** toolbar is a **Synchronize Files** icon as well as a checkbox labeled **Recursive**. DotNetNuke stores information about each folder and file in the database. Throughout the application, if a list of folders or files is required the list is generated from the information in the database, rather than the actual list of files on the server's filesystem. Clicking this button ensures that any files that may have been uploaded using an **FTP (File Transfer Protocol)** client are added to the database. Checking the **Recursive** checkbox before clicking the **Synchronize Files** icon will cause any child folders of the currently selected folder to also be synchronized. By default, DNN performs automatic synchronization of your filesystem with the database at regular intervals. The option to control this auto-sync is available in the **Host Settings** page.

On the bottom of the admin **File Manager** page are some options you can set to allow other users to upload files, which is shown in the following screenshot:

In the **Folder Security Settings** section:

- Check the boxes next to the roles allowed to upload files.
- Clicking the box a second time allows you to specifically deny roles from viewing or uploading to the currently selected folder.
- Click on **Update** to save your settings.

Recycle Bin

The **Recycle Bin** allows you to recover modules or pages that have been deleted.

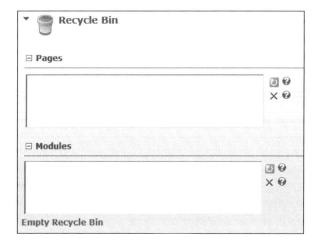

- To restore a page or module to its original location, highlight it and click on the restore icon. Be aware that a module cannot be restored if the page it was on has also been deleted. Restore the page before restoring the module.

- To delete a page or module permanently, highlight it and click on the delete icon.

- Clicking the **Empty Recycle Bin** button will permanently delete all of the modules and pages currently listed in the **Recycle Bin**.

 Pages may not be restored to the same location in the menu as they were before being deleted. If you restore a page and it does not show in the menu, use the **Pages** module to locate the page and move it to the desired position in the menu.

Event Viewer

The **Log viewer** gives an administrator of the portal or allowed users the ability to monitor all events that occur on the portal. When adding this tool to a page, select the **Log Viewer** module and be sure to set the permissions appropriately. This module contains sensitive data that you do not want to share with all users of your site.

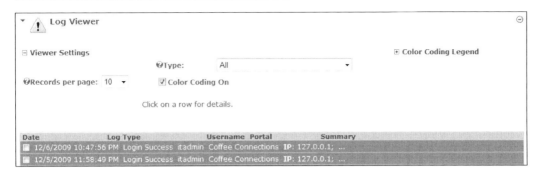

General Exception Errors will only show up in the log viewer when you are signed on as a superuser (host). These types of exceptions are normally logged on when a module raises an unhandled exception, or logs an exception using the generic `LogException` method. These logging methods are discussed in the subsequent chapters on module development.

The log will track many different pieces of information; among them the most useful are the exceptions. To view the details for any log entry just click on the row. This will give you a detailed explanation of the log entry.

This information is very helpful when attempting to track down errors generated by your portal. To alert you to errors happening to other users, DotNetNuke gives you the ability to send error notices to any e-mail address. To set up this, expand the **Send Exceptions** section at the bottom of the **Log Viewer**.

It is important to note that the e-mails will not be encrypted when sent. So be careful if sensitive data is involved.

- **Email Address**: The e-mail address of the person you would like the error notification to be sent to. This will send the addressee the detailed error message, including the stack trace. To send to more than one address, separate them with a semicolon (;).

- **Message**: A message to accompany the exception.

- Click on the **Send Selected Exceptions** link to save your settings.

Site Wizard

We will discuss this tool in more detail in *Chapter 10, Creating Multiple Portals*.

Google Analytics

This feature is new in DotNetNuke 5 and allows you to enable Google's Analytics on your portal. **Google Analytics** provides advanced site traffic analysis that includes metrics such as search keywords used to find your site, the length of time a visitor spent on your site, and much more. A complete discussion on **Google Analytics** is beyond the scope of this book. Detailed information on what **Google Analytics** provides and how to use it can be found on Google's website.

> The module only offers the basic **Google Analytics** features. There are several third-party modules that allow you to use more advanced features.

Host tools

To access the host tools, you will first need to log in as the host for your portal. Once you have done this, you will see the host menu. We will cover each of the tools that are available to you as a superuser.

Host Settings

The first menu item on the host menu is **Host Settings**. They are separated into **Basic Settings** and **Advanced Settings**. The **Host Settings** cover a very wide range of services for your portal. Because of this, we will walk through each item on the **Host Settings** page and either describe its functionality or point you to where you can find the information in this book.

Basic Settings

As we have seen when we looked at the admin **Site Settings**, the **Basic Settings** on the **Host Settings** page give you the ability to customize your hosting environment.

The **Site Configuration** section (shown in the next screenshot) covers information about your current installation of DotNetNuke, such as the DNN Version Number, .NET Framework Version Number, Data Provider, Host Name, and so on.

Starting with DotNetNuke 5.2 .NET Framework version 3.5 is required.

 If the **Check For Upgrades** checkbox is checked, DotNetNuke will notify you that a newer version is available by placing an **Upgrade Available** image on this page as well as on the control panel of each page.

The **Host Details** section (shown in the next screenshot) covers the contact information for your portal.

The various fields are as described in the following list:

- **Host Portal**: The portal that serves as the host for all other parent or child portals that you create.

- **Host Title**: The text for the hyperlink that is displayed. The **Host Title** is used by the host skin object and would typically be located on the footer of the skin. This would be used for something like a "Powered By" link for example.

- **Host URL**: The location to which the user will be taken to when the **Host Title** hyperlink is clicked.

- **Host Email**: The e-mail address used when sending out certain administration e-mails.

- **Fallback Skin Doctype**: This setting is used if the selected skin does not provide a specific doctype.

- **Enable Remember me on login controls?**: Allows users to select the **Remember Me** option while logging in to a portal. By selecting this option, a cookie is created for the user to prevent them from needing to log in when they return to the site. The cookie is a persistent cookie with a timeout duration that can be controlled through the `web.config` file.

The **Appearance** section (refer to the next screenshot) controls the basic look and feel of the site:

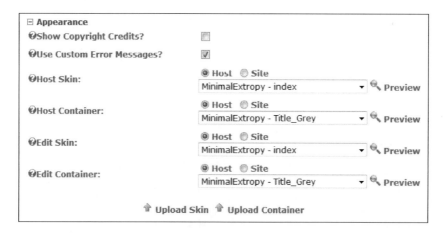

The various fields are as described in the following list:

- **Show Copyright Credits?**: Unchecking this box will remove the DotNetNuke copyright from the footer and the (DNN 5.X) from the IE header.

- **Use Custom Error Messages?**: DotNetNuke uses a custom provider for its error handling. If you would like to turn this feature off and use the default ASP.NET error handling, uncheck this box.

- **Host Skin**, **Host Container**, **Edit Skin**, and **Edit Container**: This section allows you to select a skin for your portal. There are different sections for edit and portal skins because edit sections of the site usually use only one frame and portal sections utilize three or more. This section also provides the option to upload a skin or container.

- **Payment Settings**: This section allows you to set up a payment processor for your site and gives you the ability to charge for hosting multiple DotNetNuke sites.

Advanced Settings

The **Advanced Settings** section is used to allow fine grain control over aspects such as caching, authentication, site log, and so on that are advanced administrative tasks.

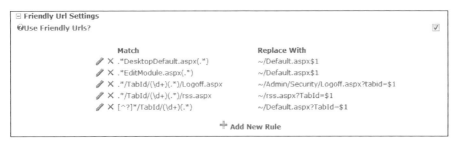

Checking the **Use Friendly Urls** box (default) will create URLs that are search engine friendly. Search engines, for the most part, prefer URLs without query strings. This option will create the URL in a friendlier version, allowing your site to perform better on search sites. Human friendly URLs are enabled by default starting in DNN 5.1 which further simplifies the URLs used to navigate to pages. This feature was available in previous versions of DotNetNuke, but required a change to the configuration file to enable the feature.

The last screenshot displays a list of regular expressions that are used to configure how to rewrite the URLs. A discussion of regular expressions is beyond the scope of this book, but if you know how to write regular expressions then you can provide very precise control over how this feature works. However, make sure you don't play around with the preconfigured rules or add new ones, unless you know what you are doing. An incorrect rule here might render your portal totally inaccessible.

Beginning in DNN 4.5.3, a Request Filter system has been available to take a specified action based on values in the request. This system works similar to how the friendly URL settings work. However, instead of simply redirecting the request to the correct page, this system can be configured to take other actions. For example, if you would like to block a particular IP address from accessing your site, you could return a "404 Not Found" error on every request from that address.

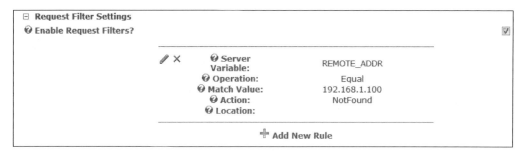

When configuring the rules for the filters, you are given the following options:

- **Server Variable**: These are variables passed with the request. A link is provided to MSDN to get a list of available values.

- **Operation**: Provides three options on how to compare the value of the specified variable. These are **Equal**, **NotEqual**, and **RegEx**. The **RegEx** option again uses regular expression like the friendly URL settings to do the comparison.

- **Action**: The action to be taken with a match is found. The options are **Redirect**, **PermanentRedirect**, and **NotFound** used to return a 404 error.

- **Location**: The URL used if one of the redirect actions are chosen.

Some intranet or Internet configurations need to use a proxy server to allow modules to make web requests to the Internet. An example of this is the RSS **Newsfeed** module, which requests data from a news feed source on the Internet. This next section allows you to configure DotNetNuke to use a proxy server:

Proxy Settings	
Proxy Server:	
Proxy Port:	-1
Proxy Username:	
Proxy Password:	
Web Request Timeout:	10000

The various fields of the **Proxy Settings** are as follows:

- **Proxy Server**: The IP address of the proxy server
- **Proxy Port**: The port that the proxy server uses to fulfill web requests
- **Proxy Username**: The username needed to connect through the proxy server
- **Proxy Password**: The password needed to connect through the proxy server
- **Web Request Timeout**: The time, in seconds, for which DotNetNuke will attempt to fulfill a web request

For the e-mail functionality to work on your portal, you will need to configure your **SMTP (Simple Mail Transfer Protocol)** server. These settings are the same settings that are available to be configured during the initial install of DotNetNuke. Once the correct information has been entered, you can click on the **Test** link to determine whether it is working. If the test succeeds, you will receive a message that says **Email Sent Successfully**. If there is an error, it will say **There has been an error trying to send the test email**. This is a generic error message; look in the **Log Viewer** for specific details.

The various fields of the **SMTP Server Settings** section are described as follows:

- **SMTP Server and port**: The address of your mail server. This can be obtained from your ISP. It is usually your domain name with `mail` replacing the `www`.

- **SMTP Authentication**: The type of authentication to use for your site. Starting with version 4.0, you now have the ability to use active directory to manage your users.

- **SMTP Enable SSL**: Allows for a secure connection to the SMTP, if required.

- **SMTP Username**: The username for your SMTP server, if required.

- **SMTP Password**: The password for your SMTP server, if required.

A **Performance Settings** section is provided to configure options used to increase the efficiency of the portals hosted by DotNetNuke. These settings are as shown in the following screenshot:

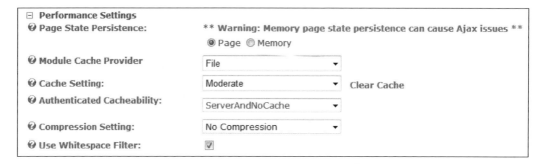

The various fields of the **Performance Settings** section are as follows:

- **Page State Persistence**: The default value is **Page** that caches the state in a hidden field on the page. The **Memory** option places state (that is, ViewState) in server memory to decrease the amount of data transferred. However, it is a known issue that **Memory** caching can cause problems with AJAX.

- **Module Cache Provider**: This setting allows you to decide whether to use memory caching or disk caching for your portal.

- **Cache Settings**: The performance settings are used to speed up the rendering of your portal. Caching stores a representation of the data contained in your page. This means that subsequent attempts to access this page (even by other users) will show the same data. Setting this to **Heavy Caching** will keep the cached data the longest and will provide the best performance. However, be advised that higher cache settings can lead to more utilization of server resources, depending upon the content on your portal. Also, heavier caching would lead to delay in time when a cached content is updated, and is displayed to the user. To clear the cache, click on the **Clear** link.

- **Authenticated Cacheability**: This setting controls how the output content is cached. Caching can improve performance as either the client or the server retains a copy of the content in its buffer. For the most part, this setting should be left at its default value. Only host users with considerable experience configuring web servers should modify this setting. The settings available include:
    - **NoCache**: No client-side caching — the browser should fetch a new copy each request
    - **Public**: Allows the output to be cached by both the client and server (including proxy servers)
    - **Private**: Allows the output to be cached on both the client and server (but not proxy servers)
    - **Server**: The output is only cached on the server
    - **ServerAndNoCache (default)**: A combination of the server and **NoCache** settings
    - **ServerAndPrivate**: A combination of the server and private settings
- **Compression Setting**: Allows HTTP compression to be used. Options are **No Compression**, **Deflate**, or **GZip** compression. Important: Make sure to use this only if IIS is not configured to compress data.
- **Use Whitespace Filter**: Removes unneeded space from the data returned to the client, but will make the source HTML harder to read. This option is not needed if you are using a compression method.

The next section is **Compression Settings** that further refines how the compression setting and whitespace filter settings are used.

The fields are described as follows:

- **Excluded Paths**: Used to disable compression for specific pages. This may become useful if a particular page begins behaving badly after enabling compression.
- **Whitespace Filter**: The regular expression used to strip whitespace from the returned HTML. The default value is usually sufficient.

The **JQuery Settings** section, as shown in the next screenshot, allows you to modify how the jQuery JavaScript library is loaded by DotNetNuke.

The fields are described as follows:

- **Installed jQuery Version**: The version of the local copy of the jQuery library.
- **Use jQuery Debug Version?**: If enabled, the standard jQuery library is used instead of the minified version. This may be helpful for troubleshooting.
- **Use Hosted jQuery Version?**: If checked, the associated URL will be used to load the JavaScript instead of the local copy.
- **Hosted jQuery URL:** The full URL to the hosted script. By default, this is set to Google's CDN, but can be changed to Microsoft's CDN or any other URL hosting the library.

The **Other Settings** section is set up to hold all the information that does not fit into any particular group.

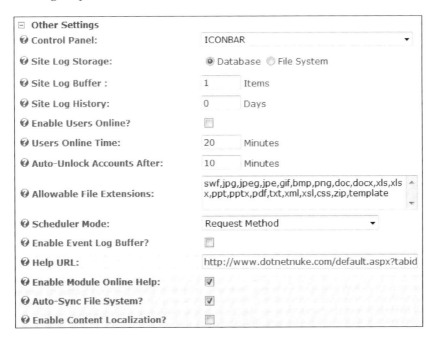

The various fields of the **Other Settings** section are described as follows:

- **Control Panel**: When signed in as host or admin, you will see a control panel at the top of the screen. If you prefer, this allows you to specify an alternative control panel to use.

- **Site Log Storage**: You can select whether you would like the site logs to be stored in your database or in the filesystem.

- **Site Log Buffer**: The site log buffer is a setting for the number of site log records that have to be reached before DotNetNuke writes them to the database. They are held in memory before they are written to the database. This can help to speed up things on a busy site. Be careful when increasing this number, because if the application is reset (that is, the application pool is recycled due to any reason like change to `bin` folder, or `web.config`, and so on) you will lose the records in the buffer. Setting the number to 1 before you reset the application will prevent this from happening.

- **Site Log History**: This tells the system how many days of history to keep for your site log. The default is 0 days.

- **Enable Users Online?** and **Users Online Time**: These settings allows the administrator to enable users and show the time period for which users have been online (in minutes) respectively.

- **Auto-Unlock Accounts After**: If a user is locked out because of successive unsuccessful logins, they will have to wait for the specified number of minutes until they can attempt again.

- **Allowable File Extensions**: This setting restricts the files that users are able to upload to your site. This is done for security purposes so that users are not able to upload malicious script files to the server. Separate file extensions (without a period) by using a comma.

- **Scheduler Mode**: This setting is used to let you set how the scheduler is activated and used. You can choose between **Timer Method**, **Request Method**, and **Disabled**.

- **Enable Event Log Buffer?**: This setting allows you to decide if the log entries are buffered before being written out to the data store.

- **Help URL**: The URL used for online help that your site will provide. By default, it is set to the DotNetNuke online help.

- **Enable Module Online Help**: This option allows you to decide if you would like to use the DotNetNuke online help for your module help. If enabled, you will have to provide this in each module setting section.

- **Auto-Sync File System?**: If checked, the database will automatically be synchronized with the filesystem. This is similar to the **Synchronize Files** button in the **File Manager** tool but is run via the scheduler.

- **Enable Content Localization?**: Allows the current users' culture settings to be passed to provide localized content.

The last item on the **Host Settings** tab is the **Upgrade Log For Version** section. When you upgrade DotNetNuke from one version to the next, it keeps a log file. To view the log files for a particular version, select the version from the drop-down and click on **Go**.

Portals

For a discussion on running multiple portals, please refer to *Chapter 10, Creating Multiple Portals*.

Module definitions

For a discussion of modules and module definitions, please see *Chapter 7, Custom Module Development*.

File Manager

The **File Manager** under the **Host Settings** functions just like the **File Manager** under the **ADMIN** menu (see the *Admin tools* section in this chapter). The only difference is that the host can manage templates, smiley images, logs, and event queue files.

Vendors

DotNetNuke comes equipped with vendor and banner advertising integration. To set up a new vendor for your site, click on the **Add New Vendor** link at the bottom of the page:

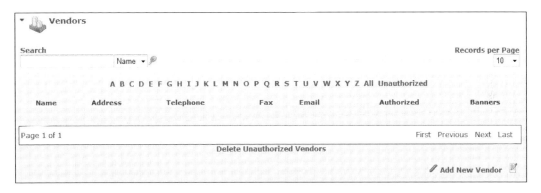

Fill out the vendor information and click on **Update** to save the vendor. Notice there are checkboxes provided next to the fields in the **Address Details** section. These are used to control which fields are required. Once you have saved the vendor information, you can add banners to this vendor by editing the vendor record.

> You might receive an error if there is a problem sending mail to the administrator or the vendor on vendor creation, but the vendor would still be created.

To add a banner to a vendor, edit the vendor, open the **Banner Advertising** section, and click on **Add New Banner**:

This allows you to add the specifications necessary to associate banner advertisements with your vendors.

The fields are described as follows:

- **Banner Name**: Enter the name of the banner. This can be anything you want. Make it descriptive to help organize your banners.

- **Banner Type**: This refers to the size of the banner. Banners can be anything from large skyscraper banners to tiny micro banners. Scripts can even be used as banners.

- **Banner Group**: To better organize your banners, type in a banner group.

The next section determines where the banner advertisement is located. You can choose between a file on your site and a URL to a file located on another site. Once you make your selection, you will be able to point to the correct file. Select the location and the name of the banner ad file:

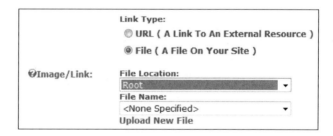

You can set the **Width** and **Height** of the banner in this section.

If you selected **URL**, you would need to enter the URL of the file.

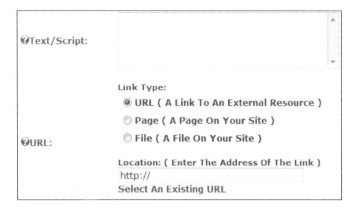

Next you will want to determine what happens when the user clicks on a banner.

- **Text/Script**: The banner text itself for text banners, and the alternate text for image banners.

- **URL**: The URL that users will be redirected to when they click on a banner advertisement. If no URL is listed here, the URL in the vendor setup will be used.

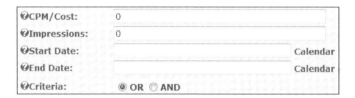

- **CPM/Cost**: The amount you will charge for every 1000 impressions. An impression is how many times the banner is displayed on the site.

- **Impressions**: The number of impressions the vendor has paid for. The default value of **0** is used to allow an unlimited number of impressions.

- **Start Date** and **End Date**: Start and end dates for the advertisement campaign.

- **Criteria**: Used to determine whether to stop the advertisements after the date has expired or the number of impressions has been reached.

When you are done adding the banner details, click on the **Update** link to save your data.

To view your banners on the portal, you will need to add a banner module to one of your pages. Once you have added a **Banner** module, select **Banner Options** from the module's drop-down menu.

To edit the banner, enter the **Banner Source** and **Banner Type** to display your banner. As the vendor was created from the host tools, you will need to select **Host** for the source. By using the information you used to set up your banner in the vendor section, you can decide the types or groups of banners you would like to be displayed. When you have finished adding the information, click on the **Update** link to save your settings.

 Note that a banner click through URL can be used to redirect the banner clicks to an intermediary page. This can be useful if you need to do custom processing for banner traffic.

SQL

Use the **SQL** host option to run SQL queries against the DotNetNuke database.

 Be extremely cautious while executing SQL against the database using this module. This SQL bypasses DNN's built-in security checks, and any SQL executed usually cannot have its effects undone after execution.

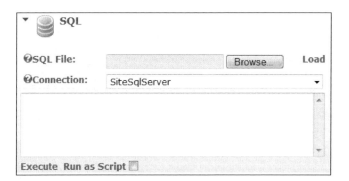

The **SQL File** control allows you to execute a SQL script located on your computer. Make sure to click the **Load** button after selecting the file, and then click the **Execute** button, if you want an external file to be executed. Alternatively, you may simply type in your SQL statement into the large textbox. Verify that the proper **Connection** is selected and click on the **Execute** link. You will then be presented with a simple tabular representation of your data. As this is part of the DotNetNuke framework, you can also run scripts that use the <objectQualifier> and <databaseOwner> tags by checking the **Run as Script** checkbox. However, in that case you would not be presented with tabular data, but just a confirmation message saying **Your script executed successfully**.

Schedule

With the addition of users online and site log in DotNetNuke 2.0, there arose a need to schedule recurring tasks. To address this, the core team developed the **scheduler**. The scheduler allows you to perform recurring actions on the portal.

Languages

Starting with DotNetNuke version 3.x, you can localize your portal to the language of your choice. Currently only English is provided by default; however, additional languages may be created, downloaded, or purchased for your DotNetNuke installations.

Search Admin

You may have noticed in the upper right-hand corner of your screen, a box with a **Search** button, as shown in the following screenshot:

DotNetNuke gives the portal visitors the ability to search the portal for relevant information. The administration for the functionality is found on the host menu.

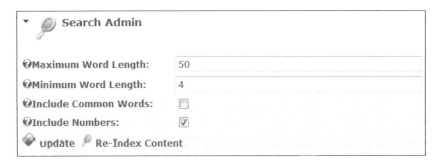

In this section, you can set parameters for the search engine to follow. You can set the maximum and minimum word length to follow, as well as decide if you want to ignore common words (and, or, the, and so on) and/or numbers. We will look further into the search functionality when we discuss custom modules in *Chapter 7, Custom Module Development*.

Lists

Many of the controls in DotNetNuke use lists to populate the information needed to fulfill a task. A good example of this is the user account registration control.

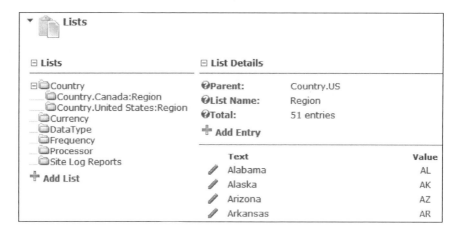

When users register for your site, they are presented with drop-down lists that allow them to select their country and region/state. This section allows the host to add items or remove items from the list. This allows you to customize the items shown in the list.

Superuser Accounts

In previous versions of DotNetNuke, only one host (superuser) account was available. This restriction was eliminated from version 3.0 onwards with the addition of the superuser section. From here, you can create additional user accounts that will have the same abilities as the host.

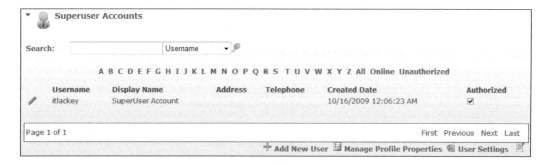

Remember that these users will have the freedom to control access to every part of every portal in the DotNetNuke installation, from creating portals to deleting users, so be careful when issuing these accounts.

Extensions

For a discussion of the host options of the **Extensions** module, please see *Chapter 7, Custom Module Development*.

Dashboard

Much like the first part of the **Basic Settings** section of the **Host Settings** tool, the **Dashboard** simply displays information about the DotNetNuke environment. However, the **Dashboard** provides information about more than just the DNN installation. By default, it includes six sections, each displaying detailed information about a different piece of the system configuration.

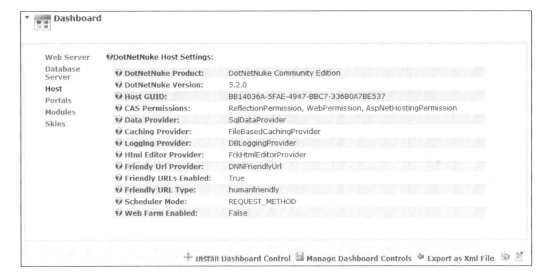

An explanation to the preceding screenshot is given as follows:

- **Web Server**: Details on the current system configuration of the computer hosting the DotNetNuke installation.

- **Database Server**: Information about the computer hosting that the database DotNetNuke is using, as well as details about the database itself.

- **Host**: Very similar to the information in **Host Settings**, but with additional details.

- **Portals**: Lists each portal along with the number of pages, roles, and users associated with the portal.

- **Modules**: Lists the currently installed modules with their version and the number of instances currently added to the pages on all portals.

- **Skins**: Lists the installed skins and if they are currently being used.

The information provided by these sections can be very useful when managing your DNN installation. However, like many parts of DotNetNuke, the **Dashboard** is designed to be extendable. So, if information is not included by default, you can add additional sections with information customized to your needs.

The **Install Dashboard Control** button will take you to a wizard that will allow you to install your custom dashboard section. In order to keep a consistent experience, the wizard used to install dashboard controls is the same one used to install all other DotNetNuke extensions.

What's New

A change log is published with each release of DotNetNuke; however, the **What's New** module allows you to view a summary of the changes directly on the portal. This makes for a convenient place to quickly browse the highlights of the release without wading through too much technical detail.

For more detailed information, a link to the DotNetNuke support site is provided where you can browse the **official change log**.

 What's New

Below is a summary of the major features for each release. For more information about a specific issue please refer to the official change log.

What's New in 05.02.00

Major Highlights

- Added Module Information to the Help page
- Added ability to view and edit the source files for a module
- Enhanced the module creation wizard to simplify creating new module definitions
- Added the ability to automatically create a test page as a step in the module creation wizard
- Added a core API to support content localization
- Added the ability to import/export page and module settings
- Added the ability to immediately run a scheduled task
- Added module caching provider API
- Converted existing module caching feature to use new provider
- Added page output caching provider API

Marketplace

The **Marketplace** tool is designed to allow portal hosts to find third-party extensions directly from the DotNetNuke portal. This is done by displaying products listed on the Snowcovered website. Snowcovered has become the official marketplace for DNN extensions and is now run by the DotNetNuke Corporation. However, the site is designed much like `Amazon.com`, in that it allows independent vendors to list their products. This enables potential customers to browse extensions developed by many different companies and individual developers in a single location.

The **Marketplace** tool provides list of the most popular, newest, and reviewed products by selecting the list type and category. After the search criteria is selected, simply click the **Go** button to display the list.

Extra options on the ADMIN menu

When you are signed in as a superuser, you may notice a few extra items in the admin tools. If you look at the **Site Settings**, you will see an extra section called **Host Settings** that allows a superuser to control certain aspects of the portal. In addition, if you view the **Log Viewer** on the **ADMIN** menu when signed in as a superuser, you will see exceptions generated by the portal. These exceptions are logged here by the framework, but are available only to the superuser. Finally, at the bottom of the **Site Settings** pane, you will see an extra section for **Portal Aliases**.

The portal alias of the site must be located in this section. When you first set up your site on a local machine, it will be added for you, but before you upload your site to a remote server, you will need to add the new URL of your site to this section.

Common Tasks

So far, we have used the icon bar at the top of the portal to work with pages and to place modules onto pages. The last section of the icon bar is used to perform common administrative tasks.

These are shortcuts to common tasks that you can find on the administrative menus and are meant to help you to be more productive. These include **Site** (a shortcut to the **Site Settings** tool), **Users**, **Roles**, **Files**, **Help**, and **Extensions**.

Summary

This chapter has covered a variety of information. It should have given you, as the administrator of a DotNetNuke portal, the skills needed to maintain your website. In the next chapter, we will delve deep into the core of the DotNetNuke architecture and find out what really makes our portal run.

6

Understanding the DotNetNuke Core Architecture

In this chapter, we will be exploring the core functionality of the DotNetNuke architecture. We will be using the Source Code version of DotNetNuke 5.2.2 that can be downloaded from the DotNetNuke CodePlex site. We will start with an overview of the architecture, touching on key concepts employed by DotNetNuke. After this, we will examine some of the major sections that make up the framework. Finally, after we learn about the objects that make up the core, we will follow a request for a page through this process to find out how each page is dynamically created.

Architecture overview

As opposed to traditional web applications that may rely on a multitude of web pages to deliver content, DotNetNuke uses a single main page called `Default.aspx`. The content for this page is generated dynamically by using a tabID value to retrieve the skin and modules needed to build the page requested, from the DotNetNuke database. Before we move on, we should discuss what is meant by a tab and a page. As you read this chapter, you will notice the word "tab" is sometimes used when referring to pages in your DotNetNuke portal. In the original IBuySpy application, pages were referred to as tabs because they resembled tabs when added to the page.

 IBuySpy application, the skeleton ASP.NET Framework, was created by Microsoft to demonstrate ASP.NET features, and DotNetNuke was originally derived from it.

This continued in the original versions of the DotNetNuke project. Starting with version 3.0, and continuing with version 5.2.x, there has been an ongoing effort to rename most of these instances to reflect what they really are: pages. Most references to "tabs" have been changed to "pages", but the conversion is not complete. For this reason, you will see both—tabs and pages—in the database, in the project files, and in this text. We will use these terms interchangeably throughout this text as we look into the core architecture of DNN.

We will begin with a general overview of what happens when a user requests a page on your DotNetNuke portal. The process for rendering a page in DotNetNuke works like this: a user navigates to a page on your portal; this calls the `Default.aspx` page, passing the `tabid` parameter in the querystring to let the application identify the page being requested. The example `http://www.dotnetnuke.com/Default.aspx?tabid=476` demonstrates this.

> DotNetNuke 3.2 introduced something called **URL rewriting**. This takes the querystring shown above and rewrites it so that it is in a format that helps increase search engine hits. We discussed this in *Chapter 3, Users Roles and Pages*, and we will cover the HTTP module that is responsible for this in more detail later in this chapter. The rewritten URL would resemble `http://localhost/DotNetNuke/Home.aspx`. This assumes that the page name for tabid 476 is `Home`.
>
> While referring to URLs in this chapter we will be using the non-rewritten version of the URL. URL rewriting can be turned off in the friendly URL section of the **Host Settings** page.

The querystring value (`?tabid=476`) is sent to the database, where the information required for the page is retrieved, as shown in the following diagram:

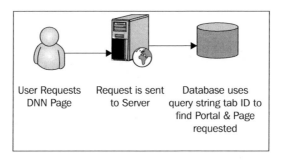

| User Requests DNN Page | Request is sent to Server | Database uses query string tab ID to find Portal & Page requested |

The portal that the user is accessing can be determined in a number of ways, but as you can see from the Tabs table (see the following screenshot), each page/tab contains a reference to the portal it belongs to in the PortalID field. Once the server has a reference to the page that the user requested (using the tabID), it can determine what modules belong to that page.

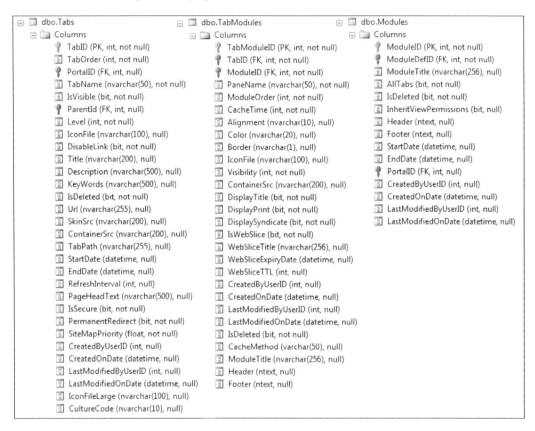

Although there are many more tables involved in this process, you can see that these tables hold not only the page and modules needed to generate the page, but also what pane to place them on (PaneName) and what container skin to apply (ContainerSrc).

All of this information is returned to the web server, and the `Default.aspx` page is constructed with it and returned to the user who requested it along with the required modules and skins, as shown in the following diagram.

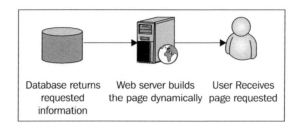

Database returns   Web server builds   User Receives
requested   the page dynamically   page requested
information

Now, this is of course a very general overview of the process, but as we work through this chapter, we will delve deeper into the code that makes this process work, and in the end, show a request work its way through the framework to deliver a page to a user.

Diving into the core

There are over 160,000 lines of code in the DotNetNuke application. There is no practical (or even possible) way to cover the entire code base. In this section, we will go in depth into what I believe are the main portions of the code base: the `PortalSettings` as well as the companion classes found in the `portals` folder; the `web.config` file including the HTTP `Modules` and `Providers`; and the `Global.asax` and `Globals.vb` files.

We will start our discussion of the core with two objects that play an integral part in the construction of the architecture. The `Context` object and the `PortalSettings` class will both be referred to quite often in the code, and so it is important that you have a good understanding of what they do.

Using the Context object in your application

ASP.NET has taken intrinsic objects like the `Request` and the `Application` objects and wrapped them together with other relevant items into an intrinsic object called `Context`.

The Context object (HttpContext) can be found in the System.Web namespace. In the following table, you will find some of the objects that make up the HttpContext object.

Title	Description
Application	Gets the HttpApplicationState object for the current HTTP request.
Cache	Gets the Cache object for the current HTTP request.
Current	Gets the HttpContext object for the current HTTP request. This is a static (shared in VB) property of the HttpContext class, through which you access all other instance properties discussed in this table, that together enable you to process and respond to an HTTP request.
Items	Gets a key-value collection that can be used to organize and share data between an IHttpModule and an IHttpHandler during an HTTP request.
Request	Gets the HttpRequest object for the current HTTP request. This is used to extract data submitted by the client, and information about the client itself (for example, IP), and the current request.
Response	Gets the HttpResponse object for the current HTTP response. This is used to send data to the client together with other response-related information such as headers, cacheability, redirect information, and so on.
Server	Gets the HttpServerUtility object that provides methods used in processing web requests.
Session	Gets the HttpSessionState instance for the current HTTP request.
User	Gets or sets security information for the current HTTP request.

Notice that most of the descriptions talk about the "current" request object, or the "current" response object. The Global.asax file, which we will look at soon, reacts on every single request made to your application, and so it is only concerned with whoever is "currently" accessing a resource.

The HttpContext object contains all HTTP-specific information about an individual HTTP request. In particular, the HttpContext.Current property can give you the context for the current request from *anywhere* in the application domain. The DotNetNuke core relies on the HttpContext.Current property to hold everything from the application name to the portal settings and through this makes it available to you.

The PortalSettings class

The portal settings play a major role in the dynamic generation of your pages and as such will be referred to quite often in the other portions of the code. The portal settings are represented by the `PortalSettings` class which you will find in the `Entities\Portal\PortalSettings.vb` file. As you can see from the private variables in this class, most of what goes on in your portal will at some point need to access this object. This object will hold everything from the ID of the portal to the default language, and as we will see later, is responsible for determining the skins and modules needed for each page.

```
Private _PortalId As Integer
Private _PortalName As String
Private _HomeDirectory As String
Private _LogoFile As String
Private _FooterText As String
Private _ExpiryDate As Date
Private _UserRegistration As Integer
Private _BannerAdvertising As Integer
Private _Currency As String
Private _AdministratorId As Integer
Private _Email As String
Private _HostFee As Single
Private _HostSpace As Integer
Private _PageQuota As Integer
Private _UserQuota As Integer
Private _AdministratorRoleId As Integer
Private _AdministratorRoleName As String
Private _RegisteredRoleId As Integer
Private _RegisteredRoleName As String
Private _Description As String
Private _KeyWords As String
Private _BackgroundFile As String
Private _GUID As Guid
Private _SiteLogHistory As Integer
Private _AdminTabId As Integer
Private _SuperTabId As Integer
Private _SplashTabId As Integer
Private _HomeTabId As Integer
Private _LoginTabId As Integer
Private _UserTabId As Integer
Private _DefaultLanguage As String
Private _TimeZoneOffset As Integer
Private _Version As String
Private _ActiveTab As TabInfo
Private _PortalAlias As PortalAliasInfo
Private _AdminContainer As SkinInfo
```

```
Private _AdminSkin As SkinInfo
Private _PortalContainer As SkinInfo
Private _PortalSkin As SkinInfo
Private _Users As Integer
Private _Pages As Integer
```

The `PortalSettings` class itself is simple. It is filled by using one of the constructors that accepts one or more parameters. These constructors then call the private `GetPortalSettings` method. The method is passed a tabID and a `PortalInfo` object. You already know that the tabID represents the ID of the page being requested, but the `PortalInfo` object is something new. This class can be found in the same folder as the `PortalSettings` class and contains the basic information about a portal such as `PortalID`, `PortalName`, and `Description`.

However, from the `PortalSettings` object, we can retrieve all the information associated with the portal. If you look at the code inside the constructors, you will see that the `PortalController` object is used to retrieve the `PortalInfo` object. The `PortalInfo` object is saved in cache for the time that is specified on the **Host Settings** page.

A drop-down box on the **Host Settings** page (`DesktopModules\Admin\HostSettings\HostSettings.ascx`) is used to set the cache.

- No caching: **0**
- Light caching: **1**
- Moderate caching: **3**
- Heavy caching: **6**

The value in this dropdown ranges from **0** to **6**; the code in the `DataCache` object takes the value set in the drop-down and multiplies it by 20 to determine the cache duration. Once the cache time is set, the method checks if the `PortalSettings` object already resides there. Retrieving these settings from the database for every request would cause your site to run slowly, so placing them in a cache for the duration you select helps increase the speed of your site. Recent versions of DotNetNuke have focused heavily on providing an extensive caching service. An example of this can be seen in the following code:

```
Dim cacheKey As String = String.Format(DataCache.PortalCacheKey,
PortalId.ToString())

Return CBO.GetCachedObject(Of PortalInfo)
(New CacheItemArgs(cacheKey, DataCache.PortalCacheTimeOut,
DataCache.PortalCachePriority, PortalId),
AddressOf GetPortalCallback)
```

We can see in the previous code that the CBO object is used to return an object from the cache. CBO is an object that is seen frequently throughout the DotNetNuke core. This object's primary function is to return the populated business object. This is done in several ways using different methods provided by CBO. Some methods are used to map data from an IDataReader to the properties of a business object. However, in this example, the GetCachedObject method handles the logic needed to determine if the object should be retrieved from the cache or from the database. If the object is not already cached, it will use the GetPortalCallback method passed to the method to retrieve the portal settings from the database. This method is located in the PortalController class (Entities\Portal\PortalController.vb) and is responsible for retrieving the portal information from the database.

```
Dim portalID As Integer = DirectCast(cacheItemArgs.ParamList(0),
Integer)

Return CBO.FillObject(Of PortalInfo)(DataProvider.Instance _
.GetPortal(portalID, Entities.Host.Host.ContentLocale.ToString))
```

This will fill the PortalInfo object (Entities\Portal\PortalInfo.vb), which as we mentioned, holds the portal information. This object in turn is returned to the GetCachedObject method. Once this is complete, the object is then cached to help prevent the need to call the database during the next request for the portal information. There is also a section of code (not shown) that verifies whether the object was successfully stored in the cache and adds an entry to the event log if the item failed to be cached.

```
' if we retrieved a valid object and we are using caching
If objObject IsNot Nothing AndAlso timeOut > 0 Then

' save the object in the cache
DataCache.SetCache(cacheItemArgs.CacheKey, objObject, _
cacheItemArgs.CacheDependency, Cache.NoAbsoluteExpiration, _
TimeSpan.FromMinutes(timeOut), cacheItemArgs.CachePriority, _
cacheItemArgs.CacheCallback)
…
End If
```

After the portal settings are saved, the properties of the current tab information are retrieved and populated in the ActiveTab property. The current tab is retrieved by using the tabID that was originally passed to the constructor. This is handled by the VerifyPortalTab method and done by getting a list of all of the tabs for the current portal. Like the portal settings themselves, the tabs are saved in cache to boost performance. The calls to the caching provider, this time, are handled by the TabController (Entities\Tabs\TabController.vb). In the last VerifyPortalTab method, the code will loop through all of the host and non-host tabs, returned by the TabController, for the site until the current tab is located.

```
' find the tab in the portalTabs collection
If TabId <> Null.NullInteger Then
    If portalTabs.TryGetValue(TabId, objTab) Then
     'Check if Tab has been deleted (is in recycle bin)
       If Not (objTab.IsDeleted) Then
          Me.ActiveTab = objTab.Clone()
          isVerified = True
       End If
    End If
End If


' find the tab in the hostTabs collection
If Not isVerified AndAlso TabId <> Null.NullInteger Then
    If hostTabs.TryGetValue(TabId, objTab) Then
     'Check if Tab has been deleted (is in recycle bin)
       If Not (objTab.IsDeleted) Then
          Me.ActiveTab = objTab.Clone()
          isVerified = True
       End If
    End If
End If
```

If the tab was not found in either of these collections, the code attempts to use the splash page, home page, or the first page of the non-host pages. After the current tab is located, further handling of some of its properties is done back in the GetPortalSettings method. This includes formatting the path for the skin and default container used by the page, as well as collecting information on the modules placed on the page.

```
Me.ActiveTab.SkinSrc = _
SkinController.FormatSkinSrc(Me.ActiveTab.SkinSrc, Me)
Me.ActiveTab.SkinPath = _
SkinController.FormatSkinPath(Me.ActiveTab.SkinSrc)
...
For Each kvp As KeyValuePair(Of Integer, ModuleInfo) In _
objModules.GetTabModules(Me.ActiveTab.TabID)

' clone the module object _
( to avoid creating an object reference to the data cache )

    Dim cloneModule As ModuleInfo = kvp.Value.Clone

    ' set custom properties
    If Null.IsNull(cloneModule.StartDate) Then
        cloneModule.StartDate = Date.MinValue
```

```
        End If
        If Null.IsNull(cloneModule.EndDate) Then
            cloneModule.EndDate = Date.MaxValue
        End If

        ' container
        If cloneModule.ContainerSrc = "" Then
            cloneModule.ContainerSrc = Me.ActiveTab.ContainerSrc
        End If
        cloneModule.ContainerSrc = _
SkinController.FormatSkinSrc(cloneModule.ContainerSrc, Me)

        cloneModule.ContainerPath = _
SkinController.FormatSkinPath(cloneModule.ContainerSrc)

        ' process tab panes
        If objPaneModules.ContainsKey(cloneModule.PaneName) = False Then
            objPaneModules.Add(cloneModule.PaneName, 0)
        End If

        cloneModule.PaneModuleCount = 0

        If Not cloneModule.IsDeleted Then

            objPaneModules(cloneModule.PaneName) = _
objPaneModules(cloneModule.PaneName) + 1

            cloneModule.PaneModuleIndex = _
objPaneModules(cloneModule.PaneName) - 1
        End If

        Me.ActiveTab.Modules.Add(cloneModule)

    Next
```

We have now discussed some of the highlights of the `PortalSettings` object as well as how it is populated with the information it contains. In doing so, we also saw a brief example of the robust caching service provided by DotNetNuke. You will see the `PortalSettings` class referenced many times in the core DotNetNuke code, so gaining a good understanding of how this class works will help you to become more familiar with the DNN code base. You will also find this object to be very helpful while building custom extensions for DotNetNuke.

The caching provider itself is a large topic, and reaches beyond the scope of this chapter. However, simply understanding how to work with it in the ways shown in these examples should satisfy the needs of most developers. It is important to note that, you can get any type of object cached by DNN by passing in a key for your object to `DataCache.SetCache` method, together with the data, and some optional arguments.

While fetching the object back from `DataCache.GetCache`, you pass in the same key, and check the result. A non-null (non-Nothing in VB) return value means you have fetched the object successfully from the cache, otherwise you would need to fetch it from the database.

Working with the configuration files

Next, we will continue our exploration of the DotNetNuke architecture by looking at a couple of files in the main DotNetNuke folder. The DotNetNuke Source Code version download is broken up into many different projects. This has been done so that you can open up only the files that you are concerned with. In this section, we will work with the website project along with the `Providers` used by the core. If you open the solution file in the Source Code download, you will find that the website project will start with `http://localhost/DotNetNuke_Community`.

Expand the website project to expose two very important files, the `web.config` file, and the `Global.aspx` file. You will need to rename the `release.config` file to `web.config` before we begin.

If this is the first time you have worked with the download, you will notice that there is no `web.config` file. The `web.config` file will originally be called `release.config`. This has been done to help ensure that during an upgrade you don't overlay the original `web.config`. As DotNetNuke uses encryption keys to store user passwords in the database, if you overlay this file your users will not be able to log in.

It is a recommended strategy to always back up your entire site including the `web.config` file for your production installation in a secure place after installation, and after each upgrade to the core.

The web.config file

The web.config file is an XML-based file that contains configuration information that is specific to your web application. At runtime, ASP.NET stores this configuration information in cache so that it can be easily retrieved by your application. If changes are made to this file, ASP.NET will detect the changes and automatically apply the new configuration. The web.config file is very extensible; it allows you to define new configurations and write handlers to process them. DotNetNuke takes full advantage of this ability, which we will discover as we move through this file.

> Please be aware that any modification to web.config file leads ASP.NET to recycle the complete application domain for your website together with all cached data (possibly), and rebuild it from scratch, which can take a significant time for the first request after the app-domain was recycled.

We will only touch on the areas of the web.config file that are specifically used in DotNetNuke. In the DotNetNuke website project, open up the web.config file, which was renamed from release.config. The first section in the file is the local configuration settings. Here we find the settings for our provider models. For our providers to work, we need a configuration section and configuration section handler.

Configuring the providers used in DotNetNuke

<configSections> is broken into separate groups. The group named <dotnetnuke>, describes the providers that are available to the application, as shown in the following code snippet:

```
<sectionGroup name="dotnetnuke">
  <!-- the requirePermission attribute will cause a syntax warning -
    please ignore - it is required for Medium Trust support-->
  <section name="data"
    requirePermission="false"
    type="DotNetNuke.Framework.Providers.
      ProviderConfigurationHandler, DotNetNuke"/>
  <section name="logging"
    requirePermission="false"
    type="DotNetNuke.Framework.Providers.
      ProviderConfigurationHandler, DotNetNuke"/>
  <section name="scheduling"
    requirePermission="false"
    type="DotNetNuke.Framework.Providers.
      ProviderConfigurationHandler, DotNetNuke"/>
```

```xml
<section name="htmlEditor"
   requirePermission="false"
   type="DotNetNuke.Framework.Providers.
      ProviderConfigurationHandler, DotNetNuke"/>
<section name="navigationControl"
   requirePermission="false"
   type="DotNetNuke.Framework.Providers.
      ProviderConfigurationHandler, DotNetNuke"/>
<section name="searchIndex"
   requirePermission="false"
   type="DotNetNuke.Framework.Providers.
      ProviderConfigurationHandler, DotNetNuke"/>
<section name="searchDataStore"
   requirePermission="false"
   type="DotNetNuke.Framework.Providers.
      ProviderConfigurationHandler, DotNetNuke"/>
<section name="friendlyUrl"
   requirePermission="false"
   type="DotNetNuke.Framework.Providers.
      ProviderConfigurationHandler, DotNetNuke"/>
<section name="caching"
   requirePermission="false"
   type="DotNetNuke.Framework.Providers.
      ProviderConfigurationHandler, DotNetNuke"/>
<section name="authentication"
   requirePermission="false"
   type="DotNetNuke.Framework.Providers.
      ProviderConfigurationHandler, DotNetNuke"/>
<section name="members"
   requirePermission="false"
   type="DotNetNuke.Framework.Providers.
      ProviderConfigurationHandler, DotNetNuke"/>
<section name="roles"
   requirePermission="false"
   type="DotNetNuke.Framework.Providers.
      ProviderConfigurationHandler, DotNetNuke"/>
<section name="profiles"
   requirePermission="false"
   type="DotNetNuke.Framework.Providers.
      ProviderConfigurationHandler, DotNetNuke"/>
<section name="permissions"
   requirePermission="false"
   type="DotNetNuke.Framework.Providers.
      ProviderConfigurationHandler, DotNetNuke"/>
<section name="moduleCaching"
```

```
        requirePermission="false"
        type="DotNetNuke.Framework.Providers.
            ProviderConfigurationHandler, DotNetNuke"/>
    <section name="outputCaching"
        requirePermission="false"
        type="DotNetNuke.Framework.Providers.
            ProviderConfigurationHandler, DotNetNuke"/>
</sectionGroup>
```

This custom configuration section handles the different providers integrated into the framework. Providers give the developer the ability to have a pluggable architecture. The data provider, for example, lets us decide which data store to use (Access or SQL Server), while the logging provider allows us to decide what logger we would like to use for our web application. The framework separates the act of logging from the type of logger being used. To change the logging, or any of the other providers, you would need to write your own provider to handle the functions as you see fit (or choose from the providers that ship with the core).

The first declaration states the name that you will use when you refer to this section in your configuration file. In other words, you will need the following tag to look for in your `web.config` file in order to see the providers that will handle this functionality:

```
name="data"
```

It also includes the type, which is the configuration section handler. This should include the **Global Assembly Cache (GAC)** location information for the class.

```
type="DotNetNuke.Framework.Providers.ProviderConfigurationHandler,
    DotNetNuke"
```

The `type` declaration follows the following configuration:

```
type="configuration section handler class, assembly"
```

The providers serve some of the following functions:

- The `data` provider: Gives the ability to decide which datastore type you would like to use. The DotNetNuke framework is prepackaged with SQL, but there are others, such as MySQL and Oracle, which are available from third-party providers.
- The `logging` provider: Used for all logging associated with the core framework. This handles, among other things, exception logging.
- The `scheduling` provider: One of the newer features; along with the logging, this provider helps to facilitate recurring functionality.

- The `htmlEditor` provider: The default HTML WYSIWYG editor is the FCKEditor. This configuration setting allows you to substitute other rich textbox components for the FCKEditor.

- The `searchIndex` provider: The default provides, if implemented, the ability to search the content of the modules located on your portal.

- The `searchDataStore` provider: The default provides the ability to search for information inside the datastore you have selected as your data provider.

- The `friendlyUrl` provider: The default provides the ability to rewrite the URL in a manner that is friendly to search engines.

Handling the providers

The configuration section only tells the application where each provider will be handled. The configuration section has a companion section in the `web.config` file. This defines the configuration section handlers. You will find two handler sections in the `web.config` file, one for each group we just described. The first handler section we will look at is the `<dotnetnuke>` section. This corresponds to the `sectionGroup` name in the configuration section.

The <dotnetnuke> group

Within the `<dotnetnuke>` section (as shown in the next code snippet), we see the handlers for our individual providers, beginning with the HTML provider. The first node in this section defines the default provider. The `defaultProvider` attribute is advised, but is optional. If it's left out, the first provider in the list will serve as the default. The default provider for the `htmlEditor` is the `FckHtmlEditorProvider`.

The next node starts the provider section; it is followed by a `<clear/>` node. This node is used to clear out the providers from the configuration settings that may have been added in the `machine.config` file. The final node is the `<add/>` node. This node is used to add our provider to the list of available providers. This list is used by the DotNetNuke core to tell it what is handling each section that uses a provider. DNN chooses one of the providers based on the `defaultProvider` attribute, if specified, or the first one, for each section in `web.config` that uses the provider model. Inside this node, we need to define a few attributes that are as follows:

- `name`: This is the friendly name of our provider. This can be any name that you like, preferably something meaningful.

- `type`: This again follows the `[namespace.class]`, `[assembly name]` format.

- `providerPath`: This attribute points to where the provider class can be found within the application structure.

After the end of the `<add/>` node, the structure is completed with the closing tags for add, providers, and htmlEditor.

```
<dotnetnuke>
    <htmlEditor defaultProvider="FckHtmlEditorProvider">
        <providers>
            <clear/>
            <add name="FckHtmlEditorProvider"
                type="DotNetNuke.HtmlEditor.
FckHtmlEditorProvider.FckHtmlEditorProvider, DotNetNuke.
FckHtmlEditorProvider"
                providerPath="~/Providers/
HtmlEditorProviders/Fck/"
                CustomConfigurationPath="~/Providers/
HtmlEditorProviders/Fck/custom/FCKConfig.js"
                EnhancedSecurityDefault="false"
                SecureConfigurationPath="~/Providers/
HtmlEditorProviders/Fck/custom/FCKConfigSecure.js"
                ImageGalleryPath="~/Providers/
HtmlEditorProviders/Fck/fckimagegallery.aspx"
                ImageUploadPath="~/Providers/HtmlEditorProviders/
Fck/fckimagegallery.aspx"
                ImageAllowedFileTypes="gif,png,bmp,jpg"
                FlashGalleryPath="~/Providers/
HtmlEditorProviders/Fck/fckimagegallery.aspx"
                FlashUploadPath="~/Providers/HtmlEditorProviders/
Fck/fckimagegallery.aspx"
                FlashAllowedFileTypes="fla,swf"
                LinksGalleryPath="~/Providers/
HtmlEditorProviders/Fck/fcklinkgallery.aspx"
                DynamicStylesGeneratorPath="~/Providers/
HtmlEditorProviders/Fck/FCKStyles.aspx"
                DynamicStylesCaseSensitive="true"
                DynamicStylesGeneratorFilter="controlpanel|
filemanager|mainmenu|wizard"
                StaticStylesFile="~/Providers/
HtmlEditorProviders/Fck/FCKeditor/fckstyles.xml"
                StylesDefaultMode="Static"
                DynamicCSSGeneratorPath="~/Providers/
HtmlEditorProviders/Fck/FCKCSS.aspx"
                StaticCSSFile="~/Providers/HtmlEditorProviders/
Fck/FCKeditor/editor/css/fck_editorarea.css"
                CSSDefaultMode="static"
                spellCheck="ieSpell"
```

```
                     AvailableToolbarSkins="Office2003,Silver"
                     DefaultToolbarSkin="Office2003"
                     AvailableToolBarSets="DNNDefault,Default,
NoGallery,Basic"

                     DefaultToolbarSet="DNNDefault"
                     DefaultImageGallerySkin="Default"
                     DefaultFlashGallerySkin="Default"
                     DefaultLinksGallerySkin="Default"
                     FCKDebugMode="false"
                     UseFCKSource="false"
                     OptionsOpenMode="ShowModalDialog"
                     CustomOptionsDialog="Admin"/>
            </providers>
        </htmlEditor>
```

This is followed by the <navigationControl> handler. This allows you to decide what control you would like to use for your menu navigation. The default is SolpartMenu.

The next two configuration handlers are for the search facility built into the DotNetNuke framework. The searchIndex and searchDataStore follow the same configuration as the htmlEditor. This is followed by the data provider.

```
<data defaultProvider="SqlDataProvider">
  <providers>
    <clear/>
    <add name="SqlDataProvider"
        type="DotNetNuke.Data.SqlDataProvider, DotNetNuke.
          SqlDataProvider"
        connectionStringName="SiteSqlServer"
          upgradeConnectionString=""
          providerPath="~\Providers\DataProviders\SqlDataProvider\"
          objectQualifier=""
          databaseOwner="dbo"/>
  </providers>
</data>
```

The data provider has some additional attributes, which we did not see in the HTML provider. They are as follows:

- connectionStringName: This provides the name of the connection string you will use for your portal. This string can be found in the <appSettings> section of the web.config file. <appSettings> section for connection string is used by only legacy modules. DNN core together with most modules now use the connection strings defined in the <connectionString> section in web.config.

- upgradeConnectionString: This connection string is used for installation and updates. It is only used to run the upgrade scripts. This can be used to run the updates using a database user with more privileges.

- objectQualifier: The objectQualifier is used to allow multiple DotNetNuke installations to run inside the same database. For example, if you added CC1 in the object qualifier before you installed DotNetNuke, all the tables and stored procedures would be prefixed with CC1. This would allow you to run another DotNetNuke implementation inside the same database by setting the object qualifier in the second one to CC2. Inside the database, you would have two of every stored procedure and table. Each pair would be named according to the pattern CC1_users, CC2_users, which would keep them separate. While developing your custom modules, you would also need to take care of this, and prefix each database object reference with the object qualifier.

- databaseOwner: The databaseOwner is set to dbo. This is the default database owner in SQL Server. Some hosting companies will require you to change this to reflect your user.

The next configuration handler is for the logging provider. The logging provider handles all logging, including errors, associated with the portal.

```
<logging defaultProvider="DBLoggingProvider">
        <providers>
            <clear/>
            <add name="DBLoggingProvider"
                type="DotNetNuke.Services.Log.EventLog.
DBLoggingProvider.DBLoggingProvider, DotNetNuke.Provider.
DBLoggingProvider"
                providerPath="~\Providers\LoggingProviders\
DBLoggingProvider\"/>
        </providers>
    </logging>
```

This is followed by the handler for the DNNScheduler:

```
<scheduling defaultProvider="DNNScheduler">
        <providers>
            <clear/>
            <add name="DNNScheduler"
                type="DotNetNuke.Services.Scheduling.
DNNScheduling.DNNScheduler, DotNetNuke.DNNScheduler"
                providerPath="~\Providers\SchedulingProviders\
DNNScheduler\"
                debug="false"
                maxThreads="1"/>
        </providers>
    </scheduling>
```

The scheduler has a few additional attributes which we have not seen so far. They are as follows:

- debug: When set to true, it will add additional log entries to aid in debugging scheduler problems.
- maxThreads: This sets the maximum number of thread-pool threads to be used by the scheduler (1-10). Setting it to -1 tells the scheduler to determine this on its own.

The next handler for this section is for handling friendly URLs. We will be looking further into this functionality when we discover the HTTP modules that DotNetNuke employs, later in this chapter.

```
<friendlyUrl defaultProvider="DNNFriendlyUrl">
        <providers>
            <clear/>
            <add name="DNNFriendlyUrl"
                type="DotNetNuke.Services.Url.FriendlyUrl.
DNNFriendlyUrlProvider, DotNetNuke.HttpModules"
                includePageName="true"
                regexMatch="[^a-zA-Z0-9 _-]"
                urlFormat="humanfriendly"/>
        </providers>
    </friendlyUrl>
```

The following handlers in this section are mainly concerned with authentication and caching. We will be looking further into the authentication functionality later in this chapter.

The <system.web> group

The `<system.web>` section of the `web.config` file is where most of the configuration of your ASP.NET web application is placed. However, the most common configurations are added to the `machine.config` when the .NET Framework is installed. The configurations will be automatically applied unless overridden in the `web.config` file.

You should take particular care while specifying `HttpModules`, and `HttpHandlers` in this section. IIS 6 and earlier use `<system.web>`, whereas IIS uses `<system.webServer>` sections for the purpose.

A good rule of thumb is to specify your `HttpHandlers` and `HttpModules` in both sections to make sure they run on any version of IIS.

A discussion of ASP.NET configuration is far beyond the scope of this book. If you would like to have a better understanding of how the framework handles the configuration settings, please check MSDN for the latest information.

We will be discussing some of the information that can be contained in this section (including the HTTP modules) but for now, we'll concentrate on the providers that are defined in this section. As we saw in the `<dotnetnuke>` section earlier, here we see the information needed to configure the ASP.NET providers. One of the providers we find in the `<system.web>` section is the `AspNetSqlMembership` provider. The setup is similar to those we have already seen with the exception of the additional attributes.

This section may also contain the configuration for the members, roles, and profile providers. They all follow the same pattern as the Membership provider, inheriting from the Microsoft provider and overriding the `ApplicationName` property using the corresponding XML attribute.

HTTP modules

Located at the beginning of the `<system.web>` section is the `HttpModules` section, as shown in the following screenshot:

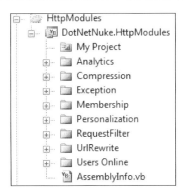

HTTP modules give you the ability to intercept the request for a page and modify the request in some way. In DotNetNuke, they have been added to abstract some of the code that used to reside inside the `Global.asax.vb` file, which is located in the `App_Code` folder of the website. This gives a greater degree of modularity and allows developers to change behavior without affecting the core architecture. An HTTP module is a class that implements the `IHttpModule` interface. This interface has the following two methods that you need to implement:

1. `Init`: This method allows an HTTP module to register its event handlers to the events in the `HttpApplication` object.

2. `Dispose`: This method gives the HTTP module an opportunity to perform any cleanup before the object gets garbage collected.

These methods are called when they are hooked into the HTTP pipeline. The HTTP pipeline refers to the path followed by each request made to your application. The following diagram shows the path that a typical request takes through the pipeline:

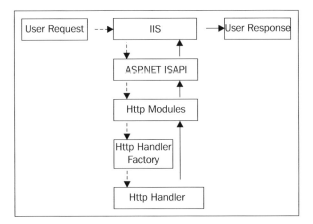

For more information on how HTTP modules work within the HTTP pipeline, check out this great MSDN article by George Sheperd at `http://msdn.microsoft.com/en-us/magazine/cc301362.aspx`.

HTTP modules plug themselves into the ASP.NET request process by adding entries into the `web.config` file. This allows them to intercept the request before it is returned in order to modify the request to perform certain actions. DotNetNuke uses this process for a number of things.

To see an example of this, we will look at the `Exception` module, shown in the following code snippet. It is declared in the `web.config` file, along with the other HTTP modules.

```
<add name="Exception"  type="DotNetNuke.HttpModules.Exceptions.
ExceptionModule, DotNetNuke.HttpModules"/>
```

The last line of code will place the `ExceptionModule` in the HTTP pipeline, allowing it to intercept each request. Let's take a look at the `ExceptionModule` class found in the `DotNetNuke.HttpModules` project, along with the other core HTTP modules. As we learned earlier, the `Init` method is called when the module is hooked into the pipeline with a declaration in the `web.config` file. In this method, we add an event handler to the `application.Error` event that is raised whenever an unhandled exception happens in your application, as shown in the following code snippet:

```
Public Class ExceptionModule

    Implements IHttpModule
    Public ReadOnly Property ModuleName() As String
        Get
            Return "ExceptionModule"
        End Get
    End Property

    Public Sub Init(ByVal application As HttpApplication) _
                        Implements IHttpModule.Init
        AddHandler application.Error, AddressOf Me.OnErrorRequest
    End Sub
```

The `OnErrorRequest` method is then called and the error is passed to the `Error` provider designated in the `web.config` file. The actual logging of the error is done by the logging provider. The default implementation of DotNetNuke comes with a `DBLoggingProvider`, but you may write your own provider to fit your needs.

```
Public Sub OnErrorRequest(ByVal s As Object, ByVal e As EventArgs)

        Try
                Dim Context As HttpContext = HttpContext.Current
                Dim Server As HttpServerUtility = Context.Server
                Dim Request As HttpRequest = Context.Request

                'exit if a request for a .net mapping that isn't a
content page is made i.e. axd
                If Request.Url.LocalPath.ToLower.EndsWith(".aspx") =
False _
                        AndAlso Request.Url.LocalPath.ToLower.
EndsWith(".asmx") = False _
                        AndAlso Request.Url.LocalPath.ToLower.
EndsWith(".ashx") = False Then
                        Exit Sub
                End If
                Dim lastException As Exception = Server.GetLastError()

                'HttpExceptions are logged elsewhere
                If Not (TypeOf lastException Is HttpException) Then
                        Dim lex As New Exception("Unhandled Error: ",
Server.GetLastError)
                        Dim objExceptionLog As New Services.Log.EventLog.
ExceptionLogController
                        Try
                                objExceptionLog.AddLog(lex)
                        Catch
                        End Try
                End If
        Catch ex As Exception
                ' it is possible when terminating the request for the
context not to exist
                ' in this case we just want to exit since there is
nothing else we can do
        End Try

        End Sub

        Public Sub Dispose() Implements IHttpModule.Dispose
        End Sub

    End Class
```

The `UrlRewrite` module is quite extensive. The first thing that is needed is a designation in the `HttpModules` section of the `web.config` file.

```
<add name="UrlRewrite" type="DotNetNuke.HttpModules.UrlRewriteModule,
DotNetNuke.HttpModules"/>
```

As pointed in the beginning of this action, please ensure that you register your module in both the `<system.web>` and `<system.webServer>` sections.

If you are using Windows Vista, Windows 7, or Window Server 2008, then you definitely need the module registered in the `<system.webServer>` section.

You can view the `UrlRewriteModule` by looking in the `DotNetNuke.HttpModules` project under the `UrlRewrite` folder. This class is responsible for taking a URL and querystring that looks like this:

```
http://www.dotnetnuke.com/Default.aspx?tabid=476
```

and converting it to look like this:

```
http://localhost/DotNetNuke/Home.aspx
```

There are a few reasons why you would want to rewrite your URLs; among them are a cleaner appearance or hiding the physical page names, but probably the most important reason for DotNetNuke is to increase traffic to your site. Search engines crawl your site with bots that look to catalog your pages. Search bots prefer non-dynamic web pages with descriptive URLs. By using URL rewriting, you can increase the popularity of your links on the major search engines.

As you look at this module, you can see that although the code that does the URL rewriting is extensive, it is hooked into the pipeline in the same fashion as the other modules. The `Init` method is used to add an event handler to `Application.BeginRequest`, which fires every time a user requests a page on your site, so that on every request to your site the `OnBeginRequest` method is called and the URL is rewritten before it is sent on its way.

```
Public Sub Init(ByVal application As HttpApplication) _
Implements IHttpModule.Init
        AddHandler application.BeginRequest, _
AddressOf Me.OnBeginRequest
End Sub
```

The rest of the HTTP modules follow this same pattern, and although they differ in complexity, they all accomplish their task by intercepting the request.

Application settings

Let's look at one of the remaining sections of `web.config`. Below `<configSettings>` you will find a section called `<appSettings>`. This section holds three items that are of interest to us—`SiteSqlServer`, `InstallProcedure`, and `InstallTemplate`:

```
<appSettings>
        <!-- Connection String for SQL Server 2005/2008 Express - kept
for backwards compatability - legacy modules   -->
        <add key="SiteSqlServer"
            value="Data Source=.\SQLExpress;Integrated
Security=True;User Instance=True;AttachDBFilename=|DataDirectory|Data
base.mdf;"/>
        <!-- Connection String for SQL Server 2005/2008 - kept for
backwards compatability - legacy modules
    <add key="SiteSqlServer" value="Server=(local);Database=DotNetNuke
;uid=;pwd=;"/>
    -->
        <add key="InstallTemplate"
            value="DotNetNuke.install.config"/>
        <add key="AutoUpgrade"
            value="true"/>
        <add key="UseInstallWizard"
            value="true"/>
        <add key="InstallMemberRole"
            value="true"/>
        <add key="ShowMissingKeys"
            value="false"/>
        <add key="EnableWebFarmSupport"
            value="false"/>
        <add key="EnableCachePersistence"
            value="false"/>
        <add key="HostHeader"
            value=""/>
        <!-- Host Header to remove from URL so "www.mydomain.com/
johndoe/Default.aspx" is treated as "www.mydomain.com/Default.aspx"
-->
        <add key="RemoveAngleBrackets"
            value="false"/>
        <!--optionally strip angle brackets on public login and
registration screens-->
        <add key="PersistentCookieTimeout"
            value="0"/>
        <!--use as persistent cookie expiration. Value is in minutes,
and only active if a non-zero figure-->
        <!-- set UsePortNumber to true to preserve the port number if
you're using a port number other than 80 (the standard)
    <add key="UsePortNumber" value="true" /> -->
    </appSettings>
```

The `SiteSqlServer` is used for backwards compatibility for older modules. It holds the connection string for your data store. In .NET 2.0 and later versions, these settings are now held in the `<connectionStrings>` section. The next few keys help you decide how your portal is installed. `IntallTemplate` allows you to set which template to use when your portal is created.

The `AutoUpgrade` key allows you to determine if the application will automatically upgrade your portal if the database version is different than your file version. If this is set to `false`, you will have to manually navigate to the install URL as discussed in the *Upgrading* section of *Chapter 2, Installing DotNetNuke*.

So if the hosting environment will not allow you to run the scripts necessary to install the membership provider on your own, you can use this key to turn this off so that the scripts can be run by your hosting provider manually.

The rest of the keys allow you to customize your portal to work in special environments.

The global files

The `Global.asax.vb` and `Globals.vb` files share similar names but the parts they play in DotNetNuke are vastly different. The `Global.asax.vb` is used by DotNetNuke to handle application-level events raised by the ASP.NET runtime. The `Globals.vb` file, on the other hand, is a public module (which is the same as a static class in C#) that contains global utility functions. Before we take a look at these files, we first want to look at what object is being passed around in these transactions.

Global.asax.vb

Much of the logic that used to reside in the `Global.asax.vb` file has now been abstracted to the HTTP modules. We will look into the code that remains.

Application_Start

When the first request is made to your application (when the first user accesses the portal), a pool of `HttpApplication` instances are created and the `Application_Start` event is fired. This will (theoretically) fire just once and on the first `HttpApplication` object in the pool. When there is inactivity on your portal for a certain amount of time, the application (or **application pool**) will be recycled. When the pool is recycled, your application will restart (and this event will fire again) when the next request is made for your application.

As the new version of DotNetNuke uses the .NET website structure, you will find the `Global.asax.vb` file in the `App_Code` folder.

In the `Application_Start`, we are loading all of the configured providers to ensure they are available to the rest of the framework when needed. These are performed in the `Application_Start` because we want them to be called only once.

```
Private Sub Application_Start(ByVal Sender As Object, ByVal E As
EventArgs)
            If Config.GetSetting("ServerName") = "" Then
                ServerName = Server.MachineName
            Else
                ServerName = Config.GetSetting("ServerName")
            End If

            ComponentFactory.Container = New SimpleContainer()

            'Install most Providers as Singleton LifeStyle
            ComponentFactory.InstallComponents _
(New ProviderInstaller("data", GetType(DotNetNuke.Data.DataProvider)))
            ComponentFactory.InstallComponents _
(New ProviderInstaller("caching", GeType(Services.Cache.
CachingProvider)))
            ComponentFactory.InstallComponents _
(New ProviderInstaller("logging", GetType(Services.Log.EventLog.
LoggingProvider)))
            ComponentFactory.InstallComponents _
(New ProviderInstaller("scheduling", GetType(Services.Scheduling.
SchedulingProvider)))
            ComponentFactory.InstallComponents _
(New ProviderInstaller("searchIndex", GetType(Services.Search.
IndexingProvider)))
            ComponentFactory.InstallComponents _
(New ProviderInstaller("searchDataStore", GetType(Services.Search.
SearchDataStoreProvider)))
            ComponentFactory.InstallComponents_
(New ProviderInstaller("friendlyUrl", GetType(Services.Url.
FriendlyUrl.FriendlyUrlProvider)))
            ComponentFactory.InstallComponents _
(New ProviderInstaller("members", GetType(DotNetNuke.Security.
Membership.MembershipProvider)))
            ComponentFactory.InstallComponents _
(New ProviderInstaller("roles", GetType(DotNetNuke.Security.Roles.
RoleProvider)))
```

```vb
        ComponentFactory.InstallComponents _
(New ProviderInstaller("profiles", GetType(DotNetNuke.Security.
Profile.ProfileProvider)))
        ComponentFactory.InstallComponents _
(New ProviderInstaller("permissions", GetType(DotNetNuke.Security.
Permissions.PermissionProvider)))
        ComponentFactory.InstallComponents _
(New ProviderInstaller("outputCaching", GetType(DotNetNuke.Services.
OutputCache.OutputCachingProvider)))
        ComponentFactory.InstallComponents _
(New ProviderInstaller("moduleCaching", GetType(DotNetNuke.Services.
ModuleCache.ModuleCachingProvider)))
        Dim provider As DotNetNuke.Security.Permissions.
PermissionProvider =  _
DotNetNuke.ComponentModel.ComponentFactory.GetComponent _
(Of DotNetNuke.Security.Permissions.PermissionProvider)()
        If provider Is Nothing Then
            ComponentFactory.RegisterComponentInstance _
(Of DotNetNuke.Security.Permissions.PermissionProvider) _
(New DotNetNuke.Security.Permissions.PermissionProvider())
        End If


        'Install Navigation and Html Providers as NewInstance
Lifestyle (ie a new instance is generated each time the type is
requested, as there are often multiple instances on the page)
        ComponentFactory.InstallComponents _
(New ProviderInstaller("htmlEditor",  _
GetType(Modules.HTMLEditorProvider.HtmlEditorProvider), _
ComponentLifeStyleType.Transient))
        ComponentFactory.InstallComponents _
(New ProviderInstaller("navigationControl", _
GetType(Modules.NavigationProvider.NavigationProvider), _
ComponentLifeStyleType.Transient))
        End Sub
```

In previous versions of DotNetNuke, there was a great deal happening in this method. However, this code has been moved into various methods inside of the `Initialize` class. This was done to support the integrated pipeline mode of IIS 7.

 If you would like to take a look at what is happening inside of the `Initialize` class, it can be found in the `\Common` folder of the `DotNetNuke.Library` project.

Examining Application_BeginRequest

The `Application_BeginRequest` is called for each request made to your application. In other words, this will fire every time a page (tab), or other web request handlers such as a web service or an ashx handler, is accessed in your portal. This section is used to implement the scheduler built into DotNetNuke. Starting in version 2.0, two items, "users online" and "site log", require recurring operations. Also in this method is the call to the `Initialize.Init()` method that was moved out of the `Application_Startup` method as mentioned previously.

You can find out more about the scheduler by looking at the `DotNetNuke Scheduler.pdf` document (only if you download the documentation pack).

Also note that, there is a host setting that defines the running mode of a scheduler, you can check for a scheduler run on every request to your portal, or run the scheduler in a timer mode. More information can be found about this in *Chapter 5, Host and Admin Tools.*

```
Private Sub Global_BeginRequest(ByVal sender As Object, _
ByVal e As EventArgs) Handles Me.BeginRequest
   Dim app As HttpApplication = CType(sender, HttpApplication)
   Dim Request As HttpRequest = app.Request

    If Request.Url.LocalPath.ToLower.EndsWith("scriptresource.axd") _
    OrElse Request.Url.LocalPath.ToLower.EndsWith("webresource.axd") _
    OrElse Request.Url.LocalPath.ToLower.EndsWith("gif") _
    OrElse Request.Url.LocalPath.ToLower.EndsWith("jpg") _
    OrElse Request.Url.LocalPath.ToLower.EndsWith("css") _
    OrElse Request.Url.LocalPath.ToLower.EndsWith("js") Then
    Exit Sub
    End If

    ' all of the logic which was previously in Application_start
    ' was moved to Init() in order to support IIS7 integrated pipeline
mode
    ' ( which no longer provides access to HTTP context within
Application_Start )
    Initialize.Init(app)

    'run schedule if in Request mode
    Initialize.RunSchedule(Request)

    End Sub
```

The Globals.vb file

As part of the namespace-reorganization effort associated with DotNetNuke version 3.0, general utility functions, constants, and enumerations have all been placed in a public module (as just mentioned, module here refers to VB.NET module keyword, not a DotNetNuke module) named **Globals**. As items in a .NET module are inherently shared, you do not need to instantiate an object in order to use the functions found here. In this module, you will find not only global constants, as shown in the following code:

```vb
Public Const glbRoleAllUsers As String = "-1"
        Public Const glbRoleSuperUser As String = "-2"
        Public Const glbRoleUnauthUser As String = "-3"
        Public Const glbRoleNothing As String = "-4"

        Public Const glbRoleAllUsersName As String = "All Users"
        Public Const glbRoleSuperUserName As String = "Superuser"
        Public Const glbRoleUnauthUserName As String =
"Unauthenticated Users"
        Public Const glbDefaultPage As String = "Default.aspx"
        Public Const glbHostSkinFolder As String = "_default"

        Public Const glbDefaultControlPanel As String = "Admin/
ControlPanel/IconBar.ascx"
        Public Const glbDefaultPane As String = "ContentPane"
        Public Const glbImageFileTypes As String = "jpg,jpeg,jpe,gif,
bmp,png,swf"
        Public Const glbConfigFolder As String = "\Config\"
        Public Const glbAboutPage As String = "about.htm"
        Public Const glbDotNetNukeConfig As String = "DotNetNuke.
config"


        Public Const glbSuperUserAppName As Integer = -1

        Public Const glbProtectedExtension As String = ".resources"

        Public Const glbEmailRegEx As String = "\b[a-zA-Z0-9._%\-
+']+@[a-zA-Z0-9.\-]+\.[a-zA-Z]{2,4}\b"

        Public Const glbScriptFormat As String = "<script type=""text/
javascript"" src=""{0}"" ></script>"
```

but a tremendous number of public functions to help you do everything, from retrieving the domain name, as shown:

```
Public Function GetDomainName(ByVal Request As HttpRequest, ByVal
ParsePortNumber As Boolean) As String
```

to setting the focus on a page:

```
Public Sub SetFormFocus(ByVal control As Control)
```

This one file contains a wealth of information for the developer. As there are more than 3070 lines in the file and the methods are fairly straightforward, we will not be stepping through this code.

The `Globals.vb` file can now be found in the `DotNetNuke.Library` project in the `\Common` folder.

Putting it all together

We have spent some time looking at some of the major pieces that make up the core architecture. You might be asking yourself how all this works together. In this section, we will walk you through an overview version of what happens when a user requests a page on your portal.

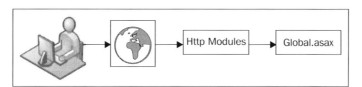

A shown in the preceding diagram, when a user requests any page on your portal, the **HTTP Modules** that have been declared in the `web.config` file are hooked into the pipeline. Typically, these modules use the `Init` method to attach event handlers to application events.

The request then goes through the `Global.asax` page. As just mentioned, some of the events fired here will be intercepted and processed by the HTTP modules, but the call to run the scheduler will happen in this file.

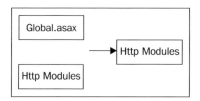

Next, the page that was requested, `Default.aspx`, will be processed. As we stated at the beginning of this chapter, all requests are sent to the `Default.aspx` page and all the controls and skins needed for the page are created dynamically by reading the tabID from the requested URL. So let's begin by looking at the HTML for this page.

The HTML of the page is pretty simple and straightforward. The attributes at the top of the page tell us that the HTML page inherits from the `DotNetNuke.Framework.` `CDefault` class, which is found in the `Default.aspx.vb` code-behind page. We will be examining this class soon.

```
<%@ Page Language="vb" AutoEventWireup="false" Explicit="True"
    Inherits="DotNetNuke.Framework.DefaultPage" CodeFile="Default.
aspx.vb" %>
```

The title and meta tags are populated dynamically from variables in the `PortalSettings` class via a method in the code-behind file:

```
<head id="Head" runat="server">
    <meta content="text/html; charset=UTF-8" http-equiv="Content-
Type"/>
    <meta content="text/javascript" http-equiv="Content-Script-Type"/>
    <meta content="text/css" http-equiv="Content-Style-Type"/>
    <meta id="MetaRefresh" runat="Server" http-equiv="Refresh"
name="Refresh" />
    <meta id="MetaDescription" runat="Server" name="DESCRIPTION" />
    <meta id="MetaKeywords" runat="Server" name="KEYWORDS" />
    <meta id="MetaCopyright" runat="Server" name="COPYRIGHT" />
    <meta id="MetaGenerator" runat="Server" name="GENERATOR" />
    <meta id="MetaAuthor" runat="Server" name="AUTHOR" />
    <meta name="RESOURCE-TYPE" content="DOCUMENT" />
    <meta name="DISTRIBUTION" content="GLOBAL" />
    <meta id="MetaRobots" runat="server" name="ROBOTS" />
    <meta name="REVISIT-AFTER" content="1 DAYS" />
    <meta name="RATING" content="GENERAL" />
    <meta http-equiv="PAGE-ENTER" content="RevealTrans(Duration=0,Tra
nsition=1)" />
```

After the meta tags, placeholders are set to hold CSS and favicons. These are declared in this manner so that the actual files can be determined by the skin being used on the site. This is followed by a script declaration for the file; this declaration is responsible for the module drag-and-drop capability of DotNetNuke 3.0 and later.

```
<style type="text/css" id="StylePlaceholder" runat="server"></style>
<asp:placeholder id="CSS" runat="server" />
</head>
```

The body of the HTML is relatively bare. The important code in this section is the `SkinPlaceholder`, used to inject the selected skin into the body of the page.

```
  <body id="Body" runat="server" >
    <dnn:Form id="Form" runat="server" ENCTYPE="multipart/form-data" >
        <asp:Label ID="SkinError" runat="server" CssClass="NormalRed"
Visible="False"></asp:Label>
        <asp:PlaceHolder ID="SkinPlaceHolder" runat="server" />
        <input id="ScrollTop" runat="server" name="ScrollTop"
type="hidden" />
        <input id="__dnnVariable" runat="server" name="__dnnVariable"
type="hidden" />
    </dnn:Form>
  </body>
</html>
```

Now we will venture into the code-behind class for this file. If you look past the `Imports` statements, you will see that this class inherits from the `DotNeNuke.Framework.PageBase` base class.

```
Partial Class DefaultPage
  Inherits DotNetNuke.Framework.CDefault
```

Its base class handles the localization for the page and of course, as this is a web page, inherits from `System.Web.UI.Page`.

The first procedure that is run in the page is the `Page_Init` method. Most of the action required to generate the response to our request resides in this section. As shown in the next diagram, the first action the `Page_init` method takes is to call the `InitializePage`, which generates the information to fill the meta tags. After initializing the page, the `Page_Init` method begins configuring the skin by setting the **DOCTYPE** for the page and verifies that the requested page is enabled.

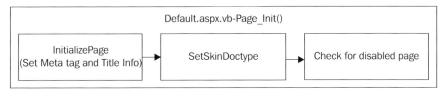

If you look at a couple of pieces of code, we can see some of the files we looked at earlier in use. In the `InitializePage` method, we make use of both the `PortalSettings` class and the `Current` property of the `HttpContext` object to retrieve the `TabName`:

```
objTab = objTabs.GetTabByName(Request.QueryString("TabName"),
CType(HttpContext.Current.Items("PortalSettings"), PortalSettings).
PortalId)
```

Once the properties of the page are retrieved, the process of loading the skin begins. The process starts by retrieving a skin control from the `GetSkin` method of the `Skin` object that will do the work of loading the skin.

```
' load skin control
    Dim ctlSkin As DotNetNuke.UI.Skins.Skin = _
    DotNetNuke.UI.Skins.Skin.GetSkin(Me)
```

After determining whether the request is a skin preview, the code moves on to load the skin. There are three possible outcomes when loading the skin: it is for an admin page, it is for a regular page, or there was an error and it loads the default skin. Regardless of which section is invoked, the skin is loaded using the `LoadSkin` method.

```
ctlSkin = LoadSkin(Page, skinSource)
```

This method reads the physical path of the skin control and loads it into our `ctlSkin` variable. And finally, there are calls to `ManageStyleSheets` and `ManageFavicon`, and the control is added to the page by using the `SkinPlaceholder` that we looked at earlier in the HTML page:

```
        ' add CSS links
        ManageStyleSheets(False, ctlSkin)

        ' add skin to page
        SkinPlaceHolder.Controls.Add(ctlSkin)

        ' add CSS links
        ManageStyleSheets(True, ctlSkin)

        ' add Favicon
        ManageFavicon()

        ' ClientCallback Logic
        DotNetNuke.UI.Utilities.ClientAPI _
    .HandleClientAPICallbackEvent(Me)
```

At this point, you may be thinking to yourself, "I understand how the skin is dynamically added to the page for a user's request, but how are the modules dynamically added?" Well, to get the answer to that question, we will need to look at the skin control itself. You can find the skin control (skin.vb) in the UI\Skins folder of the DotNetNuke.Library project. We will not look at this entire class, but if you look closely at the OnInit method, which is called when the control is instantiated, you will see how the modules are created. First, all of the panes for the skin are loaded into the Skin object's Panes property. Then a check is made to determine if the requested page is an admin/edit view. Based on this information, one of two methods are called to load the modules for the request.

```
'Load the Module Control(s)
If Not IsAdminControl() Then
    ' master module
    bSuccess = ProcessMasterModules()
Else
    ' slave module
    bSuccess = ProcessSlaveModule()
End If
```

These methods determine which modules should be loaded and verify that the requesting user has access to the module(s), determines which pane to place the module, and finally inject the module into the skin.

```
'try to inject the module into the pane
bSuccess = InjectModule(pane, objModule)
```

This procedure will be repeated for all of the modules associated with that page, and the request is finally completed and presented to the user. Of course, we did not cover every piece of code that is called in the process, but hopefully have given you a path to follow to continue researching the core architecture on your own.

Summary

In this chapter, we have taken a look at how the core of DotNetNuke works. We looked at a general overview, examined important pieces of the framework, and finally followed a request through its paces. We will be expanding on this knowledge as we venture into the world of custom-module creation in the next chapter.

7
Custom Module Development

DotNetNuke is an application framework that is designed to be extended through the creation of custom modules.

In this chapter, we will be creating a custom module for the Coffee Connections portal. A custom module consists of one or more custom web controls.

In this chapter, we will cover the following topics:

- Setting up the development environment
- Creating a "Hello World!" view control
- Creating a "Hello Edit" edit control
- Navigation between controls in a module
- Localizing modules to display content in different languages

The Coffee Shop Listing module

In the next few chapters, we will go through the process of creating a DotNetNuke module. Although we go through quite a bit of code in this chapter, we do not cover every single line. To help you as you work through the chapter, the complete source code is available for download from the publisher's site at `http://www.packtpub.com/files/code/9928_Code.zip`.

One of the main features of the Coffee Shop Listing module is that users are able to search, by zip code, for coffee shops in their area. After searching, the users are presented with the shops in their area, as shown in the following screenshot:

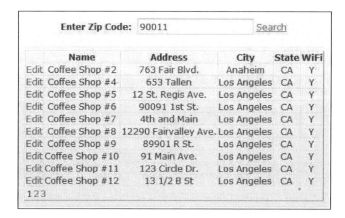

This is accomplished using the view control.

In addition, the module is configurable to allow certain users to add coffee shops using the edit control, as shown in the next screenshot:

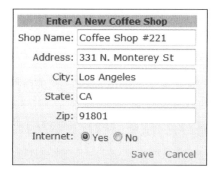

The administrator of the site is able to configure the number of coffee shops that will display on each page in the results, using the settings control as shown in the following screenshot:

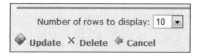

Finally, we will create a Silverlight version of the view control (as shown in the next screenshot), that will present a dynamic **GridView** to unauthenticated users who communicate with the DotNetNuke site using web services.

The development environment

To develop modules for DotNetNuke, you must first have a DotNetNuke installation running on the computer on which you intend to develop them.

DotNetNuke comes in two versions, a source version and an install version. The install version is also packaged as the DotNetNuke Starter Kit. They are functionally the same.

Surprisingly, it is recommended that you use the install version to develop modules. The reason for this is that the source version should only be used if you intend to change the DotNetNuke core code. This is not recommended as it may not allow you to properly upgrade your DotNetNuke site in the future.

Follow the instructions in the earlier chapters of this book to set up DotNetNuke.

To develop the module, Visual Studio 2010 will be used (hereafter, referred to as Visual Studio); however, the instructions apply to all versions of Visual Studio 2008 and all versions of Visual Studio 2010.

If you are using Visual Studio 2008, you will also need to install Microsoft® Silverlight™ 3 Tools for Visual Studio 2008, available at `http://Microsoft.com`.

Creating the view control

Our first example will be the traditional *Hello World!* example. Later, we will alter this control to complete the Coffee Shop Listing module.

Open Visual Studio and select **File** from the toolbar, then select **Open Web Site**, as shown in the next screenshot:

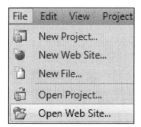

Next, select the root directory of the DotNetNuke website and click the **Open** button. The website will open and display in the **Solution Explorer** window, as shown in the following screenshot:

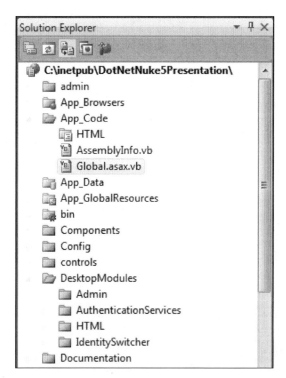

If a box appears offering to upgrade to Framework 4.0, click **No**.

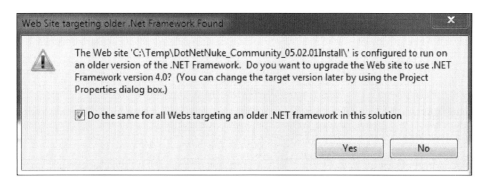

In the **Solution Explorer**, right-click on the DesktopModules folder and select **New Folder**. Name the folder CoffeeShopCSharp if using C#, and CoffeeShopVB if you are creating the module in Visual Basic (hereafter referred to as VB), as shown in the following screenshot:

 The remaining screenshots will show the C# version. Some file and folder names will be different in the VB version. These changes will be indicated.

Next, right-click on the Coffee Shop Listing folder and select **Add New Item**. This directs you to the **Add New item** window, as shown in the following screenshot:

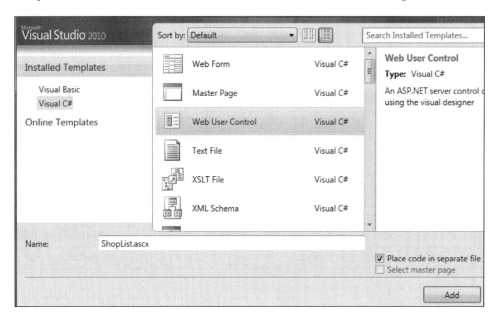

When the **Add New Item** menu appears, select the **Web User Control** and enter ShopList.ascx in the **Name** box and check the box next to **Place code in separate file**. Also, ensure that the proper language is selected under the **Installed Templates** section.

Click the **Add** button.

The ShopList.ascx file will now appear under the Coffee Shop Listing folder.

The source for the ShopList.ascx will also appear in the main window. If the page is in the design view, click the **Source** button in the lower lefthand corner of the window to switch to the **Source** view.

We will now create code to display "Hello World".

Replace all the code with the following code:

C#:

```
<%@ Control language="C#" AutoEventWireup="true"
Inherits="CoffeeShopCSharp.ShopList"
CodeFile="ShopList.ascx.cs"%>
<asp:Label ID="Label1" runat="server" Text="Label"></asp:Label>
```

VB:

```
<%@ Control Language="VB" AutoEventWireup="false"
  Inherits="CoffeeShopVB.ShopList"
  CodeFile="ShopList.ascx.vb" %>
<asp:Label ID="Label1" runat="server" Text="Label"></asp:Label>
```

 You may see wavy lines that indicate errors. These errors will be cleared up when we replace the code in the code behind file in the next step.

Now, right-click on the `ShopList.ascx` file and select **View Code**, as shown in the next screenshot:

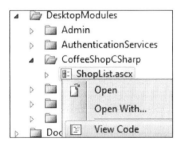

Replace all the code with the following code:

C#:

```
using System;
using DotNetNuke;
using DotNetNuke.Entities.Modules;
using DotNetNuke.Services.Exceptions;

namespace CoffeeShopCSharp
{
  partial class ShopList : PortalModuleBase
  {
    protected void Page_Load(object sender, EventArgs e)
    {
      try
      {
        Label1.Text = "Hello World!";
      }
      catch (Exception exc)
      {
```

```
        Exceptions.ProcessModuleLoadException(this, exc);
      }
    }
  }
}
```

VB:

```
Imports System
Imports DotNetNuke
Imports DotNetNuke.Entities.Modules
Imports DotNetNuke.Services.Exceptions

Namespace CoffeeShopVB

  Partial Class ShopList
    Inherits PortalModuleBase

    Protected Sub Page_Load(ByVal sender As    _
                            System.Object, _
                            ByVal e As System.EventArgs) _
                            Handles MyBase.Load
        Try
            Label1.Text = "Hello World!"
        Catch exc As Exception
            Exceptions.ProcessModuleLoadException(Me, exc)
        End Try
      End Sub
    End Class
End Namespace
```

Displaying the module

We will now walk through the steps needed to configure the module and view it in your DotNetNuke website.

In the **Solution Explorer**, right-click on the `Default.aspx` file and select **View in Browser** to launch the website, as shown:

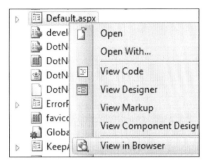

Log in as the host account. From the **HOST** menu, select **Module Definitions**.

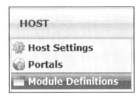

At the bottom of the **Module Definitions** page, select **Create New Module**.

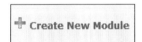

Select **Control** for the **Create Module From** drop-down menu.

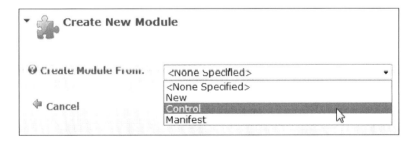

Here, select `CoffeeShopCSharp` if using C#, or `CoffeeShopVB` if using VB for the **Module Folder** drop-down list. Enter `CoffeeShopCSharp` for the **Module Name** if using C#, or `CoffeeShopVB` if using VB. Select `ShopList.ascx` for the **Resource**. Then, click **Create Module**.

Navigate to a page in your DotNetNuke website and place the module on the page by selecting it in the **Module** dropdown at the top of the page (see the next screenshot) and then clicking the **Add Module To Page** link.

The module will display, as shown in the next screenshot:

Next, we will intentionally generate an error to explore the functionality of the **Log Viewer**. Leave the website open and return to Visual Studio. In Visual Studio, add the following line of code directly under the line `Label1.Text = "Hello World!"`:

C#:

```
throw new Exception("Something didn't work right.");
```

VB:

```
Throw New Exception("Something didn't work right.")
```

Save the page and return to the site in the web browser and refresh the page. The page will now show an error, as shown in the following screenshot:

Select **Event Viewer** from the **ADMIN** menu. Locate the most recent entry for **Module Load Exception** and click on it to expand it. We can see that it indicates that the error is in the `ShopList` file and provides additional details, as shown:

Return to Visual Studio and remove the `throw new Exception("Something didn't work right.")` line. Save the page.

View control summary

We have just explored a few core concepts of DotNetNuke module development, which are as follows:

- The DotNetNuke module folder structure
- Inheriting from `PortalModuleBase`
- Module configuration
- Diagnosing errors using the **Log Viewer**

The module folder structure

A DotNetNuke module is made up of web controls and their associated code behind files that reside in folders in the `DesktopModules` directory. Optionally, other code files for the module that are not associated with a web control (for example, **Data Access Layer (DAL)** and **Business Logic Layer (BLL)** code) reside in the `App_Code` directory. In later steps, we will create code that will reside in the `App_Code` directory.

Inheriting from PortalModuleBase

The most important item for making your web control integrate well with the DotNetNuke framework is this:

C#:

```
: PortalModuleBase
```

VB:

```
Inherits Entities.Modules.PortalModuleBase
```

Inheriting from `PortalModuleBase` is essential because it is the base class for most custom web controls in DotNetNuke. Using this base class is what gives our control consistency in its appearance with the portal it resides in and provides functionality such as the menu and portal access security.

This class also gives us access to useful items such as the current user and the current `ModuleID`. In later steps, you will see how these items allow the web control to interact with the DotNetNuke framework to provide most of the functionality you desire.

From the toolbar in Visual Studio, select **View** and then **Object Browser**. When the **Object Browser** window opens, click on the plus symbol next to the **DotNetNuke** node to expand it. Next, expand the **DotNetNuke.Entities.Modules** node. Finally, click on the **PortalModuleBase** node to see the various properties that are available to your web control when you inherit from this class. Refer to the following screenshot:

Module configuration

Creating a module definition makes the module appear in the control panel's module drop-down menu. It connects your controls to the portal framework. In the walk-through, we configured the module to have one web control. In later steps, we will create and configure additional web controls.

Diagnosing errors using the Log Viewer

The ProcessModuleLoadException method of the DotNetNuke.Services. Exceptions class offers a simple way to send errors to the **Log Viewer**.

```
Exceptions.ProcessModuleLoadException(this, exc)
```

This is useful during module development as well as to assist an administrator in diagnosing problems when the module is deployed to production.

Navigation

Because a DotNetNuke module is a collection of web controls, you will need to navigate between them. We will now implement two forms of navigation:

1. **NavigateURL**: Used to create links that navigate between web controls
2. **IActionable**: Used to display a menu that will also navigate between web controls

To demonstrate this, we will create an Edit web control. For now it will just say *Hello Edit!*. Later we will alter it to complete the Coffee Shop Listing module.

NavigateURL

The following code will demonstrate how to create links that use `NavigateURL`.

In Visual Studio, right-click on the Coffee Shop Listing folder and select **Add New Item**.

When the **Add New Item** menu comes up, select **Web User Control** and enter `EditShopList.ascx` in the **Name** box. Ensure that the **Place code in separate file** box is checked, and the proper language is selected, then click the **Add** button.

When the page comes up in source view, replace all the code with the following code:

C#:

```
<%@ Control language="C#" AutoEventWireup="true"
Inherits="CoffeeShopCSharp.EditShopList"
CodeFile="EditShopList.ascx.cs"%>
<asp:Label id="Label1" runat="server" text="Label" />
<br />
<br />
<asp:LinkButton id="cmdReturn" runat="server" text="Return" />
```

VB:

```
<%@ Control Language="VB" AutoEventWireup="false"
Inherits="CoffeeShopVB.EditShopList"
CodeFile="EditShopList.ascx.vb" %>
<asp:Label id="Label1" runat="server" text="Label" />
<br />
<br />
<asp:LinkButton id="cmdReturn" runat="server" text="Return" />
```

Right-click on `EditShopList.ascx` in the **Solution Explorer** and select **View Code**. When the source code is displayed, replace all the code with the following code:

C#:

```csharp
using System;
using DotNetNuke;
using DotNetNuke.Entities.Modules;
using DotNetNuke.Services.Exceptions;
using DotNetNuke.Services.Localization;

namespace CoffeeShopCSharp
{
  partial class EditShopList : PortalModuleBase
  {
    protected void Page_Load(System.Object sender,
                              System.EventArgs e)
    {
      Label1.Text = "Hello Edit!";
    }

    protected void cmdReturn_Click(object sender, EventArgs e)
    {
      // Redirect back to the portal
      Response.Redirect(DotNetNuke.Common.Globals.NavigateURL());
    }
  }
}
```

VB:

```vb
Imports System
Imports DotNetNuke
Imports DotNetNuke.Entities.Modules
Imports DotNetNuke.Services.Exceptions

Namespace CoffeeShopVB

  Partial Class EditShopList
    Inherits PortalModuleBase

      Protected Sub Page_Load(ByVal sender As System.Object, _
        ByVal e As System.EventArgs) Handles MyBase.Load

          Label1.Text = "Hello Edit!"
```

```
            End Sub

        Protected Sub cmdDelete_Click( _
          ByVal sender As System.Object, _
            ByVal e As System.EventArgs) Handles cmdReturn.Click

              ' Redirect back to the portal
              Response.Redirect(NavigateURL())
            End Sub
        End Class
    End Namespace
```

Save the page.

IActionable

Now we will create a menu that will navigate to the EditShopList control.

Right-click on ShopList.ascx and select **View Code** and make the following changes to indicate that we will implement the IActionable interface:

C#:

Alter the line:

```
    partial class EditShopList : PortalModuleBase
```

to:

```
    partial class EditShopList : PortalModuleBase , IActionable
```

VB:

Alter the line:

```
    Inherits PortalModuleBase
```

to:

```
    Inherits PortalModuleBase
    Implements Entities.Modules.IActionable
```

 The preceding code indicates that we will implement the IActionable interface. As we have not yet done, you will see wavy lines on the page indicating an error. This will be fixed in the next step.

Now, we will implement the `IActionable` interface. Add the following method to the class:

C#:

```csharp
DotNetNuke.Entities.Modules.Actions.ModuleActionCollection
IActionable.ModuleActions
{
  get
  {
    DotNetNuke.Entities.Modules.Actions.ModuleActionCollection
      objActions = new DotNetNuke.Entities.Modules.Actions.
                ModuleActionCollection();
    objActions.Add(GetNextActionID(),
              "Add Coffee Shop",
              DotNetNuke.Entities.Modules.Actions.
              ModuleActionType.AddContent,
              "",
              "",
              EditUrl(),
              false,
              DotNetNuke.Security.SecurityAccessLevel.Edit,
              true,
              false
              );
    return objActions;
  }
}
```

VB:

```vb
Public ReadOnly Property ModuleActions() As _
      DotNetNuke.Entities.Modules.Actions.ModuleActionCollection _
      Implements DotNetNuke.Entities.Modules.IActionable.ModuleActions
      Get
          Dim Actions As New _
          Entities.Modules.Actions.ModuleActionCollection
          Actions.Add(GetNextActionID, _
              "Add Coffee Shop", _
              Entities.Modules.Actions.ModuleActionType.AddContent, _
              "", "", _
              EditUrl(), _
              False, _
              DotNetNuke.Security.SecurityAccessLevel.Edit, _
              True, False)
          Return Actions
      End Get
    End Property
```

Save the page.

Updating the configuration

We will now update the module configuration to add the `EditShopList` control as follows:

- In your web browser, log in to your DotNetNuke site as host
- From the **HOST** menu, select **Module Definitions**
- From the **Module Definitions** page, click the edit symbol next to the `CoffeeShopCSharp` entry to select it (or `CoffeeShopVB` if using VB)
- The module will show up on the **Module Definitions** page. Click the **Add Module Control** link
- When the control configuration screen appears, configure it with the following settings:
  - Enter **Edit** for **Key**
  - Enter **Edit Shoplist** for **Title**
  - Use the drop-down to select `DesktopModules/CoffeeShopCSharp/EditShopList.ascx` (or `DesktopModules/CoffeeShopVB/EditShopList.ascx` if using VB) for **Source.**
  - Use the dropdown to select **Edit** for **Type**
  - Click the **Update** button

Navigating from ShopList to EditShopList

Now, navigate to the Coffee Shop Listing module in the DotNetNuke site. You will see that there is a link to **Add Coffee Shop**, as shown in the next screenshot:

Click on the link and you will navigate to the **Edit** page.

Hello Edit!

Return

Click the **Return** link and you will navigate back to the ShopList page. Click the menu icon in the corner of the Coffee Shop Listing module and notice that there is also an **Add Coffee Shop** link there.

Navigation summary

We have explored the following features of the DotNetNuke **application programming interface (API)**:

- NavigateURL
- IActionable

NavigateURL

If you want to create a simple link, you can use code such as Response.Redirect(NavigateURL()). The NavigateURL function works in conjunction with DotNetNuke URL rewriting. URL rewriting is a function DotNetNuke performs to create URL's that are more easily indexed by search engines.

We can see in the Visual Studio object browser that the NavigateURL() method has multiple overloads, as shown in the next screenshot:

```
NavigateURL() As String
NavigateURL(Integer) As String
NavigateURL(Integer, Boolean) As String
NavigateURL(Integer, Boolean, DotNetNuke.Entities.Portals.PortalSettings, String, ParamArray String()) As String
NavigateURL(Integer, Boolean, DotNetNuke.Entities.Portals.PortalSettings, String, String, ParamArray String()) As String
NavigateURL(Integer, DotNetNuke.Entities.Portals.PortalSettings, String, ParamArray String()) As String
NavigateURL(Integer, String) As String
NavigateURL(Integer, String, ParamArray String()) As String
NavigateURL(String) As String
NavigateURL(String, ParamArray String()) As String
```

We will see more implementations of this function in code presented later in this chapter.

IActionable

We only implemented the IActionable interface in one place in the code, yet the **Add Coffee Shop** link shows up in two places on the module. It shows up on the ShopList page and on the module's menu. This demonstrates the benefit of the DotNetNuke API. The link and the menu item not only show up in standardized places, but they also show up based on the security roles that you indicate. For example, currently the **Add Coffee Shop** link will only show up if you are logged in as the host or administrator.

To add an **Action** menu item to the module's **Action** menu, we create an instance of a ModuleActionCollection. This is done in the ModuleActions property declaration.

We then use the Add method of this object to add an item to the menu. The parameters of the Actions.Add method are:

Parameter	Type	Description
ID	Integer	The GetNextActionID function (found in the ActionsBase.vb file) will retrieve the next available ID for your ModuleActionCollection. This works like an auto-increment field, adding one to the previous action ID.
Title	String	The title is what is displayed in the context menu from your module.
CmdName	String	If you want your menu item to call client-side code (JavaScript), then this is where you will place the name of the command. This is used for the delete action on the context menu. When the delete item is selected, a message asks you to confirm your choice before executing the command. For the menu items we are adding, we will leave this blank.
CmdArg	String	This allows you to add additional arguments for the command.
Icon	String	This allows you to set a custom icon to appear next to your menu option.

Parameter	Type	Description
URL	String	This is where the browser will be redirected to when your menu item is clicked. You can use a standard URL or use the EditURL function to direct it to another module. The EditURL function finds the module associated with your view module by looking at the key passed in. You will notice that the first example passes in "Options" and the second one passes nothing. This is because the default key is "Edit". These keys are entered in the **Module Definition**. We will learn how to add these manually later.
ClientScript	String	As the name implies, this is where you would add the client-side script to be run when this item is selected. This is paired with the CmdName attribute. We are leaving this blank for your actions.
UseActionEvent	Boolean	This determines if the user will receive notification when a script is being executed.
Secure	SecurityAccessLevel	This is an Enum that determines the access level for this menu item.
Visible	Boolean	Determines whether this item will be visible.
New Window	Boolean	Determines whether information will be presented in a new window.

Localization

In the final exercise for this chapter, we will create resource files that can be used to replace the text in your module to allow it to display in multiple languages. This is called **localization**.

First, we will localize the link on the **EditShopList** control.

Localizing static content

Right-click on the Coffee Shop Listing folder and select **Add ASP.NET Folder** and then `App_LocalResources`.

When the `App_LocalResources` folder appears, right-click on it and select **Add New Item**.

When the **Add New Item box** comes up, select **Resource File** as the template, enter `EditShopList.ascx.resx` in the **Name** box, select the appropriate language, and click the **Add** button.

The resource file will be created, as shown in the preceding screenshot.

The resource editor window will appear. When it does, enter **cmdReturn.Text** in the **Name** column and **Return** in the **Value** column, as shown in the next screenshot:

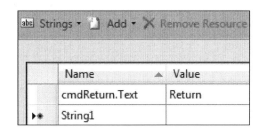

Save the file and close it.

In the source code for the `EditShopList.ascx` page, you will now create a resource key in the `Linkbutton` that will point to the entry you just created in the resource file. Change the code for the `Linkbutton` to:

C# and VB:

```
<asp:LinkButton id="cmdReturn" runat="server" text="Return"
   resourcekey="cmdReturn" onclick="cmdReturn_Click" />
```

Save the file and close it.

Next, we will localize the menu item on the **ShopList** control.

Localizing dynamic content

The content for the **Add Coffee Shop** link is in the code behind file. This is considered *dynamic content*. To localize it, we will replace the words **Add Coffee Shop** with code that will retrieve the **localized** content.

Use the previous example to create a resource file named ShopList.ascx.resx. Create a key with **AddContent.Action** in the **Name** column and a **Add Coffee Shop** in the **Value** column.

Save the file and close it. You will now have two resource files in the App_LocalResources folder, as shown in the following screenshot:

Locate **Add Coffee Shop** in the code behind the ShopList.ascx file (ShopList.ascx.cs for C# and ShopList.ascx.vb for VB) and replace it with the following code:

C# and VB:

```
DotNetNuke.Services.Localization.Localization.GetString(DotNetNuke.
  Entities.Modules.Actions.ModuleActionType.AddContent,
  LocalResourceFile)
```

Save the page.

Localizing the content

We will now localize the module to display some of the text in a different language.

In your web browser, log in to your DotNetNuke site as host. From the **ADMIN** menu, select **Languages**. At the bottom of the screen, select **Add New Language**. You will be directed to the following page:

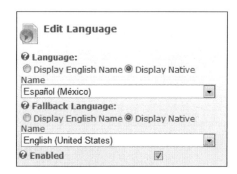

Here, select a language in the **Language** dropdown and a language in the **Fallback Language**. Check the box next to **Enabled** and click the **Update** link. This will redirect you to the main **Languages** page. Select the language you just added in the **Available Locales** dropdown, as shown in the following screenshot:

In the **Language Editor** tree, navigate to the page you want to translate and click on the file.

Enter a translation for the **Localized Value** and click the **Save Resource File** link.

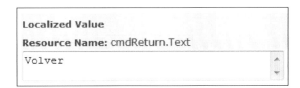

You will now see flags representing the available translations, as shown in the following screenshot:

When you click on a flag, you will see localized content, as shown in the screenshot below:

Summary

The module is not complete, however, we have covered many important concepts that you will most likely use in every module you create. Essentially a DotNetNuke module is made up of web controls that are inherited from `Entities.Modules.PortalModuleBase`. Navigation and localization were covered and their proper use will allow you to create modules that integrate well into your portal. In addition, we covered exception handling that will also aid you in your module development. In the next chapter, we will cover connecting your module to the database.

Connecting to the Database

8

In this chapter, we are going to continue developing the custom module for the Coffee Connections portal. In the previous chapter, we set up our development environment and created custom web controls. In this chapter, we will connect the module to the database. The areas that will be covered are:

- Comparing data access layers
- Create the LINQ to SQL `DataContext` class
- Complete the Coffee Shop Listing module
    - The `Settings` page
    - The `EditShopList` page
    - The `ShopList` page

The DAL, DAL+, and LINQ to SQL

This chapter will demonstrate using LINQ to SQL to connect the module to the database. However, the DotNetNuke core code uses a method called the **data access layer (DAL)** to connect to the database and also provides another method to connect to the database called the **DAL+**.

The DAL

The DAL's purpose is to allow the DotNetNuke core code and add-on modules to communicate with any data source. It is a **design pattern** that consists of an **Abstract Data Provider** and a **Concrete Data Provider**. The DAL allows your module to run on different data sources by simply replacing the Concrete Data Provider. Developers have created providers to allow the DotNetNuke Core to run on Oracle and MySQL (by creating Concrete Data Providers for those databases).

Module developers can use the DAL pattern to develop modules. Many of the modules sponsored by the DotNetNuke Core, such as the **Survey** module, use the DAL pattern. However, this pattern requires a lot of code to implement. In response to the concern as to the amount of code required to implement the DAL, and the complexity in implementing it, the DotNetNuke Core team provided an alternative pattern called the DAL+.

The DAL+

The DAL+ is an alternative method of communicating with the database. With the DAL+, developers do not need to write code for an Abstract Data Provider or a Concrete Data Provider. Instead, they use a subset of methods that are a part of the Core DAL. These methods will still allow you to create modules that can communicate with an alternative database. However, unlike the traditional DAL, the DAL+ is not 100 percent portable to other data sources.

The reason it is not 100 percent portable is that a situation can exist where one stored procedure or SQL statement is needed to perform an action using one data source (for example, Microsoft SQL Server), but more than one is needed for another data source (for example, MySQL). In such cases, the DAL+ will not work. The traditional DAL will work in all situations with all data sources.

LINQ to SQL

ASP.NET 3.5 provides a valuable tool for connecting to the database called LINQ to SQL. LINQ to SQL is directly integrated into all versions of Visual Studio 2010 and Visual Studio 2008. LINQ to SQL provides a fast, easy to use method to connect to the database because you can use the **Object Relational Designer (O/R Designer)** to automatically create the data access code.

The primary disadvantage of LINQ to SQL is that it only works with modules that connect to a Microsoft SQL database. The Coffee Shop Listing module in this tutorial uses Microsoft SQL server, so it will be used for this module.

Another disadvantage of using LINQ to SQL with DotNetNuke is that it does not work with the optional **object qualifier** and **database owner** settings in the web.config file. DotNetNuke allows you to specify an object qualifier setting in the web.config file to allow you to install more than one DotNetNuke instance in a single database, or install DNN instance within the same database that is used by other application(s) of yours. It also allows you to specify a database owner other than dbo. **Brandon Haynes** has created an open source project **DotNetNuke Linq to Sql Model Adapter** (http://dnnlinqtosqladapter.codeplex.com) that overcomes these two limitations.

Summary of the data connection methods

The differences can be summarized as follows:

- **DAL**: A more robust data access method that allows your modules to have 100 percent *portability*. However, it requires a significant amount of code to implement.

- **DAL+**: A simplified data access method that still allows your module to support multiple data sources. However, it is not 100 percent *portable* to all data sources.

- **LINQ to SQL**: The fastest and easiest method to connect to the database. However, it works only with SQL server.

The database scripts

We will create an SQL script that will create the table needed for the module. We will also create an uninstallation script. Later when we package this module in a .zip file that can be used to install the module in another DotNetNuke portal, the installation script will be executed by the DotNetNuke installer to create the table in the database, and the uninstallation script will be executed to remove the table when the module is uninstalled.

By convention, the database scripts should be named in the following manner:

Type of script	Description	Example
Installation script	Concatenate the version number of your module with the type of provider the script represents, for example, Sql.	01.00.00.SqlDataProvider
Uninstallation script	Concatenate the word uninstall with the type of provider the script represents.	uninstall.SqlDataProvider

The first step in creating the installation scripts will be to create the folder that will contain them. We will place them in the Coffee Shop Listing folder that is under the DesktopModules folder.

In Visual Studio, in the **Solution Explorer**, right-click on the Coffee Shop Listing folder, that is under the DesktopModules folder (CoffeeShopCSharp if using C# and CoffeeShopVB if using VB) and select **New Folder**. Name the folder Sql.

We will now create the installation scripts. We will create an install script (01.00.00.SqlDataProvider) and an uninstall script (uninstall.SqlDataProvider). The install script will be processed by the DotNetNuke installation when the module is installed, and the uninstall script will be processed by the DotNetNuke installation when the module is uninstalled.

Right-click on the Sql folder and select **Add New Item**. Select **Text File** as the template and enter 01.00.00.SqlDataProvider in the **Name** field and click the **Add** button.

Right-click on the 01.00.00.SqlDataProvider file and select **Open**. When the file opens in the editor window, enter the following code and save the file:

```
IF NOT EXISTS (SELECT * FROM dbo.sysobjects
WHERE id = OBJECT_ID(N'[dbo].[CoffeeShopInfo]')
AND OBJECTPROPERTY(id, N'IsUserTable') = 1)
BEGIN
CREATE TABLE [dbo].[CoffeeShopInfo](
  [coffeeShopID] [int] IDENTITY(1,1) NOT NULL,
  [moduleID] [int] NOT NULL,
  [coffeeShopName] [nvarchar](100) NOT NULL,
  [coffeeShopAddress] [nvarchar](150) NULL,
  [coffeeShopCity] [nvarchar](50) NULL,
  [coffeeShopState] [nvarchar](2) NULL,
  [coffeeShopZip] [nvarchar](11) NULL,
  [coffeeShopWiFi] [nvarchar](2) NOT NULL,
 CONSTRAINT [PK_CoffeeShopInfo] PRIMARY KEY CLUSTERED
(
  [coffeeShopID] ASC
) ON [PRIMARY]
) ON [PRIMARY]
END
```

Right-click on the Sql folder and select **Add New Item**. Select **Text File** as the template and enter uninstall.SqlDataProvider in the **Name** field and click the **Add** button. Right-click on the uninstall.SqlDataProvider file and select **Open**, as shown in the following screenshot:

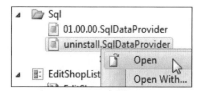

When the file opens in the editor window, enter the following code and save the file:

```
IF  EXISTS (SELECT * FROM dbo.sysobjects WHERE id = OBJECT_ID(N'[dbo].
[CoffeeShopInfo]') AND OBJECTPROPERTY(id, N'IsUserTable') = 1)
DROP TABLE [dbo].[CoffeeShopInfo]
```

Executing the install script

You will now execute the database script that will create the `CoffeeShopInfo` table that the module will use to store the coffee shops.

Log in to your DotNetNuke website using the host account, and select **SQL** from the **HOST** menu.

Copy the script from the `01.00.00.SqlDataProvider` file and paste it into the textbox, as shown in the following screenshot:

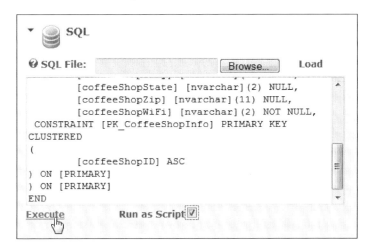

Select the **Run as Script** checkbox and click the **Execute** link.

The screen will display **The Query completed successfully!**.

> Please note that this step is only required when you are developing your module. After your module is ready, and you zip it up for installation, the DNN module installer would automatically execute the scripts from the `.zip` folder during module installation, and you do not need to do it manually.

Creating the LINQ to SQL DataContext class

You will now create the Linq to SQL `DataContext` class that the module code will use to connect to the database.

In Visual Studio, in the **Solution Explorer,** right-click on the `App_Code` folder and select **New Folder**. Name the folder `CoffeeShopCSharp` if using C# or `CoffeeShopVB` if using VB.

```
<codeSubDirectories>
    <add directoryName="CoffeeShopCSharp" />
</codeSubDirectories>
```

Open the `web.config` file and add the following line to the `<codeSubDirectories>` section, as shown in the previous screenshot:

C#:

```
<add directoryName="CoffeeShopCSharp" />
```

VB:

```
<add directoryName="CoffeeShopVB" />
```

This is required to instruct ASP.NET that there will be code created in a language other than VB.NET (which is the language of the main DotNetNuke project).

It is also customary to do this even if your module is coded in VB because the DotNetNuke installer will always create the entry in the `web.config` when installing a module that has code in the `App_Code` directory.

Right-click on the Coffee Shop Listing directory located under the `App_Code` directory (`CoffeeShopCSharp` if using C# and `CoffeeShopVB` if using VB) and select **Add New Item**.

In the **Add New Item** window, select the **LINQ to SQL Classes** template and for the Name, enter `CoffeeShopCSharp.dbml` if using C# or `CoffeeShopVB.dbml` if using VB. Select **Visual C#** for the **Language** if using Visual C#, and **Visual Basic** if using VB, and click the **Add** button.

Open the .dbml file, and in the **Object Relational Designer**, click on the **Server Explorer** link to open the **Server Explorer**.

In the **Server Explorer**, right-click on the **Data Connections** icon and select **Add Connection**, as shown in the following screenshot:

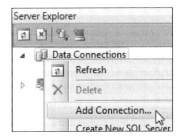

In the **Add Connection** dialog, enter the information to connect to the database that the DotNetNuke site is running on.

This will not be the connection that the module will use when it runs (you will set that connection in a later step). This is only a connection to allow you to use the Object Relational Designer.

Click the **OK** button.

When the connection shows up in the **Server Explorer**, click the plus icon to expand its object tree to display the tables.

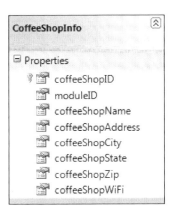

Locate the `CoffeeShopInfo` table, click on it, and drag-and-drop it on the **design surface** of the Object Relational Designer.

Click in the whitespace on the design surface of the Object Relational Designer, and in its **Properties**, set the **Connection** to **SiteSqlServer**. This step is required to instruct the LINQ to SQL `DataContext` class to use the **SiteSqlServer** setting in the `web.config` file to connect to the database at runtime.

Save the file and close it.

The Settings page

We will now create the **Settings** page that will allow the administrator to set the number of coffee shops to be displayed.

When we click on the Coffee Shop Listing module's menu and select **Settings**, we are able to navigate to the module's standard settings.

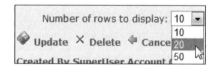

We will now create a page, which when configured, will display a section at the bottom of the **Settings** page of the Coffee Shop Listing module that will allow us to set the number of coffee shops to display.

Creating the Settings page

We will now create the **Settings** page. In Visual Studio, right-click on the Coffee Shop Listing folder that is under the `DesktopModules` folder (`CoffeeShopCSharp` if using C# or `CoffeeShopVB` if using VB) and select **Add New Item**.

When the **Add New Item** window comes up, select **Web User Control** and enter
Settings.ascx in the **Name** box. Ensure that the proper language is selected for
Installed Templates, and that the **Place code in a separate file** box is checked.

Click the **Add** button.

The Settings.ascx file will now appear in the **Solution Explorer** under the Coffee
Shop Listing folder.

The source for the Settings.ascx will also appear in the edit window.

Replace all the code with the following code:

C#:

```
<%@ Control Language="C#"
AutoEventWireup="true"
CodeFile="Settings.ascx.cs"
Inherits="CoffeeShopCSharp.Settings" %>
<asp:Label ID="lblNumberOfRows" runat="server"
  resourcekey="lblNumberOfRows"
  Text="Number of Rows" />:
<asp:DropDownList ID="ddlNumberOfRows"
  runat="server">
  <asp:ListItem>10</asp:ListItem>
  <asp:ListItem>20</asp:ListItem>
  <asp:ListItem>50</asp:ListItem>
  <asp:ListItem>100</asp:ListItem>
</asp:DropDownList>
```

VB:

```
<%@ Control Language="VB"
AutoEventWireup="true"
CodeFile="Settings.ascx.vb"
Inherits="CoffeeShopVB.Settings" %>
<asp:Label ID="lblNumberOfRows"
  runat="server"
  resourcekey="lblNumberOfRows"
  Text="Number of Rows" />:
<asp:DropDownList ID="ddlNumberOfRows"
  runat="server">
  <asp:ListItem>10</asp:ListItem>
  <asp:ListItem>20</asp:ListItem>
  <asp:ListItem>50</asp:ListItem>
  <asp:ListItem>100</asp:ListItem>
</asp:DropDownList>
```

You may see wavy lines that indicate errors. These errors will be cleared up when we replace the code in the code behind file in the next step.

Right-click on the `Settings.ascx` file and select **View Code**. When the source code is displayed, replace all the code with the following code:

C#:

```csharp
using System;
using System.Web.UI;
using DotNetNuke.Entities.Modules;
using DotNetNuke.Services.Exceptions;

namespace CoffeeShopCSharp
{
  public partial class Settings : ModuleSettingsBase
  {
    DotNetNuke.Entities.Modules.ModuleController objModules =
      new DotNetNuke.Entities.Modules.ModuleController();

    #region LoadSettings
    public override void LoadSettings()
    {
      try
      {
        if (!Page.IsPostBack)
        {
          if ((((string)(ModuleSettings["NumberOfRows"])) != null))
          {
            ddlNumberOfRows.SelectedValue =
            ((string)(ModuleSettings["NumberOfRows"]));
          }
          else
          {
            objModules.UpdateModuleSetting(ModuleId,
            "NumberOfRows", "10");
          }
        }
      }
      catch (Exception exc)
      {
        // Module failed to load
        Exceptions.ProcessModuleLoadException(this, exc);
```

```
      }
    }
    #endregion

    #region UpdateSettings
    public override void UpdateSettings()
    {
      objModules.UpdateModuleSetting(ModuleId, "NumberOfRows",
        ddlNumberOfRows.SelectedValue);
    }
    #endregion
  }
}
```

VB:

```
Imports System
Imports System.Web.UI
Imports DotNetNuke.Entities.Modules
Imports DotNetNuke.Services.Exceptions

Namespace CoffeeShopVB
  Partial Public Class Settings
    Inherits ModuleSettingsBase
    Private objModules As New DotNetNuke.Entities.Modules.
ModuleController()
  Public Overloads Overrides Sub LoadSettings()
    Try
      If Not Page.IsPostBack Then
        If ((DirectCast((ModuleSettings("NumberOfRows")), _
          String)) <> Nothing) Then
          ddlNumberOfRows.SelectedValue = _
          (DirectCast((ModuleSettings("NumberOfRows")), String))
        Else
          objModules.UpdateModuleSetting(ModuleId, _
          "NumberOfRows", "10")
        End If
      End If
      Catch exc As Exception
      ' Module failed to load
        Exceptions.ProcessModuleLoadException(Me, exc)
    End Try
  End Sub
  Public Overloads Overrides Sub UpdateSettings()
```

```
        objModules.UpdateModuleSetting(ModuleId, "NumberOfRows", _
            ddlNumberOfRows.SelectedValue)
    End Sub
End Class
End Namespace
```

Save and close the file.

The Settings page

The code for the **Settings** page covers the following concepts and controls:

- Inheriting from ModuleSettingsBase
- Overriding LoadSettings and UpdateSettings
- Storing values in ModuleSettings

Inheriting from ModuleSettingsBase

Unlike the other web user controls, the **Settings** page inherits from ModuleSettingsBase. ModuleSettingsBase inherits from PortalModuleBase and contains all of its useful properties such as ModuleId, but it also has two abstract methods that we implement: LoadSettings and UpdateSettings.

Overriding LoadSettings and UpdateSettings

LoadSettings is called when the **Module Settings** page is accessed, and UpdateSettings is called when the **Update** button is clicked on the **Module Settings** page. In the LoadSettings method, we load the NumberOfRows value and bind it to the ddlNumberOfRows dropdown. In the UpdateSettings method we save the NumberOfRows value.

> LoadSettings would be called on a PostBack. Therefore, it is important to check for the page's IsPostBack property, and set the values on controls only if it is false. Otherwise, you would overwrite the user submitted values on PostBack.

Storing values in ModuleSettings

The DotNetNuke API allows modules to store values in ModuleSettings. Values are stored in ModuleSettings by passing the current ModuleId, a key, and a value to the UpdateModuleSetting method. They are retrieved by passing the same key to the ModuleSettings method.

Updating the configuration

In your web browser, log in to your DotNetNuke site as the host account and perform the following steps:

- From the **HOST** menu select **Module Definitions**
- On the **Module Definitions** page, click the edit symbol next to the Coffee Shop Listing module (`CoffeeShopCSharp` if using C# or `CoffeeShopVB` if using VB) to select it
- Click the **Add Module Control** link towards the bottom of the module definition
- When the control configuration screen appears, configure it with the following settings:
    - Enter **Settings** for **Key**
    - Enter **CoffeeShop Settings** for **Title**
    - Use the dropdown to select `DesktopModules/CoffeeShopCSharp/Settings.ascx` if using C# or `DesktopModules/CoffeeShopVB/Settings.ascx` if using VB for **Source**
    - Use the dropdown to select **Edit** for **Type**
- Click the **Update** button

The EditShopList page

The `EditShopList` web user control will be used by the portal administrator to insert, edit, and delete coffee shops. We will replace all the existing code created in *Chapter 7, Custom Module Development*, with new code that will use the LINQ to SQL `DataContext` class to connect to the database.

Although we will go through quite a bit of code in this section, we do not cover every single line. To help you as you work through the section, the complete source code is available for download from the publisher's site (`http://www.packtpub.com/files/code/9928_Code.zip`).

The EditShopList.ascx file

In Visual Studio, under the Coffee Shop Listing folder that is under the DesktopModules folder (CoffeeShopCSharp if using C# and CoffeeShopVB if using VB) right-click on the EditShopList.ascx file, and select **Open**. The page will open in the edit window. Replace all the code with the following code:

C#:

```
<%@ Control Language="C#"
AutoEventWireup="true"
CodeFile="EditShopList.ascx.cs"
Inherits="CoffeeShopCSharp.EditShopList"
%>
```

VB:

```
<%@ Control Language="VB"
AutoEventWireup="True"
Inherits="CoffeeShopVB.EditShopList"
CodeFile="EditShopList.ascx.vb"
%>
```

This code creates the standard control header that indicates that there is a code behind file associated with this control.

Add the remaining code to the previous code. The first part represents the main form.

C# and VB :

```
<table>
  <tr>
    <td align="center" bgcolor="#CCCCCC" colspan="2">
      <asp:Label ID="lblNewCoffeeShop"
        runat="server" Font-Bold="True"
        Text="Enter A New Coffee Shop" />
      <asp:Label ID="lblUpdateCoffeeShop"
        runat="server" Font-Bold="True"
        Text="Update Coffee Shop" />
    </td>
  </tr>
  <tr>
    <td align="right">
      <asp:Label ID="lblShopName"
        runat="server" Text="Shop Name:" />
    </td>
```

```
        <td>
          <asp:TextBox ID="txtCoffeeShopName"
            runat="server" />
        </td>
      </tr>
      <tr>
        <td align="right">
          <asp:Label ID="lblAddress"
            runat="server" Text="Address:" />
        </td>
        <td>
          <asp:TextBox ID="txtCoffeeShopAddress"
            runat="server" />
        </td>
      </tr>
      <tr>
        <td align="right">
          <asp:Label ID="lblCity"
            runat="server" Text="City:" />
        </td>
        <td>
          <asp:TextBox ID="txtcoffeeShopCity"
            runat="server" />
        </td>
      </tr>
      <tr>
        <td align="right">
          <asp:Label ID="lblState"
            runat="server" Text="State:" />
        </td>
        <td>
          <asp:TextBox ID="txtcoffeeShopState"
            runat="server" />
        </td>
      </tr>
      <tr>
        <td align="right">
          <asp:Label ID="lblZip"
            runat="server" Text="Zip:" />
        </td>
        <td>
          <asp:TextBox ID="txtcoffeeShopZip"
            runat="server" />
        </td>
```

```
      </tr>
      <tr>
        <td align="right">
          <asp:Label ID="lblInternet"
            runat="server" Text="Internet:" />
        </td>
        <td>
          <asp:RadioButtonList ID="rblWiFi"
            runat="server" RepeatDirection="Horizontal">
          <asp:ListItem Value="Y"
            Text="Yes" Selected="True" />
          <asp:ListItem Value="N"
            Text="No" />
          </asp:RadioButtonList>
        </td>
      </tr>
```

The following code represents the command buttons for the form.

C# and VB:

```
      <tr>
        <td align="right">
           
        </td>
        <td align="right">
          <asp:LinkButton ID="cmdSave"
            runat="server" BorderStyle="none" Text="Save"
            onclick="cmdSave_Click" />
          <asp:LinkButton ID="cmdUpdate"
            runat="server" BorderStyle="none" Text="Update"
            onclick="cmdUpdate_Click" />
             <asp:LinkButton ID="cmdDelete"
            runat="server" BorderStyle="none" Text="Delete"
            onclick="cmdDelete_Click"
            OnClientClick='if (!confirm("Are you sure you want to
              delete?")){return false;}' />
             <asp:LinkButton ID="cmdCancel" runat="server"
            BorderStyle="none" CausesValidation="False"
            Text="Cancel" OnClick="cmdCancel_Click" />
        </td>
      </tr>
    </table>
```

This code creates all the elements of the EditShopList page. The code consists of a standard HTML table with labels, textboxes, radio buttons, and link buttons.

 You may see wavy lines that indicate errors. These errors will be cleared up when we replace the code in the code behind file in the next step.

Save the page. Click the **Design** button in the lower left-hand corner of the edit window to view the page, which appears as shown in the following screenshot:

The EditShopList code behind file

Right-click on the EditShopList.ascx file, and select **View Code**. The EditShopList.ascx.cs file will display in the edit window if using C# or the EditShopList.ascx.vb file will display if using VB.

Replace all the code with the following code:

C#:

```
using System;
using DotNetNuke.Common;
using DotNetNuke.Entities.Modules;
using System.Linq;
using System.Web.UI.WebControls;

namespace CoffeeShopCSharp
{
  public partial class EditShopList : PortalModuleBase
  {

  }
}
```

VB:

```
Imports System
Imports DotNetNuke.Common
Imports DotNetNuke.Entities.Modules
Imports System.Linq
Imports System.Web.UI.WebControls

Namespace CoffeeShopVB
  Partial Public Class EditShopList
    Inherits PortalModuleBase
  End Class
End Namespace
```

This declares the namespaces we will be using and creates the code behind class that inherits from PortalModuleBase.

Add the following method to the class:

C#:

```
protected void Page_Load(object sender, EventArgs e)
{
  if (!Page.IsPostBack)
  {
    if (Request.QueryString["CoffeeShopID"] != null)
    {
      // A CoffeeShipID was passed. Show the record
      ShowExistingCoffeeShop(Convert.ToInt32(Request.
        QueryString["CoffeeShopID"]));
    }
    else
    {
      // Set Save Mode
      cmdUpdate.Visible = false;
      cmdDelete.Visible = false;
      lblUpdateCoffeeShop.Visible = false;
    }
  }
}
```

VB:

```
Protected Sub Page_Load(ByVal sender As Object, ByVal e As EventArgs)
  If Not Page.IsPostBack Then
    If Request.QueryString("CoffeeShopID") <> Nothing Then
      ' A CoffeeShipID was passed. Show the record

  ShowExistingCoffeeShop(Convert.ToInt32(Request.QueryString("CoffeeSho
  pID")))
    Else
      ' Set Save Mode
      cmdUpdate.Visible = False
      cmdDelete.Visible = False
      lblUpdateCoffeeShop.Visible = False
    End If
  End If
End Sub
```

The `Page_Load` method checks to see if the page is in `PostBack` mode to determine if it should detect if a `CoffeeShopID` parameter has been passed to the control. If it has, it will pass that value to the `ShowExistingCoffeeShop` method; if not, it assumes the form is in the "add coffee shop" mode and hides the update and delete controls.

Add the following `ShowExistingCoffeeShop` method to the class:

C#:

```
private void ShowExistingCoffeeShop(int coffeeShopID)
{
    // Set Update Mode
    cmdSave.Visible = false;
    lblNewCoffeeShop.Visible = false;
    lblNewCoffeeShop.Visible = false;
    CoffeeShopCSharpDataContext objCoffeeShopCSharpDataContext = new
CoffeeShopCSharpDataContext();

    CoffeeShopInfo objCoffeeShop = (from CoffeeShop in
objCoffeeShopCSharpDataContext.CoffeeShopInfos
    where CoffeeShop.moduleID == ModuleId
    where CoffeeShop.coffeeShopID == coffeeShopID
    select CoffeeShop).FirstOrDefault();

    txtCoffeeShopAddress.Text = objCoffeeShop.coffeeShopAddress;
    txtcoffeeShopCity.Text = objCoffeeShop.coffeeShopCity;
    txtcoffeeShopName.Text = objCoffeeShop.coffeeShopName;
    txtcoffeeShopState.Text = objCoffeeShop.coffeeShopState;
```

```
        rblWiFi.SelectedValue = objCoffeeShop.coffeeShopWiFi;
        txtcoffeeShopZip.Text = objCoffeeShop.coffeeShopZip;

        // Set the CoffeeShopID as the CommandArgument on the Update and
    Delete buttons
        cmdUpdate.CommandArgument = objCoffeeShop.coffeeShopID.ToString();
        cmdDelete.CommandArgument = objCoffeeShop.coffeeShopID.ToString();

    }
```

VB:

```
    Private Sub ShowExistingCoffeeShop(ByVal coffeeShopID As Integer)
     ' Set Update Mode
     cmdSave.Visible = False
     lblNewCoffeeShop.Visible = False
     lblNewCoffeeShop.Visible = False

     Dim objCoffeeShopVBDataContext As New CoffeeShopVBDataContext()

     Dim objCoffeeShop As CoffeeShopInfo = _
     (From CoffeeShop In objCoffeeShopVBDataContext.CoffeeShopInfos _
      Where CoffeeShop.moduleID = ModuleId _
      Where CoffeeShop.coffeeShopID = coffeeShopID _
      Select CoffeeShop).FirstOrDefault()

     txtCoffeeShopAddress.Text = objCoffeeShop.coffeeShopAddress
     txtcoffeeShopCity.Text = objCoffeeShop.coffeeShopCity
     txtcoffeeShopName.Text = objCoffeeShop.coffeeShopName
     txtcoffeeShopState.Text = objCoffeeShop.coffeeShopState
     rblWiFi.SelectedValue = objCoffeeShop.coffeeShopWiFi
     txtcoffeeShopZip.Text = objCoffeeShop.coffeeShopZip
     ' Set the CoffeeShopID as the CommandArgument on the Update and
    Delete buttons
     cmdUpdate.CommandArgument = objCoffeeShop.coffeeShopID.ToString()
     cmdDelete.CommandArgument = objCoffeeShop.coffeeShopID.ToString()
    End Sub
```

This method retrieves an existing coffee shop from the database by instantiating the LINQ to SQL DataContext and performing a query. It then takes the values retrieved and assigns them to the controls we placed in the EditShop.ascx page in the earlier step.

The remaining methods for EditShopList

You will need to consult the full source code that is available for download from the publisher's site (`http://www.packtpub.com/files/code/9928_Code.zip`) for the remaining methods:

- `cmdSave_Click`: Saves a new coffee shop
- `cmdUpdate_Click`: Updates an existing coffee shop
- `cmdDelete_Click`: Deletes an existing coffee shop
- `cmdCancel_Click`: Navigates back to the `ShopList` web control without making any changes

After you complete entering the code and have saved the pages, log in to the website as an **administrator** who has **Edit** permission to the Coffee Shop Listing module, and click on the **Add Coffee Shop** link. You will see the following form to add a coffee shop:

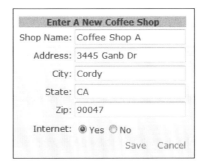

The form will allow you to add a coffee shop, but you will not be able to see any coffee shops added until you complete the `ShopList` page in the next step.

The ShopList page

The `ShopList` web user control will display existing coffee shops as well as display an edit link for the portal administrators to edit existing coffee shops. We will replace and add methods to the code created in *Chapter 7, Custom Module Development*.

We will cover code that will connect to the databases as well as the following DotNetNuke core API methods:

- `Personalization` (`SetProfile`/`GetProfile`): Used to store and retrieve data for a user
- `GetModuleSettings`: Used to retrieve module values

Although we will go through quite a bit of code in this section, we do not cover every single line. To help you as you work through the section, the complete source code is available for download from the publisher's site (`http://www.packtpub.com/files/code/9928_Code.zip`).

The ShopList.ascx file

In Visual Studio, under the Coffee Shop Listing folder that is under the `DesktopModules` folder (`CoffeeShopCSharp` if using C# and `CoffeeShopVB` if using VB), right-click on the `ShopList.ascx` file, and select **Open**. The page will open in the edit window. Replace all the code with the following code:

C#:

```
<%@ Control language="C#" AutoEventWireup="true"
Inherits="CoffeeShopCSharp.ShopList"
CodeFile="ShopList.ascx.cs"
%>
<asp:LinqDataSource ID="LDSCoffeeShop"
  runat="server"
  ContextTypeName="CoffeeShopCSharp.CoffeeShopCSharpDataContext"
  TableName="CoffeeShopInfos"
  OnSelecting="LDSCoffeeShop_Selecting">
</asp:LinqDataSource>
```

VB:

```
<%@ Control Language="VB" AutoEventWireup="true"
Inherits="CoffeeShopVB.ShopList"
CodeFile="ShopList.ascx.vb"
%>
<asp:LinqDataSource ID="LDSCoffeeShop"
  runat="server"
  ContextTypeName="CoffeeShopVB.CoffeeShopVBDataContext"
  TableName="CoffeeShopInfos"
  OnSelecting="LDSCoffeeShop_Selecting">
</asp:LinqDataSource>
```

This code not only adds the standard control header code but also inserts a `LinqDataSource` control that calls the `LDSCoffeeShop_Selecting` method on its `OnSelecting` event. This event is fired when the control is loaded. It retrieves a collection of coffee shops and binds them to the `gvCoffeeShops` GridView.

Add the following code. The first part of the code creates a `LinqDataSource` control and a search box with a search button.

C# and VB:

```
<asp:Panel ID="pnlASPDataGrid" runat="server">
<table align="center">
  <tr>
    <td>
       
    </td>
  </tr>
  <tr>
    <td align="center">
      <asp:Label ID="lblZipCode" runat="server"
        Text="Enter Zip Code:" Font-Bold="True" />
         <asp:TextBox ID="txtZipSearch" runat="server">
      </asp:TextBox> <asp:LinkButton ID="LinkButton1"
        runat="server" Font-Underline="True"
        OnClick="lnkSearch_Click">Search</asp:LinkButton>
    </td>
  </tr>
  <tr>
    <td>
       
    </td>
  </tr>
</tr>
```

This code creates a `GridView` to display the results of the search.

C# and VB:

```
<tr>
  <td align="center">
   <asp:GridView ID="gvCoffeeShops"
     runat="server"
     AutoGenerateColumns="False"
     DataSourceID="LDSCoffeeShop"
     AllowPaging="True"
     OnRowDataBound="gvCoffeeShops_RowDataBound">
     <Columns>
       <asp:TemplateField ShowHeader="False">
         <ItemTemplate>
```

```
            <asp:LinkButton ID="lnkEditCoffeeShop"
              runat="server" CausesValidation="False"
              CommandArgument='<%# Eval("coffeeShopID") %>'
              CommandName="Select" Text="Edit"
              OnClick="lnkEditCoffeeShop_Click">
            </asp:LinkButton>
          </ItemTemplate>
        </asp:TemplateField>
        <asp:BoundField DataField="coffeeShopName"
          HeaderText="Name" ReadOnly="True"
          SortExpression="coffeeShopName"
          ItemStyle-HorizontalAlign="Left" />
          <asp:BoundField DataField="coffeeShopAddress"
            HeaderText="Address" ReadOnly="True"
            SortExpression="coffeeShopAddress" />
          <asp:BoundField DataField="coffeeShopCity"
            HeaderText="City" ReadOnly="True"
            SortExpression="coffeeShopCity" />
          <asp:BoundField DataField="coffeeShopState"
            HeaderText="State" ReadOnly="True"
            SortExpression="coffeeShopState" />
          <asp:BoundField DataField="coffeeShopWiFi"
            HeaderText="WiFi" ReadOnly="True"
            SortExpression="coffeeShopWiFi" />
      </Columns>
    </asp:GridView>
  </td>
</tr>
</table>
</asp:Panel>
```

This code creates the remaining elements of the `ShopList` page. The code consists of a standard HTML table in a `Panel` with labels, textboxes, link buttons, and a GridView.

 You may see wavy lines that indicate errors. These errors will be cleared up when we replace the code in the code behind file in the next step.

Save the page. Click the **Design** button in the lower left-hand corner of the edit window to view the page that appears as shown in the following screenshot:

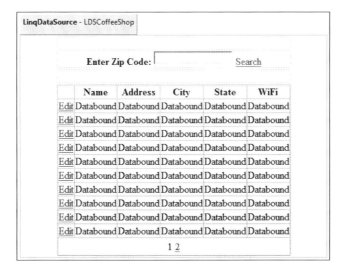

The ShopList code behind file

Right-click on the ShopList.ascx file, and select **View Code**. The ShopList.ascx.cs file will display in the editing window if using C# or the ShopList.ascx.vb file will display if using VB.

Remove the existing Page_Load method and enter the following code:

C#:

```
bool boolCanEdit;
protected void Page_Load(object sender, EventArgs e)
{
 if (!Page.IsPostBack)
 {
  GetLastZipCodeUsed();
  SetPageSize();
 }

 // Set the boolCanEdit value to determine if this user has
 // Edit permission
 boolCanEdit =
 ModulePermissionController.CanEditModuleContent(
 this.ModuleConfiguration);
}
```

VB:

```
Private boolCanEdit As Boolean
Protected Sub Page_Load(ByVal sender As Object, ByVal e As EventArgs)
    If Not Page.IsPostBack Then
GetLastZipCodeUsed()
SetPageSize()
    End If

    ' Set the boolCanEdit value to determine if this user has Edit
permission
    boolCanEdit = _
ModulePermissionController.CanEditModuleContent(Me.
ModuleConfiguration)
End Sub
```

First we create a global boolCanEdit variable (that will be used in the gvCoffeeShops_RowDataBound method) to determine if the **Edit** link will show. The DotNetNuke core API method, ModulePermissionController. CanEditModuleContent, sets the value of the boolCanEdit variable. It determines if the current user has been configured with **Edit** permission in the module settings on the **Settings** page.

The Page_Load method also calls the GetLastZipCodeUsed method to attempt to load the last zip code a logged-in user has searched for. It also calls the SetPageSize method to set the number of rows specified on the **Settings** page.

Add the following method to the class:

C#:

```
protected void LDSCoffeeShop_Selecting(object sender,
LinqDataSourceSelectEventArgs e)
{
  // When the LinqDataSource control is Selecting,
  // perform this query instead of the default query
  CoffeeShopCSharpDataContext
  objCoffeeShopCSharpDataContext =
    new CoffeeShopCSharpDataContext();

    var colCoffeeShops = from CoffeeShop in
      objCoffeeShopCSharpDataContext.CoffeeShopInfos
    where CoffeeShop.moduleID == ModuleId
    select CoffeeShop;
    // Only add the ZipCode criteria if a value is entered
    if (txtZipSearch.Text.Trim().Length > 0)
```

```
    {
        colCoffeeShops = from CoffeeShop in colCoffeeShops
        where CoffeeShop.coffeeShopZip ==
        txtZipSearch.Text.Trim()
        select CoffeeShop;
    }
    e.Result = colCoffeeShops;
}
```

VB:

```
Protected Sub LDSCoffeeShop_Selecting(ByVal sender As Object, ByVal e
As LinqDataSourceSelectEventArgs)
    ' When the LinqDataSource control is Selecting,
    'perform this query instead of the default query
    Dim objCoffeeShopVBDataContext As New    CoffeeShopVBDataContext()

    Dim colCoffeeShops = From CoffeeShop In
objCoffeeShopVBDataContext.CoffeeShopInfos _
 Where CoffeeShop.moduleID = ModuleId _
 Select CoffeeShop

    ' Only add the ZipCode criteria if a value is entered
    If txtZipSearch.Text.Trim().Length > 0 Then
colCoffeeShops = From CoffeeShop In colCoffeeShops _
 Where CoffeeShop.coffeeShopZip = txtZipSearch.Text.Trim() _
 Select CoffeeShop
    End If

    e.Result = colCoffeeShops
End Sub
```

This method is fired by the LinqDataSource control. It returns coffee shops to the control filtered by ModuleId and by zip code (if one is entered, otherwise it returns all coffee shops).

Add the following method to the class:

C#:

```
protected void gvCoffeeShops_RowDataBound(object sender,
GridViewRowEventArgs e)
{
    LinkButton lnkEditCoffeeShop =
(LinkButton)e.Row.FindControl("lnkEditCoffeeShop");
```

```
        if (lnkEditCoffeeShop != null)
        {
    // Show the Edit link only if the
    // user has edit permission for the module
    lnkEditCoffeeShop.Visible = boolCanEdit;
        }
    }
```

VB:

```
    Protected Sub gvCoffeeShops_RowDataBound(ByVal sender As Object, ByVal
    e As GridViewRowEventArgs)
        Dim lnkEditCoffeeShop As LinkButton = _
    DirectCast(e.Row.FindControl("lnkEditCoffeeShop"), LinkButton)

        If Not lnkEditCoffeeShop Is Nothing Then
         ' Show the Edit link only if the user
         'has edit permission for the module
         lnkEditCoffeeShop.Visible = boolCanEdit
        End If
    End Sub
```

This method is fired each time a row is bound to the GridView that displays the coffee shops. If the boolCanEdit global variable is true, the **Edit** link is displayed. Clicking this link will allow the user to edit the coffee shop entry.

Add the following method to the class:

C#:

```
    protected void lnkEditCoffeeShop_Click(object sender, EventArgs e)
    {
        // Get an instance of the Edit button
        LinkButton onjLinkButton = (LinkButton)sender;

        // Navigate to the Edit page passing the
        // selected CoffeeShopID and the ModuleId
        Response.Redirect(
        Globals.NavigateURL(PortalSettings.ActiveTab.TabID,
        "Edit",
        String.Format("mid={0}&CoffeeShopID={1}",
        ModuleId.ToString(),
        onjLinkButton.CommandArgument)));
    }
```

VB:

```
Protected Sub lnkEditCoffeeShop_Click(ByVal sender As Object, ByVal e
As EventArgs)
    ' Get an instance of the Edit button
    Dim onjLinkButton As LinkButton = DirectCast(sender, LinkButton)

    ' Navigate to the Edit page passing the
    'selected CoffeeShopID and the ModuleId
    Response.Redirect(Globals.NavigateURL( _
    PortalSettings.ActiveTab.TabID, _
    "Edit", [String].Format("mid={0}&CoffeeShopID={1}", _
    ModuleId.ToString(), onjLinkButton.CommandArgument)))
End Sub
```

This method is fired when the **Edit** link next to a coffee shop entry is clicked. Each coffee shop entry has its `CoffeeShopID` from the `CoffeeShopInfo` table bound to its `LinkButton`. This method gets that value from the `LinkButton` and then uses `NavigateURL` to navigate to the `EditShopList` web user control, passing the `CoffeeShopID` (so that the `EditShopList` web user control will know what coffee shop entry to display).

SetProfile/GetProfile

The DotNetNuke core `Personalization` API provides methods to store data for logged-in users. This API is recommended rather than using session variables because it works with server farms and values are persisted to the database so they are not lost if the server restarts.

 The `Personalization` API works only for logged-in users.

Add the following methods to the class:

C#:

```
protected void lnkSearch_Click(object sender, EventArgs e)
{
    // Only save last ZipCode if the user is logged in
    if (UserId > -1)
    {
     Personalization.SetProfile(ModuleId.ToString(),
     "ZipCode", txtZipSearch.Text);
    }
```

```
    // Refresh the list of Coffee Shops
    gvCoffeeShops.DataBind();
}

private void GetLastZipCodeUsed()
{
    // Only get last ZipCode if the user is logged in
    // and there is a zipCode stored in the user's profile
    if (!(Personalization.GetProfile(ModuleId.ToString(),
    "ZipCode") == null) & (UserId > -1))
    {
     string strZipCode = (string)(
     Personalization.GetProfile(
     ModuleId.ToString(),"ZipCode"));
     txtZipSearch.Text = strZipCode;
    }
}
```

VB:

```
Protected Sub lnkSearch_Click(ByVal sender As Object, ByVal e As
EventArgs)
    ' Only save last ZipCode if the user is logged in
    If UserId > -1 Then
     Personalization.SetProfile(ModuleId.ToString(), _
     "ZipCode", txtZipSearch.Text)
    End If

    ' Refresh the list of Coffee Shops
    gvCoffeeShops.DataBind()
End Sub

Private Sub GetLastZipCodeUsed()
    ' Only get last ZipCode if the user is logged in
    'and there is a zipCode stored in the user's profile
    If Not (Personalization.GetProfile(ModuleId.ToString(), _
       "ZipCode") = Nothing) And (UserId > -1) Then
        Dim strZipCode As String = DirectCast(( _
        Personalization.GetProfile(ModuleId.ToString(), _
        "ZipCode")), String)
        txtZipSearch.Text = strZipCode
    End If
End Sub
```

The `lnkSearch_Click` method calls the `Personalization.SetProfile` method to store the last zip code the user entered. It then calls `gvCoffeeShops.DataBind` that will cause the `LinqDataSource` control to refresh the search.

The `GetLastZipCodeUsed` method uses `Personalization.GetProfile` to retrieve the last used zip code (if any) and displays it in the `txtZipSearch` textbox.

GetModuleSettings

The DotNetNuke core `GetModuleSettings` method allows modules to retrieve values stored for that module instance.

Add the following method to the class:

C#:

```
private void SetPageSize()
{
    // Get an instance of the Module Controller
    DotNetNuke.Entities.Modules.ModuleController objModules =
     new DotNetNuke.Entities.Modules.ModuleController();

    // Get the value of the NumberOfRows key
    if ((((string)(objModules.GetModuleSettings
     (ModuleId)["NumberOfRows"])) != null))
    {
    // Set the page size on the GridView
    gvCoffeeShops.PageSize =
     (Convert.ToInt32(
      objModules.GetModuleSettings(ModuleId)["NumberOfRows"]
     ));
    }
}
```

VB:

```
Private Sub SetPageSize()
    ' Get an instance of the Module Controller
    Dim objModules As New _
     DotNetNuke.Entities.Modules.ModuleController()

    ' Get the value of the NumberOfRows key
    If ((DirectCast((objModules.GetModuleSettings _
     (ModuleId)("NumberOfRows")), String)) <> Nothing) Then
     ' Set the page size on the GridView
```

```
    gvCoffeeShops.PageSize = _
    (Convert.ToInt32( _
     objModules.GetModuleSettings(ModuleId)("NumberOfRows") _
    ))
  End If
End Sub
```

The `SetPageSize` method first instantiates an instance of the `ModuleController`
class, then it calls the `GetModuleSettings` method to retrieve the value for
`NumberOfRows`. It then sets this value (if any) on the `PageSize` property of the
`gvCoffeeShops` GridView.

The remaining methods for ShopList

You will need to consult the full source code that is available for download from
the publisher's site (`http://www.packtpub.com/files/code/9928_Code.zip`) for
the remaining methods. After you have entered the full source code and saved the
pages, log in to the website using your web browser. You will see any coffee shops
that you have added using the `EditShopList` page, which appears as shown in the
following screenshot:

Enter Zip Code:	90011				Search

	Name	Address	City	State	WiFi
Edit	Coffee Shop A	3445 Ganb Dr	Cordy	CA	N
Edit	Coffee Shop #2	32543 Toller Blvd	Alhambra	CA	Y

If you are an administrator who has **Edit** permission to the Coffee Shop Listing
module, you will see an edit link next to each coffee shop entry that will navigate
to the `EditShopList` page.

You can filter the coffee shops by entering a zip code and clicking the search link.

Summary

We have covered a lot of code in the last two chapters, including setting up our
development environment, creating controls, and the data access layer. In the next
module development chapter, we will modify the module to display a Silverlight
control that will also allow users to search coffee shops. We will also demonstrate
how to package the module so it can be distributed and deployed to another
DotNetNuke installation.

9
Silverlight Coffee Shop Viewer

In this chapter, we are going to complete the custom module for the Coffee Connections portal. We will create a Silverlight version of the Coffee Shop Listing module that will allow users to search for coffee shops. The functionality will be the same as the search page created in the previous chapter, but it will demonstrate passing data between a Silverlight application and DotNetNuke.

In this chapter, we will cover the following:

- Creating the web service that will be consumed by the Silverlight application
- Creating the Silverlight Coffee Shop Viewer application
- Displaying the Silverlight Coffee Shop Viewer in the DotNetNuke Coffee Shop Viewer module
- Packaging the module for distribution to another DotNetNuke site

Although we will go through quite a bit of code in this chapter, we do not cover every single line. To help you as you work through the section, the complete source code is available for download from the publisher's site at `http://www.packtpub.com/files/code/9928_Code.zip`.

Silverlight and DotNetNuke

Silverlight is a web browser plugin. It does not run inside a DotNetNuke module, rather it is "launched" by a DotNetNuke module. Once the Silverlight application has been launched by a DotNetNuke module, it communicates with the DotNetNuke website using web services.

We will now create the web service that the Silverlight application will use to communicate with the DotNetNuke website.

Creating the web service

We could use **Windows Communication Foundation (WCF)** to create the web service methods, but WCF requires that the web service responds on a single web address. This can cause problems with DotNetNuke sites that are configured with multiple portals on different addresses. We will create the web service using a standard .asmx web service instead.

Open the DotNetNuke website in Visual Studio. Right-click on the Coffee Shop Listing directory located under the App_Code directory (CoffeeShopCSharp if using C# and CoffeeShopVB if using VB) and select **Add New Item**.

In the **Add New Item** window, select the **Class** template, and enter WebService.cs if using C# or WebService.vb if using VB for the **Name**. Select **Visual C#** for the **Language** if using Visual C#, or **Visual Basic** if using VB, and click the **Add** button.

The web service file will now appear in the **Solution Explorer** under the Coffee Shop Listing folder, as shown in the following screenshot:

The source for the file will also appear in the edit window.

Replace all the code with the following code:

C#:

```csharp
using System;
using System.Collections.Generic;
using System.Linq;
using System.Web;
using System.Web.Services;
using DotNetNuke.Services.Personalization;
using DotNetNuke.Entities.Users;

namespace CoffeeShopCSharp
{
    [WebService(Namespace = "http://ADefWebserver.com/")]
```

```
    [WebServiceBinding(ConformsTo = WsiProfiles.BasicProfile1_1)]
    public class WebService : System.Web.Services.WebService
    {

    }
}
```

VB:

```
Imports System
Imports System.Collections.Generic
Imports System.Linq
Imports System.Web
Imports System.Web.Services
Imports DotNetNuke.Services.Personalization
Imports DotNetNuke.Entities.Users

Namespace CoffeeShopVB
    <WebService([Namespace]:="http://ADefWebserver.com/")> _
    <WebServiceBinding(ConformsTo:=WsiProfiles.BasicProfile1_1)> _
    Public Class WebService
        Inherits System.Web.Services.WebService
    End Class
End Namespace
```

This code adds namespaces that will be used in the subsequent code, and provides a "shell" for the remaining web service methods.

Getting coffee shops

First, we will create the web service method that will allow the Silverlight application to search for coffee shops.

Add the following method to the class:

C#:

```
[WebMethod]
public List<CoffeeShopInfo> GetCoffeeShops(int ModuleID, string
  ZipCode)
{
  CoffeeShopCSharpDataContext objCoffeeShopCSharpDataContext = new
    CoffeeShopCSharpDataContext();
  var colCoffeeShops = from CoffeeShop in
  objCoffeeShopCSharpDataContext.CoffeeShopInfos
  where CoffeeShop.moduleID == ModuleID
```

```
      select CoffeeShop;
      // Only add the ZipCode criteria if a value is entered
      if (ZipCode.Trim().Length > 0)
      {
        colCoffeeShops = from CoffeeShop in colCoffeeShops
        where CoffeeShop.coffeeShopZip == ZipCode.Trim()
        select CoffeeShop;
      }
      // Get the current user
      UserInfo objUserInfo = UserController.GetCurrentUserInfo();
      // Only store the last ZipCode used if the user is logged in
      // If the user is not -1 they are logged in
      if (objUserInfo.UserID > -1)
      {
        // Get the users Personalization Info
        PersonalizationController PersonalizationController =
        new PersonalizationController();
        PersonalizationInfo PersonalizationInfo =
        new PersonalizationInfo();
        PersonalizationInfo = PersonalizationController.LoadProfile(
          objUserInfo.UserID, objUserInfo.PortalID);
        //  Store the last ZipCode used in the users profile
        DotNetNuke.Services.Personalization.Personalization.SetProfile(
          PersonalizationInfo, ModuleID.ToString(),
          "LastZipCode", ZipCode);
        PersonalizationController.SaveProfile(
        PersonalizationInfo, objUserInfo.UserID, objUserInfo.PortalID
        );
      }
      return colCoffeeShops.ToList();
    }
```

VB:

```
<WebMethod()> _
    Public Function GetCoffeeShops(ByVal ModuleID As Integer, ByVal
ZipCode As String) _
    As List(Of CoffeeShopInfo)
Dim objCoffeeShopVBDataContext As New CoffeeShopVBDataContext()

Dim colCoffeeShops = From CoffeeShop In _
        objCoffeeShopVBDataContext.CoffeeShopInfos _
        Where CoffeeShop.moduleID = ModuleID _
        Select CoffeeShop
```

```
' Only add the ZipCode criteria if a value is entered
If ZipCode.Trim().Length > 0 Then
    colCoffeeShops = From CoffeeShop In colCoffeeShops _
        Where CoffeeShop.coffeeShopZip = ZipCode.Trim _
        Select CoffeeShop
End If


' Get the current user
Dim objUserInfo As UserInfo = UserController.GetCurrentUserInfo()


' Only store the last ZipCode used if the user is logged in
' If the user is not -1 they are logged in
If objUserInfo.UserID > -1 Then
    ' Get the users Personalization Info
    Dim PersonalizationController As New PersonalizationController()
    Dim PersonalizationInfo As New PersonalizationInfo()
    PersonalizationInfo = PersonalizationController.LoadProfile( _
        objUserInfo.UserID, objUserInfo.PortalID)

    '  Store the last ZipCode used in the users profile
    DotNetNuke.Services.Personalization.Personalization.SetProfile( _
        PersonalizationInfo, ModuleID.ToString(), "LastZipCode",
ZipCode)
    PersonalizationController.SaveProfile( _
        PersonalizationInfo, objUserInfo.UserID, objUserInfo.PortalID)
End If


Return colCoffeeShops.ToList()
End Function
```

The method accepts a `ModuleID` and a `ZipCode` as parameters and returns a list of coffee shops that match the zip code (or all the coffee shops for that `ModuleID` if no `ZipCode` is passed).

The method performs the following functions:

- Queries the database for the coffee shops (for the current module instance)
- Filters the coffee shops by zip code (if a zip code was passed)
- Stores the zip code passed in the user's profile (if the user is currently logged in)

The method, `UserController.GetCurrentUserInfo()` is used to retrieve the currently logged-in user.

When a user logs in to DotNetNuke, an authentication cookie is placed in their web browser session. When the DotNetNuke module launches the Silverlight application, the cookies associated with the current web browser session are automatically sent with each request to the DotNetNuke website by the Silverlight application. This allows you to use the `UserController.GetCurrentUserInfo()` method to determine if a user is logged in.

Getting last used zip code

We will now create a web service method that will allow the Silverlight application to display the last zip code that a logged-in user entered.

Add the following method to the class:

C#:

```csharp
[WebMethod]
public string GetLastZipCodeUsed(int ModuleID)
{
  string strLastZipCode = "";
  // Get the current user
  UserInfo objUserInfo = UserController.GetCurrentUserInfo();
  // If the user is not -1 they are logged in
  if (objUserInfo.UserID > -1)
  {
    // Get the users Personalization Info
    PersonalizationController PersonalizationController =
    new PersonalizationController();
    PersonalizationInfo PersonalizationInfo =
    new PersonalizationInfo();
    PersonalizationInfo =
    PersonalizationController.LoadProfile(
    objUserInfo.UserID, objUserInfo.PortalID);
    if (!(Personalization.GetProfile(
      PersonalizationInfo, ModuleID.ToString(),
      "LastZipCode") == null))
    {
      strLastZipCode = ((string)(Personalization.GetProfile(
      PersonalizationInfo, ModuleID.ToString(),
      "LastZipCode")));
    }
  }
  return strLastZipCode;
}
```

VB:

```
<WebMethod()> _
Public Function GetLastZipCodeUsed(ByVal ModuleID As Integer) As
String
    Dim strLastZipCode As String = ""

    ' Get the current user
    Dim objUserInfo As UserInfo = UserController.GetCurrentUserInfo()

    ' If the user is not -1 they are logged in
    If objUserInfo.UserID > -1 Then
' Get the users Personalization Info
Dim PersonalizationController As New PersonalizationController()
Dim PersonalizationInfo As New PersonalizationInfo()
PersonalizationInfo = _
    PersonalizationController.LoadProfile( _
    objUserInfo.UserID, objUserInfo.PortalID)

If Not (Personalization.GetProfile( _
PersonalizationInfo, ModuleID.ToString(), "LastZipCode") _
= Nothing) Then
    strLastZipCode = (DirectCast(( _
      Personalization.GetProfile( _
      PersonalizationInfo, ModuleID.ToString(), _
      "LastZipCode")), String))
End If
    End If
    Return strLastZipCode
End Function
```

This method accepts only a `ModuleID` and returns the last used zip code (if any).

The method performs the following functions:

- Determines if the user is logged in
- If the user is logged in, it retrieves the last used zip code (if any)

Creating the WebService.asmx entry point

We will now create an `.asmx` file that will serve as an "entry point" for the web service. The Silverlight application will point to this file to call the web service methods we have just created.

Right-click on the Coffee Shop Listing directory located under the `DesktopModules` directory (`CoffeeShopCSharp` if using C# or `CoffeeShopVB` if using VB) and select **Add New Item**. The **Add New Item** window is as shown in the following screenshot:

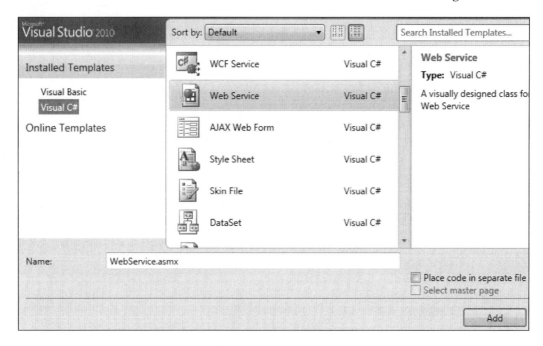

In the **Add New Item** window, select the **Web Service** template, enter `WebService.asmx` for the **Name**. Select **Visual C#** for the **Language** if using C#, or **Visual Basic** if using VB.

Ensure that **Place code in separate file** is not checked and click the **Add** button.

The file will now appear in the **Solution Explorer** under the Coffee Shop Listing folder.

The source for the `WebService.asmx` will also appear in the edit window.

Replace all the code with the following code:

C#:

```
<%@ WebService Language="C#"
  CodeBehind="~/App_Code/CoffeeShopCSharp/WebService.cs"
  Class="CoffeeShopCSharp.WebService" %>
```

VB:

```
<%@ WebService Language="VB"
  CodeBehind="~/App_Code/CoffeeShopVB/WebService.vb"
  Class="CoffeeShopVB.WebService" %>
```

This code points to the web service methods created in the earlier steps.

The Silverlight application

We will now create the Silverlight application that will be launched by the Coffee Shop Listing module.

 If you are using Visual Studio 2008, before proceeding you will need to install Microsoft® Silverlight™ 3 Tools for Visual Studio 2008 SP1 (or higher) available from `http://Silverlight.net`.

In Visual Studio, from the menu, select **File**, then **Add**, and then **New Project**, as shown in the following screenshot:

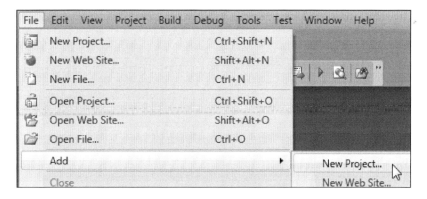

This will bring you to the **Add New Project** dialog window, as shown in the following screenshot:

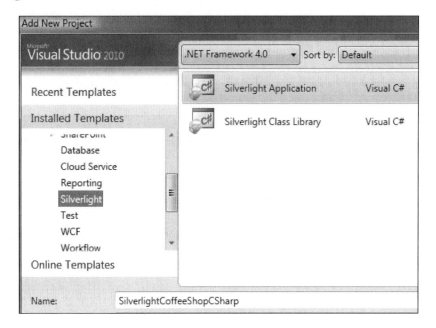

In the **Add New Project** dialog:

- Select the language you are using under **Installed Templates**
- Select **Silverlight** under **Installed Templates**
- Select the **Silverlight Application** template
- Enter `SilverlightCoffeeShopCSharp` for the **Name** if using C#, or `SilverlightCoffeeShopVB` for the **Name** if using VB
- Click the **OK** button

You will be directed to the **Add Silverlight Application** window as shown in the following screenshot:

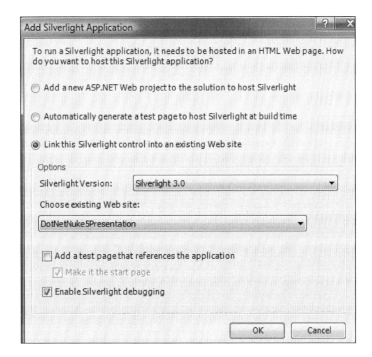

In the **Add Silverlight Application** dialog:

- Select **Link this Silverlight control into an existing Web site**
- Select **Silverlight 3.0** for **Silverlight Version**
- Select your DotNetNuke website for **Choose existing Web site**
- Uncheck all checkboxes; check only **Enable Silverlight debugging**
- Click the **OK** button

The project will be added to the **Solution Explorer**.

Adding reference to System.Windows.Controls.Data

The Silverlight application will use the Silverlight **DataGrid**. To use it, you will need to first install the **Silverlight Software Development Kit** (**SDK**) available from `http://Silverlight.net`.

Next, add a reference to the **System.Windows.Controls.Data** assembly. To add the reference, right-click on the Silverlight project and select **Add Reference**.

In the **Add Reference** dialog (shown in the next screenshot), select **System. Windows.Controls.Data** and click the **OK** button.

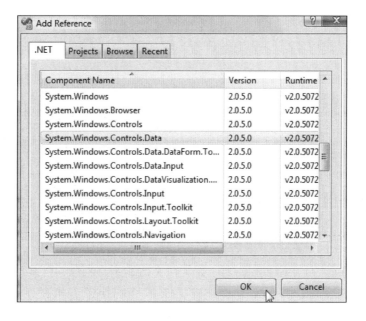

 If you do not see **System.Windows.Controls.Data** on the **.NET** tab in the **Add Reference** dialog, you will need to click the **Browse** tab and browse to select it. The **System.Windows.Controls.Data** assembly is usually installed in the ..Program Files\Microsoft SDKs\Silverlight\ v3.0\Libraries\Client\ directory by the SDK installer.

The web service proxy

We will now create a **web service proxy**. The following steps will instruct Visual Studio to create code that we will use to call the web service which we created previously.

Right-click on the Silverlight project and select **Add Service Reference**, as shown in the following screenshot:

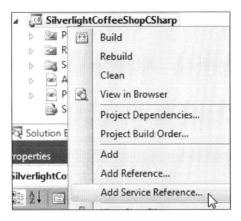

In the **Add Service Reference** dialog window that appears (see the following screenshot), click the **Discover** button to locate the web service you created in the earlier step (CoffeeShopCSharp if using C# or CoffeeShopVB if using VB).

Enter CoffeeShopCSharp if using C# or CoffeeShopVB if using VB, for the **Namespace**, as shown in the following screenshot:

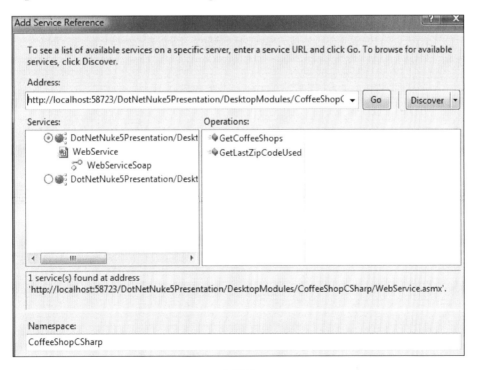

Click the **Advanced** button to go to the **Service Reference Settings** dialog, which is shown in the following screenshot:

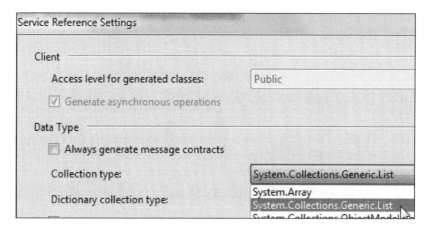

In the **Service Reference Settings** dialog, change the **Collection type** to **Systems.Collections.Generic.List** and click **OK**.

Click the **OK** button on the **Add Service Reference** dialog.

The Application_Startup page

In the Silverlight project, open the `App.xaml.cs` file if using C# or `App.xaml.vb` if using VB, and change the `Application_Startup` method to:

C#:

```
private void Application_Startup
  (object sender, StartupEventArgs e)
{
 this.RootVisual = new Page(
 e.InitParams["ModuleID"],
 e.InitParams["WebServiceURL"]);
}
```

VB:

```
Private Sub Application_Startup _
(ByVal o As Object, ByVal e As StartupEventArgs) _
Handles Me.Startup
  Me.RootVisual = New Page( _
  e.InitParams("ModuleID"), _
  e.InitParams("WebServiceURL"))
End Sub
```

You may see wavy lines that indicate errors. These errors will be cleared up when we insert the code in the code behind file in the next step.

The `Application_Startup` method is the first method executed when the Silverlight application starts. This method will be passed initialization parameters (`ModuleID` and `WebServiceURL`) from the Coffee Shop Listing module (that will later be modified to launch the Silverlight application).

The code will instantiate and pass the initialization parameters to the `Page` class that contains the majority of the code for the Silverlight application.

Save and close the file.

The Silverlight Coffee Shop Viewer UI

Right-click on the Silverlight project, select **Add** then **New Item**, and create a **Silverlight User Control**, in the appropriate language, named `Page.xaml` if one does not already exist in the Silverlight project.

 Some versions of the Visual Studio Silverlight templates automatically create a page called `Page` and some create a page called `MainPage`. If `MainPage` has been created, you can delete it, because it will not be used in this example.

Open `Page.xaml` in the Visual Studio Editor. Select the **XAML** view (as opposed to the **Design** view) and replace all the code with the following code:

C#:

```
<UserControl
  x:Class="SilverlightCoffeeShopCSharp.Page"
  xmlns="http://schemas.microsoft.com/winfx/2006/xaml/presentation"
  xmlns:x="http://schemas.microsoft.com/winfx/2006/xaml"
  xmlns:d="http://schemas.microsoft.com/expression/blend/2008"
  xmlns:mc="http://schemas.openxmlformats.org/markup-
    compatibility/2006"
  xmlns:data="clr-namespace:System.Windows.Controls;assembly=System.
Windows.Controls.Data"
  mc:Ignorable="d"
  d:DesignWidth="640" d:DesignHeight="480" Width="500" Height="300">
  <Canvas x:Name="LayoutRoot" Width="500" Height="300">
  </Canvas>
</UserControl>
```

VB:

```
<UserControl
  x:Class="SilverlightCoffeeShopVB.Page"
  xmlns="http://schemas.microsoft.com/winfx/2006/xaml/presentation"
  xmlns:x="http://schemas.microsoft.com/winfx/2006/xaml"
  xmlns:d="http://schemas.microsoft.com/expression/blend/2008"
  xmlns:mc="http://schemas.openxmlformats.org/markup-
    compatibility/2006"
    xmlns:data="clr-namespace:System.Windows.Controls;
      assembly=System.Windows.Controls.Data"
    mc:Ignorable="d"
    d:DesignWidth="640" d:DesignHeight="480" Width="500"
    Height="300">
    <Canvas x:Name="LayoutRoot" Width="500" Height="300">
    </Canvas>
</UserControl>
```

This creates a "shell" for the UI code.

Next, add the following code between the `<Canvas></Canvas>` tags.

C# and VB:

```
<TextBox x:Name="txtZipCode"
  Text="" TextWrapping="Wrap"
  Height="26" Width="73"
  Canvas.Left="231"
  Canvas.Top="19"/>

<TextBlock Width="132"
  FontSize="16"
  Text="Enter Zip Code:"
  TextWrapping="Wrap"
  Height="26" Canvas.Left="95"
  Canvas.Top="19"/>

<Button x:Name="btnSearch"
  Width="69" Content="Search"
  Click="btnSearch_Click"
  Height="26" Canvas.Left="318"
  Canvas.Top="19"/>

<data:DataGrid x:Name="dgCoffeeShops"
  Height="228" Width="458"
  Canvas.Left="24"
```

```
Canvas.Top="64"
AutoGenerateColumns="False"
GridLinesVisibility="Horizontal"
HorizontalContentAlignment="Stretch"
VerticalContentAlignment="Stretch"
IsReadOnly="True">
<data:DataGrid.Columns>
<data:DataGridTextColumn
Header="Name"
Binding="{Binding coffeeShopName}"
MinWidth="150" />
<data:DataGridTextColumn
    Header="Address"
    Binding="{Binding coffeeShopAddress}" />
    <data:DataGridTextColumn
      Header="City"
      Binding="{Binding coffeeShopCity}" />
    <data:DataGridTextColumn
      Header="State"
      Binding="{Binding coffeeShopState}" />
    <data:DataGridTextColumn
      Header="WiFi"
      Binding="{Binding coffeeShopWiFi}" />
  </data:DataGrid.Columns>
</data:DataGrid>
```

This code creates the labels, textboxes, and buttons needed to allow users to search coffee shops. It also contains the markup for the DataGrid that will display the coffee shops.

Do not worry if the XAML designer shows errors. This is usually caused by the designer not being able to properly render the DataGrid. Opening the .xaml file in a program such as **Microsoft Expression Blend** will display a design-time view properly.

The Silverlight Coffee Shop Viewer code

In the Silverlight project, open the `Page.xaml.cs` file if using C# or `Page.xaml.vb` if using VB, and replace all the code with the following code:

C#:

```
using System;
using System.Collections.ObjectModel;
using System.ServiceModel;
using System.Windows.Controls;
using SilverlightCoffeeShopCSharp.CoffeeShopCSharp;
using System.Collections.Generic;

namespace SilverlightCoffeeShopCSharp
{
  public partial class Page : UserControl
  {
    private int ModuleID;
    private string WebServiceURL;
  }
}
```

VB:

```
Imports System
Imports System.Collections.ObjectModel
Imports System.ServiceModel
Imports System.Windows.Controls
Imports SilverlightCoffeeShopVB.CoffeeShopVB

Partial Public Class Page
  Inherits UserControl
  Private ModuleID As Integer
  Private WebServiceURL As String

End Class
```

This sets up the namespaces that will be used and creates a "shell" for the remaining code.

Add the following method to the class:

C#

```csharp
public Page(string parmModuleID,
    string parmWebServiceURL)
{
    InitializeComponent();
    // Set the global values
    ModuleID = Convert.ToInt32(parmModuleID);
    WebServiceURL = parmWebServiceURL;
    GetLastZipCode();
}
```

VB:

```vb
Public Sub New(ByVal parmModuleID As String, _
 ByVal parmWebServiceURL As String)
    InitializeComponent()

    ' Set the global values
    ModuleID = Convert.ToInt32(parmModuleID)
    WebServiceURL = parmWebServiceURL

    GetLastZipCode()
End Sub
```

This is the constructor for the Page class. It is instantiated by the code in the App page (created in the previous section). The App page passes the parmModuleID (module ID) and parmWebServiceURL (web service URL) to the constructor. These values will be used to call the web service methods in the DotNetNuke website.

The method also calls the GetLastZipCode method (that will be created in the next step), that will display the last zip code the user used (if there is one).

Add the following methods to the class:

C#:

```csharp
private void GetLastZipCode()
{
    WebServiceSoapClient objWebServiceSoapClient =
        new WebServiceSoapClient();
    EndpointAddress MyEndpointAddress =
        new EndpointAddress(WebServiceURL);
    objWebServiceSoapClient.Endpoint.Address =
        MyEndpointAddress;
```

```
    objWebServiceSoapClient.GetLastZipCodeUsedCompleted +=
        new EventHandler<GetLastZipCodeUsedCompletedEventArgs>(
    objWebServiceSoapClient_GetLastZipCodeUsedCompleted);
    objWebServiceSoapClient.GetLastZipCodeUsedAsync(ModuleID);
}

void objWebServiceSoapClient_GetLastZipCodeUsedCompleted(
    object sender, GetLastZipCodeUsedCompletedEventArgs e)
{
    txtZipCode.Text = e.Result;
    CallWebService(txtZipCode.Text);
}
```

VB:

```
Private Sub GetLastZipCode()
    Dim objWebServiceSoapClient As New WebServiceSoapClient()
    Dim MyEndpointAddress As New EndpointAddress(WebServiceURL)
    objWebServiceSoapClient.Endpoint.Address = MyEndpointAddress
    AddHandler objWebServiceSoapClient.GetLastZipCodeUsedCompleted,
    AddressOf _
    objWebServiceSoapClient_GetLastZipCodeUsedCompleted
    objWebServiceSoapClient.GetLastZipCodeUsedAsync(ModuleID)
End Sub

Sub objWebServiceSoapClient_GetLastZipCodeUsedCompleted(ByVal sender
As Object, _
 ByVal e As GetLastZipCodeUsedCompletedEventArgs)
    txtZipCode.Text = e.Result
    CallWebService(txtZipCode.Text)
End Sub
```

The GetLastZipCode method calls the GetLastZipCode web service in the
DotNetNuke website. It uses the ModuleID and web service URL values
that were set to global variables in the constructor. This method makes an
asynchronous call to the web service and sets up the objWebServiceSoapClient_
GetLastZipCodeUsedCompleted method as the method to which the result of the
web service call should return to.

The objWebServiceSoapClient_GetLastZipCodeUsedCompleted method takes the
last zip code value passed and displays it in the txtZipCode textbox. The method
then calls the CallWebService method that will perform a search for coffee shops
with that zip code.

Add the following methods to the class:

C#:

```
private void CallWebService(string ZipCode)
{
  WebServiceSoapClient objWebServiceSoapClient =
    new WebServiceSoapClient();
  EndpointAddress MyEndpointAddress =
    new EndpointAddress(WebServiceURL);
  objWebServiceSoapClient.Endpoint.Address =
    MyEndpointAddress;
  objWebServiceSoapClient.GetCoffeeShopsCompleted +=
    new EventHandler<GetCoffeeShopsCompletedEventArgs>(
      objWebServiceSoapClient_GetCoffeeShopsCompleted);
  objWebServiceSoapClient.GetCoffeeShopsAsync(ModuleID, ZipCode);
}

void objWebServiceSoapClient_GetCoffeeShopsCompleted(
  object sender, GetCoffeeShopsCompletedEventArgs e)
{
  List<CoffeeShopInfo> colCoffeeShopInfo =
    (List<CoffeeShopInfo>)e.Result;
    dgCoffeeShops.ItemsSource = colCoffeeShopInfo;
}
private void btnSearch_Click(object sender,
  System.Windows.RoutedEventArgs e)
{
  CallWebService(txtZipCode.Text.Trim());
}
```

VB:

```
Private Sub CallWebService(ByVal ZipCode As String)
  Dim objWebServiceSoapClient As New WebServiceSoapClient()
  Dim MyEndpointAddress As New EndpointAddress(WebServiceURL)
  objWebServiceSoapClient.Endpoint.Address = MyEndpointAddress
  AddHandler objWebServiceSoapClient.GetCoffeeShopsCompleted,
    AddressOf _
  objWebServiceSoapClient_GetCoffeeShopsCompleted
  objWebServiceSoapClient.GetCoffeeShopsAsync(ModuleID, ZipCode)
End Sub

Sub objWebServiceSoapClient_GetCoffeeShopsCompleted(ByVal sender As
  Object, _
  ByVal e As GetCoffeeShopsCompletedEventArgs)
```

```
    Dim colCoffeeShopInfo As List(Of CoffeeShopInfo) = _
        DirectCast(e.Result, List(Of CoffeeShopInfo))
    dgCoffeeShops.ItemsSource = colCoffeeShopInfo
End Sub

Private Sub btnSearch_Click(ByVal sender As Object, _
    ByVal e As System.Windows.RoutedEventArgs)
    CallWebService(txtZipCode.Text.Trim())
End Sub
```

The following three methods handle the search for coffee shops:

- `CallWebService`: Calls the `GetCoffeeShops` web service, passing the `ModuleID` and the `ZipCode` to search

- `objWebServiceSoapClient_GetCoffeeShopsCompleted`: Handles the result from the `CallWebService` method and binds the results to the `DataGrid`

- `btnSearch_Click`: Performs a search by calling the `CallWebService` method when the user clicks the button

Building the Silverlight project and moving the .XAP

Right-click on the Silverlight project and select **Build**.

The Silverlight project will create a `.xap` package (`SilverlightCoffeeShopCSharp.xap` if using C# or `SilverlightCoffeeShopVB.xap` if using VB), and place it in the `ClientBin` directory in the DotNetNuke website, as shown in the following screenshot:

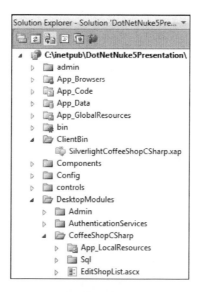

Drag the `ClientBin` directory so that it is under the Coffee Shop Viewer's directory that is under `DesktopModules` (`CoffeehopCSharp` if using C# or `CoffeeShopVB` if using VB). Your **Solution Explorer** should now appear as shown in the following screenshot:

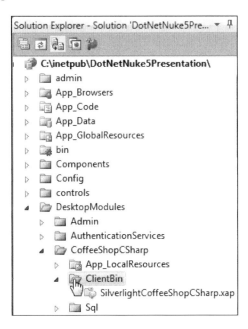

Altering Coffee Shop Viewer to launch the Silverlight application

We will now alter the DotNetNuke module code to launch the Silverlight application and pass the required initialization parameters.

You will need to consult the code download from the publisher's site (`http://www.packtpub.com/files/code/9928_Code.zip`) for the full code, but we will cover the important changes we made to the Coffee Shop Listing module created in the previous chapter.

The ShopList UI

The ShopList.ascx file was altered to add the following Panel that contains an HTML <object> tag that instantiates the Silverlight plugin control:

C# and VB:

```
<asp:Panel ID="silverlightControlHost"
align="center" runat="server">
<object data="data:application/x-silverlight-2,"
type="application/x-silverlight-2"
style="height: 300px; width: 500px">
<param name="source"
value="<%=SilverlightApplication %>" />
<param name="onError"
value="onSilverlightError" />
<param name="background"
value="white" />
<param name="minRuntimeVersion"
value="3.0.40624.0" />
<param name="autoUpgrade"
value="true" />
<param name="InitParams"
value="<%=SilverlightInitParams %>" />
<a href="http://go.microsoft.com/fwlink/?LinkID=149156&v=3.0.40624.0"
style="text-decoration: none">
<img src="http://go.microsoft.com/fwlink/?LinkId=108181"
alt="Get Microsoft Silverlight"
style="border-style: none" />
</a>
</object>
<iframe id="_sl_historyFrame"
style="visibility: hidden;
height: 0px; width: 0px;
border: 0px"></iframe>
</asp:Panel>
```

The object tag contains the code <%=SilverlightApplication %> and <%=SilverlightInitParams %> that will be replaced at runtime with the location of the .xap file and the initialization parameters respectively.

In addition, JavaScript code was added to the page that captures any errors that the Silverlight control may generate. This code is normally created by the Silverlight Visual Studio template when a new Silverlight-enabled website is created.

The ShopList code

The following code has been added to the ShopList code behind file to
enable the Silverlight HTML object and pass required parameters to it:

C#:

```
if (!boolCanEdit)
{
  // This is not a user who can edit Coffee Shops -
  //  show the Silverlight Application
  silverlightControlHost.Visible = true;
  pnlASPDataGrid.Visible = false;

  // register Silverlight.js file
  Page.ClientScript.RegisterClientScriptInclude(this.GetType(),
  "Silverlight", (
    this.TemplateSourceDirectory + "/Silverlight.js"));
    // Set the path to the .xap file
    SilverlightApplication = TemplateSourceDirectory +
    "/ClientBin/SilverlightCoffeeShopCSharp.xap";

    // Set the InitParams
    string strWebServiceURL = String.Format(@"http://{0}{1}/{2}",
    this.Context.Request.Url.Authority,
    this.Context.Request.ApplicationPath,
    "DesktopModules/CoffeeShopCSharp/WebService.asmx");

    SilverlightInitParams = string.Format("ModuleID={0},
      WebServiceURL={1}",
    ModuleId.ToString(), strWebServiceURL);
}
else
{
    // This is a user who can edit Coffee Shots
    // show the normal ASP.NET grid that allows user to edit Coffee
Shops
    silverlightControlHost.Visible = false;
    pnlASPDataGrid.Visible = true;
}
```

VB:

```vb
If Not boolCanEdit Then
  ' This is not a user who can edit
  'Coffee Shops - show the Silverlight Application
  silverlightControlHost.Visible = True
  pnlASPDataGrid.Visible = False

  ' register Silverlight.js file
  Page.ClientScript.RegisterClientScriptInclude( _
     Me.[GetType]() , "Silverlight", _
     (Me.TemplateSourceDirectory + "/Silverlight.js"))
  ' Set the path to the .xap file
  SilverlightApplication = TemplateSourceDirectory _
     + "/ClientBin/SilverlightCoffeeShopVB.xap"

  ' Set the InitParams
  Dim strWebServiceURL As String = _
     String.Format("http://{0}{1}/{2}", _
     Me.Context.Request.Url.Authority, _
     Me.Context.Request.ApplicationPath, _
     "DesktopModules/CoffeeShopVB/WebService.asmx")

  SilverlightInitParams = String.Format( _
     "ModuleID={0}, WebServiceURL={1}", _
     ModuleId.ToString(), strWebServiceURL)
           Else
  ' This is a user who can edit Coffee Shots
  ' show the normal ASP.NET grid that allows
  ' user to edit Coffee Shops
  silverlightControlHost.Visible = False
  pnlASPDataGrid.Visible = True
End If
```

This code uses the boolCanEdit variable to determine if the user will see the
Silverlight application or the non-Silverlight GridView. If the user can see the
Silverlight application, the silverlightControlHost panel that it is in is made
visible. If a user is logged in, and they have edit permission to the module, they
will see the non-Silverlight version (this will allow administrators to use the existing
functionality that allows them to edit existing coffee shops).

Next, the `RegisterClientScriptInclude` method is used to register the Silverlight JavaScript helper file. The `Silverlight.js` file contains the JavaScript required to support the Silverlight HTML `<object>` tag. This file is created by the Silverlight Visual Studio template when a new Silverlight-enabled website is created.

Lastly, the `SilverlightApplication` and `SilverlightInitParams` values are set. These values display in the HTML `<object>` tag. The `SilverlightInitParams` are passed by the HTML `<object>` tag to the `App` class in the Silverlight application.

The module is complete, as shown in the next screenshot:

Enter Zip Code: 90011		Search		
Name	Address	City	State	WiFi
Coffee Shop #1	12354 Main St #A	Los Angeles	CA	N
Coffee Shop #23	879 FairVille Ave	Deven	CA	Y

Packaging the module

It is advisable to develop your module on a separate development machine, then deploy it to production using a **Private Assembly** package (called a **PA**).

This PA package is a `.zip` file that contains all the elements needed to install the module in a DotNetNuke installation. These elements include the code and the **sql installation scripts** (that we created in *Chapter 8, Connecting to the Database*).

The version number for your sql scripts is very important. If the module is not installed, all the sql installation scripts in your module will run. If a version of the module is already installed on your portal, the framework checks the version number of the script file to determine whether to run the script. If the version number of the currently installed module is higher than the sql script, the script will not be executed. If the version number of the currently installed module is lower, or equal to the sql installation script, the script will run. In this way, you can have a single PA package work both as an installation and upgrade package.

Use the following steps to create the PA `.zip` file:

- In your web browser, log in to the DotNetNuke site as host
- From the **HOST** menu, select **Module Definitions**
- Click the edit link to navigate to the configuration settings for the Coffee Shop Listing module (`CoffeeShopListingCSharp` if using C# and `CoffeeShopListingVB` if using VB)

- Select **Create Package** (at the bottom of the page)
- Use the Wizard to create the module package

At the end of the wizard, a screen will appear indicating that the module elements have been successfully placed in the `.zip` file.

You can retrieve the `.zip` file by navigating to `\Install\Module` directory in the DotNetNuke website using the Windows **File Manager**.

Deploying the module

To upload the module, sign in as host and select **Module Definitions** in the **HOST** menu. Then select **Install Module** and use the wizard to install the module.

After the module is installed, navigate to a page in your portal and place an instance of the module on the page by selecting it in the **Module** dropdown (from the administrator control panel) and clicking the **Add Module To Page** button, as shown in the following screenshot:

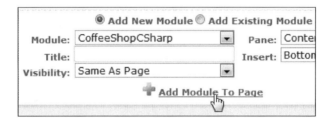

Summary

We have covered a lot of code in the last three chapters, including setting up our development environment, creating controls, the data access layer, the UI, and the Silverlight application. We then showed how to package the module so that it can be distributed to another DotNetNuke website.

We will be moving away from coding in the next chapter to explore one of DotNetNuke's most popular and powerful features. The ability to create multiple portals from a single installation is one of the many features that sets DotNetNuke apart from other content management systems. In the next chapter, we will explore this powerful feature in detail, as well as explain why we would want to use it.

10
Creating Multiple Portals

One of the more compelling reasons to use DotNetNuke is the capability to create multiple portals off one installation of DotNetNuke. All of the portals will share one database, which makes portal backup easy.

In this chapter, you will learn the following:

- Why you would want to create multiple portals
- How child portals differ from parent portals
- How to set up multiple portals
- How to create a portal template
- How to use the **Site Wizard** to update your site

In this chapter, you will see the different types of portals available, how to use the wizard to set up your portal, and how to create templates so that you never have to duplicate your work.

Multiple portals

Before we discuss how to set up multiple portals, let's understand what is meant by multiple portals and why they are important. In a typical web hosting environment, you purchase a domain name and contact a hosting provider to host your site. In normal situations, this is a one-to-one arrangement. If you then want to host another website, you follow the process again, creating another hosting account with additional fees, and set up your site. The following diagram shows the typical configuration for multiple websites:

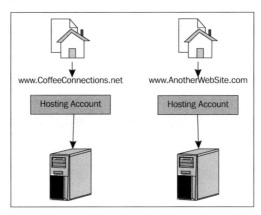

This can become time-consuming and expensive. Although this can be avoided by either spending more money to get a dedicated hosting account (you have full access to the server) or by creating subdomains and pointing to subfolders on your site, it will take some technical knowledge on your part, and, if you use subdomains, it could get kind of messy. DotNetNuke solves this dilemma by allowing you to create multiple portals easily using a single hosting account, using multiple independent domain names, subdomains, or virtual directory sort of paths, whatever suits you best. The following diagram shows the configuration for multiple websites using DotNetNuke:

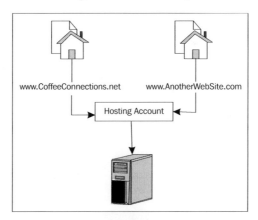

So, why would you need multiple portals? Well, let's say that you have your portal up and running, and then get a great idea for a second site dedicated to the "World of Chocolate". And then your spouse decides to sell handmade crafts and needs a website to do it. Finally, during a family dinner you decide you want to put up a website dedicated to your family tree.

Another example is in an organization where each department might want to put up its own section independently on the web. Or the company can decide to set up a domain for each of their product lines.

DNN's multiple portal feature allows you to cater to almost endless possibilities, through a single hosting account, allowing each portal administrator to independently manage his/her portal and providing the host user (super user) the central administration of all portals.

Normally, you would need to create separate hosting accounts, build the site, design the look and feel, add the needed functionality, set up the database, and finally post your site on the Web. This could take you weeks or months to set up, and the costs would be proportional to the number of sites you needed.

When you have a DotNetNuke portal up and running, there are no additional costs to create additional portals, and with the help of wizards and templates in DotNetNuke, you could have these sites up in a matter of hours or days.

It is important to note that when considering the costs of multiple portals, you need to take into account the amount of traffic each one will have. Most web hosting services sell plans based on the disk usage of your site. This may require you to purchase a plan that accommodates more traffic. Also be advised that each parent portal (discussed in the next section) would require configuration on the web server.

Also each parent portal is loaded into its own application domain by the web server. So, each parent portal would have its code and assemblies loaded independently from other parent portals into its own AppDomain, although they share the same codebase.

This is even more important if your hosting provider has imposed memory limits on your hosting account. Further discussion on adding domains is outside the scope of this book.

Parent portals versus child portals

Parent portals are sites that are defined by a unique URL (`www.CoffeeConnections.net`, `www.e-coffeehouse.com`, and so on.). Parent portals allow you to run multiple sites from the same host and same DotNetNuke installation. This means that each domain name is unique but points to the same location, though running on its own application domain. DotNetNuke handles how to route the requests depending on which domain name is entered.

On the other hand, **child portals** are subportals related to your main portal and share the domain name of their parent. A directory is created on your web server allowing the portal to be accessed through a URL address that includes a parent name and the directory name combined (for example, `www.CoffeeConnections.net/TestingPortal`).

Setting up a parent portal

The first thing that needs to be done before you attempt to set up a parent portal is to purchase a domain name or to use a subdomain of your existing domain. Purchasing domain names can be done through many different providers. Some of the most well known are `GoDaddy.com` and `Register.com`.

While working with `CoffeeConnections.net`, we realized that the sale of coffee-unique coffee beans has grown into a good-sized side business. To help this part of the company grow without overshadowing the original concept, we have decided to have a companion portal called `e-Coffeehouse.com`.

Registering your domain and setting the DNS

Setting up multiple portals on a DNN site does not mean that we have to share the same name as the original portal, although we can also use a subdomain or a subdirectory path of the original address. So, to give our new portal its own name, we need to purchase a domain name. When you purchase the domain name, you will need to tell it which **domain name server (DNS)** to point to. You will need to set up a primary and secondary DNS.

To get your domain server information, you will need to contact the company that is hosting your site or check their website to find out the name of your DNS server. You will also need to contact them to add your new domain name to your hosting account.

Most hosting providers will have a control panel that will allow you to add your domain names and find your DNS servers. You may refer to the hosting provider's website for more information or contact their support staff to assist you in the setup.

Once you set the DNS, you will need to wait a few days for it to propagate. On completing these tasks, you will be ready to set up your portal within DotNetNuke.

Creating a parent portal

In the previous chapter, we moved our local implementation of DotNetNuke to our hosting provider. Now we are going to create a parent portal from this installation. For this, log in as host and navigate to **HOST | Portals.** This will bring up a list of the portals that have already been set up. To add another portal, access the **Action** menu next to the **Portals** icon and select **Add New Portal**, as shown in the following screenshot:

You will then be presented with the **Portal Setup** dialog box, as shown in the next screenshot:

In the **Portal Setup** dialog box:

- Select the **Portal Type** you want to create. In this instance, we will be creating a **Parent** portal.

- Enter the **Portal Alias**. This is the website address of your portal (excluding `http://`).

- In **Home Directory**, if desired, you can change the location where the framework will save portal-specific information. This includes skin and container files.

- Enter the **Title** for your portal.

- Enter a **Description** and **Keywords** for your portal. The keywords entered here will be added to the metadata for your site. This helps search engines index your site more effectively.

- Select a **Template** for your portal. You can create templates for your portal so that when they are created, all the skins, containers, modules, and tabs will be created for you. You will find a sample file under the `portals/default` folder of your installation called `DotNetNuke.template`. Select **DotNetNuke**, which will create an empty shell for you.

- Enter the administrator information for this portal. This will create a user that will act as the administrator for this new portal. As a general security practice, it is recommended that you use a different username and password for each portal.

- When finished, click on **Create Portal**.

This will create a new empty portal, all ready for you to modify.

As mentioned earlier in this chapter, in order to create a parent portal, you will need to make sure that a domain name has been purchased and that the DNS is pointed to the server that is hosting this parent portal. If this is not completed, the parent portal will not work.

It is important to note that your new portal will use the default properties defined in the **Host Settings** module. Once the portal is created, these settings can be modified in the **Site Settings** module under the **ADMIN** menu.

Setting up a child portal

Child portals, as opposed to parent portals, give you a way to create separate portals without having to set up separate domain names. For this, log in as host and navigate to **HOST | Portals**. This will bring up a list of the portals that have already been set up. To add another portal, hover the cursor over the down arrow icon next to the **Portals** icon and select **Add New Portal**, as shown in the following screenshot:

You will be presented with the **Portal Setup** dialog box, as shown in the next screenshot:

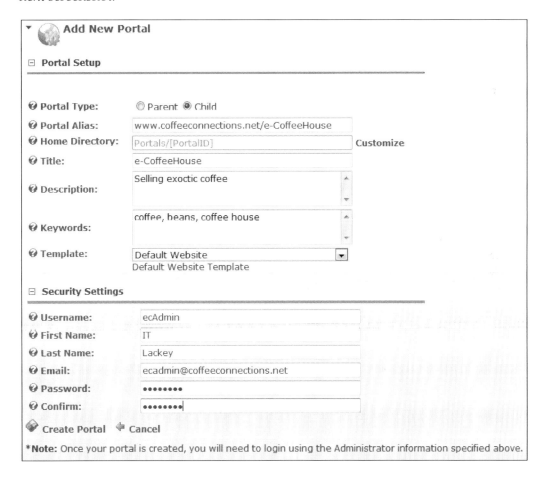

In the **Portal Setup** dialog box:

- Select the **Portal Type** you want to create. In this instance, we will be creating a **Child** portal.

- Enter the **Portal Alias**. As this is a child portal, it is run off a directory on your main site. When you select **Child** portal, it will fill in the name of your domain with a forward slash (/). Just add the directory name for your portal.

- Enter a **Title** for your portal.

- Enter a **Description** and **Keywords** for your portal.

- Select a **Template** for your portal. You can create templates for your portals so that when they are created, all of the skins, containers, modules, and tabs will be created for you. You will find a sample file under the `portals/default` folder of your installation. Select **DotNetNuke**, which will create an empty shell for you.

- Enter the administrator information for this portal. This will create a user that will act as the administrator for this new portal. Again, it is recommended that you use a different username and password for each portal.

- When finished click on **Create Portal**.

This will create a new empty portal all ready for you to modify. The new portal will use the default properties defined in the **Host Settings** module. Once the portal is created, these settings can be modified in the **Site Settings** module under the **ADMIN** menu.

Creating portal templates

In the previous examples, we created our sites using the default DotNetNuke template. While this is helpful, if you want to create a site from scratch, you usually wouldn't want to add all of the common functionality you would like on your portal each and every time you create a new one. Fortunately, DotNetNuke makes creating a portal template easy.

When you previously created new portals by going to **HOST | Portals**, you may have noticed an **Export Portal Template** button at the bottom of the screen. Clicking this button will take you to an **Export Template** section.

 Before exporting a portal's template, configure the existing portal carefully. Features such as pages, user roles, permissions, profile property definitions, and all other important aspects are exported while creating a portal's template.

The **Export Template** section appears as shown in the following screenshot:

This section allows you to save your portal configuration into a template. This includes your menu navigation, modules, and module content.

The various fields of the **Export Template** section are as follows:

- **Portal**: Select the portal you would like to export
- **Template File Name**: Enter a filename for this template
- **Template Description**: Enter a description of the kind of information this template contains
- **Include Content**: If you would like the content of the modules to be saved, check this box

Click on the **Export Template** link to save your template. This will save your template into an XML-formatted file. If you would like to see the file that is created, navigate to the location presented on the screen, which is shown in the following screenshot:

The new portal template has been saved in folder: C:\code\Dnn.Dev\Portals_default\CoffeeConnections.template

When setting up future portals, you can use this portal as a template.

Using the Site Wizard

The **Site Wizard** will allow you to customize your site by walking you through an easy to understand step-by-step process. To access this wizard, sign in as an administrator and navigate to the **Site Wizard** page under the **ADMIN** menu.

You will now be at the first step in the **Site Wizard**. The first page simply displays an overview of the purpose of the site wizard. Clicking the **Next** button will take you to the next step. This page asks you if you would like to apply a template to your site. If you did not do this when the site was set up, you can accomplish this now. If you already have content on your site, it will ask you how you want to deal with duplicate entries. For example, if you already have a home page with modules and the template has a home page with modules, how would you like to resolve this conflict? You have the following three choices:

1. **Ignore**: This will ignore any items that already exist on your site.

2. **Replace**: This will replace anything on your site with what is contained in the template.

3. **Merge**: This will merge the content in the template with what is already on your site. This may produce multiple menu items or modules, but these can be deleted later.

Click on **Next** to proceed to the next screen in the wizard.

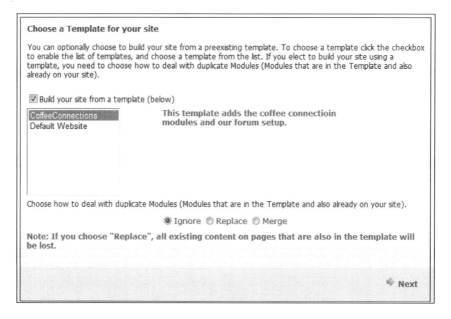

The following screen allows you to apply any available skin to your portal. If you would like to apply a certain skin, select the radio button next to the skin and click on the **Next** button.

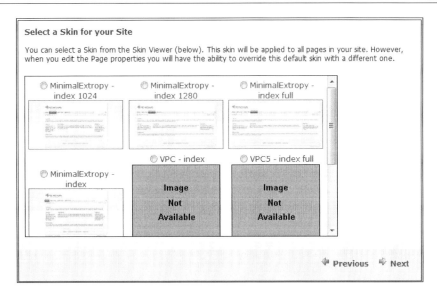

The following screen allows you to set any container that you have available to your portal as the default. If you would like to set a container skin, select the radio button next to the container and click on the **Next** button.

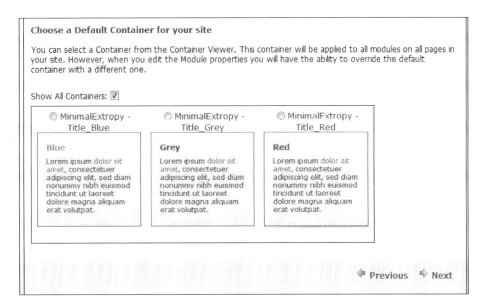

 Select the **Show All Containers** checkbox to view host level containers.

The following screen allows you to add or modify the title, description, and keywords for your portal. It also allows you to select the logo you would like to use for your site. In the default DotNetNuke skin, this would show up in the header of your portal. Click on the **Finish** button to save your settings.

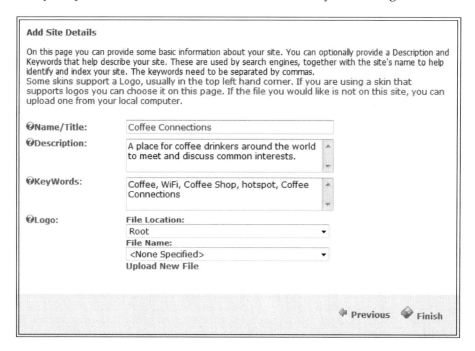

To view the changes, click on the **HOME** menu item. Any changes that you made will now be reflected on your site.

Managing multiple portals

As the host user, you will have access to every portal you create. To manage your portals, you just need to navigate to the **Portals** page by going to **HOST | Portals** from the main menu. The **Portals** page appears as shown in the following screenshot:

You can access each site by clicking on the **Portal Aliases** link or edit each site by clicking on the pencil icon next to the portal. Next to each portal, you will notice the following columns:

- **Users**: The number of users registered for the particular portal.

- **Pages**: The number of pages created for the portal.

- **Disk Space**: As each separate portal shares the same hosting environment, you can set the disk space allowed for each portal. This will limit the amount each admin will be able to upload to their particular site.

- **Hosting Fee**: If you are charging a hosting fee for each site, you can place that fee in this section.

- **Expires**: You can enforce the fees that you charge for each portal by allowing you to automatically expire (turn off) a portal when its hosting fee period ends by specifying a date for this field.

 It is important to note that even though users of each portal are kept in the same database, they are assigned only to the portal that they registered on. In a default implementation of DotNetNuke, a user would have to register for *each* portal they would like to be a part of. If you need to manage users in a multi-portal environment, there are a few good third-party modules available to make this process much easier.

All of these items can be accessed by clicking on the pencil icon next to the portal name. This will bring up the **Portal Settings** page. We have seen most of these in *Chapter 5, Host and Admin Tools*. We will just look at the **Host Settings** section, which is visible only to super users:

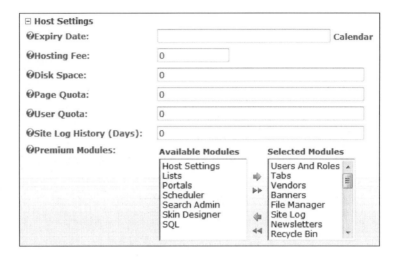

This is where you can set the information found on the **Portals** page. The two quota properties allow you to set the maximum number of users and pages respectively. Also the **Premium Modules** settings provide a way to select what modules are available to each portal.

Only a superuser (host) account is able to see all of the portals that have been created. The administrators of each portal will only be able to see the information related to their portal.

Summary

In this chapter, we learned how to create multiple portals that can all be hosted from one account. We have seen how to create and use templates, and how to use the **Site Wizard** to upgrade your site. We then finished this by showing you how to manage these portals once they have been set up. Not only will this functionality allow you to create multiple portals, but as all of the information is stored in one database, backing them up is simple.

Index

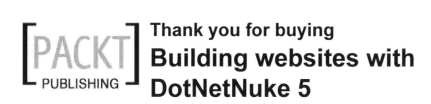

Thank you for buying
Building websites with DotNetNuke 5

Packt Open Source Project Royalties

When we sell a book written on an Open Source project, we pay a royalty directly to that project. Therefore by purchasing Building websites with DotNetNuke 5, Packt will have given some of the money received to the DotNetNuke 5 project.

In the long term, we see ourselves and you—customers and readers of our books—as part of the Open Source ecosystem, providing sustainable revenue for the projects we publish on. Our aim at Packt is to establish publishing royalties as an essential part of the service and support a business model that sustains Open Source.

If you're working with an Open Source project that you would like us to publish on, and subsequently pay royalties to, please get in touch with us.

Writing for Packt

We welcome all inquiries from people who are interested in authoring. Book proposals should be sent to author@packtpub.com. If your book idea is still at an early stage and you would like to discuss it first before writing a formal book proposal, contact us; one of our commissioning editors will get in touch with you.

We're not just looking for published authors; if you have strong technical skills but no writing experience, our experienced editors can help you develop a writing career, or simply get some additional reward for your expertise.

About Packt Publishing

Packt, pronounced 'packed', published its first book "Mastering phpMyAdmin for Effective MySQL Management" in April 2004 and subsequently continued to specialize in publishing highly focused books on specific technologies and solutions.

Our books and publications share the experiences of your fellow IT professionals in adapting and customizing today's systems, applications, and frameworks. Our solution-based books give you the knowledge and power to customize the software and technologies you're using to get the job done. Packt books are more specific and less general than the IT books you have seen in the past. Our unique business model allows us to bring you more focused information, giving you more of what you need to know, and less of what you don't.

Packt is a modern, yet unique publishing company, which focuses on producing quality, cutting-edge books for communities of developers, administrators, and newbies alike. For more information, please visit our website: www.PacktPub.com.

PUBLISHING

CMS Made Simple 1.6

ISBN: 978-1-847198-20-4 Paperback: 364 pages

Create a fully functional and professional website using CMS Made Simple

1. Learn everything there is to know about setting up a professional website in CMS Made Simple

2. Implement your own design into CMS Made Simple with the help of the easy-to-use template engine

3. Create photo galleries with LightBox and implement many other JQuery effects like interactive navigation in your website

DotNetNuke Skinning Tutorial

ISBN: 978-1-847192-78-3 Paperback: 156 pages

A simple, clear, step-by-tutorial to creating DotNetNuke skins to put you in control of the look and feel of your DotNetNuke website

1. Take control of the look and feel of your DotNetNuke website

2. Simple, clear, tutorial to creating DotNetNuke skins

3. Practical step-by-step guidance

4. No knowledge of DotNetNuke skinning required

Please check **www.PacktPub.com** for information on our titles

AJAX and PHP

ISBN: 978-1-847197-72-6   Paperback: 308 pages

Build user friendly Web 2.0 Applications with JavaScript and PHP

1. The ultimate AJAX tutorial for building modern Web 2.0 Applications

2. Create faster, lighter, better web applications by using the AJAX technologies to their full potential

3. Leverage the power of PHP and MySQL to create powerful back-end functionality and make it work in harmony with a responsive AJAX clientWrite better JavaScript code to enable powerful web features

Joomla! 1.5

ISBN: 978-1-847199-90-4   Paperback: 380 pages

Build and maintain impressive user-friendly web sites the fast and easy way with Joomla! 1.5

1. Create a web site that meets real-life requirements by following the creation of an example site with the help of easy-to-follow steps and ample screenshots

2. Practice all the Joomla! skills from organizing your content to completely changing the site's looks and feel

3. Go beyond a typical Joomla! site to make the site meet your specific needs

Please check **www.PacktPub.com** for information on our titles

Printed in Great Britain by
Amazon.co.uk, Ltd.,
Marston Gate.